MENOPAUSE

MENOPAUSE

DR. MIRIAM STOPPARD

DORLING KINDERSLEY LIMITED
LONDON • NEW YORK • STUTTGART

For my mother

A DORLING KINDERSLEY BOOK

Created and produced by
CARROLL & BROWN LIMITED
5 Lonsdale Road
London NW6 6RA

Editorial Director Amy Carroll
Project Editor Kesta Desmond

Design Director Denise Brown
Art Editor Chrissie Lloyd
Designers Julie Adams
Sandra Schneider
Mike Snell
James Arnold

Production Consultant Lorraine Baird
Production Editors Wendy Rogers
Amanda Mackie

First published in Great Britain in 1994
by Dorling Kindersley Limited,
9 Henrietta Street, London WC2E 8PS

A CIP catalogue record for this book is available from the
British Library.

ISBN 0 7513 0082 9

Reproduced by Colourscan, Singapore
Printed and bound in Great Britain by Butler and Tanner

CONTENTS

INTRODUCTION

For many women, the menopause can be a psychological, emotional, and intellectual turning point as well as a physical one, but it does not have to mean a decline. As your children leave home and you look forward to reducing your workload, you will have more time to yourself than ever before. This can be liberating and you can take the opportunity to reassess your lifestyle, your working patterns, decide what you want from the future, and make some positive changes.

Exercise is an excellent way of maintaining bone health, muscle tone, and joint mobility during the menopause and beyond.

As the menopause approaches, the ovaries begin to fail and there is a sudden dip in our female sex hormones, oestrogen and progesterone, which causes the cessation of menstruation. About three-quarters of all women have some symptoms referable to the suddenness of oestrogen withdrawal, all of which can be treated. There is no need to slide on to the sidelines or to succumb to middle-aged spread if you don't want to. A good diet, combined with exercises to maintain strong healthy bones, will enable you to keep your shape and self-confidence.

Symptoms of the menopause may be both long- and short-term. Short-term symptoms include hot flushes, night sweats, and loss of libido, and some women can experience these for ten years or more. Long-term symptoms include the thinning and drying out of the vaginal and genital skin, and urinary troubles – these may all become permanent. Fortunately, these complaints are not dangerous and can be remedied by many therapies. However, some of the other consequences of the menopause are dangerous and are like bombs waiting to explode. These are osteoporosis or brittle bones, and one in four women who is admitted to hospital with a fractured thigh bone never leaves, so it is important that we are all protected from this disease. Oestrogens depress blood cholesterol and protect us from all forms of heart and vascular disease, including heart attacks and strokes. In this respect, they are truly life-saving.

The good news is that hormone replacement therapy (HRT) can alleviate menopausal symptoms, and many different types are available, such as tablets, skin patches, creams, pessaries, and implants. This means that nearly every woman can take HRT without experiencing side-effects. With knowledge about the effects of HRT on your body, you can negotiate with your doctor on your own terms. In addition to medical help, there are many strategies that you can adopt to manage your own treatment. There is a whole range of alternative therapies, from yoga to aromatherapy.

Any discussion of the menopause will run into controversy. Although we know that 98 percent of menopausal symptoms can be relieved by HRT, hormone replacement is by no means the only way to treat symptoms, which may be related to redundancy, changing family structure, a crisis of self-confidence, or a partner who is himself at one of life's crossroads. In any case, the menopause affects every organ of a woman's body, and any treatment must be viewed in the context of what is good for the whole; that involves diet, exercise, relaxation, yoga, vitamins, minerals, and whatever change in your lifestyle you think would help. Each of the alternative therapies has its own champions.

All muscles, including the pelvic floor muscles, may slacken when oestrogen levels decline.

Far and away the two subjects that remain most hotly debated are, "is the menopause a hormone (oestrogen) deficiency disease?" and, following on from that, "should HRT be made available to any woman who wants to try it?" The first question is crucial because, if your answer is "yes", as mine is, then the inevitable conclusion is that treatment with HRT is justified. After all, no one disagrees with daily insulin injections for a person who has ceased to produce the hormone insulin.

Some medical experts claim that there is no hormone deficiency during the menopause because small amounts of oestrogen are manufactured in fat cells and during exercise. But these amounts are tiny compared to the amounts that we secrete when we are fertile, and when oestrogen falls below a certain level, symptoms such as hot flushes, and frequent, urgent urination can appear, and bone mass decreases. It's then a question of whether these symptoms should be treated. I believe that any symptom that is distressing deserves treating and, while other therapies may help, only HRT has a predictable success rate of 90 percent or above.

We also face the argument that "the menopause is natural and should be left alone". It *isn't* natural. Even it were, it shouldn't be dismissed as trivial, and by no means everything that is natural is good. The menopause is a mistake of nature. Women were never intended to forgo oestrogen. The human female wasn't meant to live beyond her fertile age. Up to the end of the last century the average woman didn't live long enough to experience the menopause. Simply because we are now able to prolong life 30 or 40 years beyond the menopause doesn't mean that women should be penalized with heart disease and osteoporosis – both natural consequences of living beyond 60 – when both these conditions can be prevented with HRT. Prevention is always better than cure. Why ignore one of the most potent tools of preventative medicine because of prejudice and woolly thinking?

HRT is available as tablets, skin patches, implants, and local vaginal creams and pessaries.

Part of the "it's natural" argument is that the menopause is said to be part of the natural ageing process. It isn't. It is due to ovarian failure. Men suffer no comparable drop in their hormones and it is unjust to expect women to tolerate sudden and almost complete withdrawal of their sex hormones.

At the menopause there is a profound hormonal change that may lead to debilitating symptoms in the short-term and fatal diseases in the long-term. In every other area doctors act to change malfunctions and correct mistakes of nature. It's inconsistent to exclude the menopause from this principle.

There still remains the controversy over *who* can take HRT. Alarming stories exist about HRT being the cause of breast cancer, uterine cancer, and blood clots, and therefore dangerous in anyone who has a history of illness related to increased coagulability of the blood, such as heart attack or stroke. In fact, with the exception of uterine cancer, no specific work has been done on the link between HRT and these conditions. Warnings about HRT are indirectly derived from studies on the contraceptive pill, which contains not just a higher dose of hormone, but also different kinds of hormone (the components of HRT are mainly natural oestrogens, whereas those in the pill rarely are). The link between HRT and uterine cancer was referable to the predominantly US habit of prescribing oestrogen without progestogen (ERT). Twenty years ago, research in Europe eradicated the possibility of uterine cancer by adding

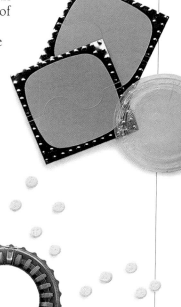

progestogen to the HRT regime. The US still lags behind the rest of the world in adhering to this safe method of prescribing HRT and retains a prejudice against HRT (still thought of as ERT).

Largely because of regulations and the possibility of litigation, drug companies still include long lists of contraindications to HRT on their pack inserts. These lists are outdated. Having performed a careful literature search, I have been unable to find an absolute ban on the use of HRT, since in the hands of a gynaecologist or doctor who is interested in and sympathetic towards you, there is always a way round the problem.

Even when facing the thorny question of previous breast cancer, the aim of HRT should be to alleviate menopausal symptoms while minimizing risks. A sensitive doctor will present the risk/benefit ratio of HRT to a woman – something doctors do every day with other medications – and help her to

There are many alternative therapies, such as herbalism, that will alleviate menopausal symptoms.

weigh up the pros and cons. The severity of a woman's symptoms, and the impact they have on her life should be considered in relation to the potential risks of HRT. This means that some women will choose to take HRT, despite theoretical risks – risks that can be vastly diminished if the doctor uses his or her imagination about the dose and method of taking HRT. For example, local vaginal oestrogen in the form of a cream or a pessary can relieve vaginal and urinary symptoms, and restore sexual pleasure, yet, because the hormones are confined to the pelvis, they will not affect the breasts. Some women find that hot flushes may be relieved by the use of a progestogenic drug called tibolone (see page 102), which will have no adverse effect on the breasts. Research trials are currently underway to evaluate the safety of adding a small daily dose of the drug tamoxifen to HRT for women who have had breast cancer. Tamoxifen is given to premenopausal women as a treatment for breast cancer. There are no longer any grounds for a doctor to deny a woman HRT or to refuse to discuss the risks and benefits with her. Not all woman need oestrogen, but I believe that all women should have the choice. Indeed, I would go further: all women have the right to a four

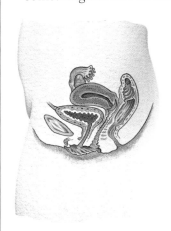

Oestrogen deficiency causes changes to the bladder, vagina, and genitals. These can be reversed by all forms of HRT.

month trial of HRT. After all, you have nothing to lose (you won't incur any risk with such short-term dosage) and everything to gain. In four months you will know if the quality of your life has improved.

To come up to the present day and the forefront of research, we have not only made it possible for all women to take HRT if they want to, but we have also defined a group of women who definitely need HRT – women who would experience a measurable benefit in terms of life expectancy. Anyone who has taken steroids in the past, has had a heart attack, or who has a family history of heart disease can be protected from conditions such as osteoporosis, heart attack, and stroke by HRT. If you are one of these women you should be demanding HRT from your doctor.

Movement therapies such as yoga keep the body supple and promote mental tranquility.

1
PREPARING
FOR THE
MENOPAUSE

*Menopause can be a psychological turning point as well as
a physical one. As children leave home, and you look
forward to reducing your workload, you can take the
opportunity to reassess your lifestyle, working patterns,
and relationships, and make some positive changes.*

PLANNING YOUR FUTURE

The menopause is an important crossroads in your life and, if viewed positively, it can be a rewarding and revealing one. Life is a series of milestones, and whereas in your younger days you rushed past the markers with your eye constantly on the lookout for the next, as you grow older, you tend to slow down, reflect on what you've done, and you may find that it is time to choose a new lifestyle. The menopause is the perfect opportunity to do this.

Making plans for the years ahead is like planning a trip. Look upon it as a reward for a lifetime of work or for bringing up a family. Think about your last big holiday. Half the fun was planning it a long way in advance – perhaps you got out guide books and maps, planned where you wanted to go, and made reservations. The further ahead you planned, the more you anticipated going, and the more you enjoyed the trip. There may have been some unexpected adventures along the way, but because you had prepared yourself thoroughly you were able to cope with any eventuality.

ATTITUDES TOWARDS THE MENOPAUSAL WOMAN
Unfortunately, society rarely views the menopause positively. It remains a taboo subject and, even when it is talked about, it may be referred to in a disparaging or negative way. It is no wonder then that some women dread the menopause. Society, with its emphasis on youth, beauty, and sex, at worst, portrays menopausal women as irrational, neurotic, matronly, or sexually neutral; women are perceived as being controlled by the changes happening within their bodies. The media, with its obsession with youth, relegates middle-aged women to the sidelines, and over a period of time we may gradually become "invisible".

Writers who should know better don't help. Years ago, Robert Wilson in his book *Feminine Forever* headed one of his chapters "Loss of Womanhood and the Loss of Good Health", and described the menopause as "living decay", "a destruction of personality," and "an aberration". Menopausal women, meanwhile, were "eunuchs" who were "dull-minded", "irrational", "deluded", and "incapacitated". Other writers, such as Dr David Reuben, the author of *Everything You Always Wanted To Know About Sex*, perpetuate the view that femininity is inextricably bound up with a woman's ovaries. Once oestrogen production wanes, a woman loses her femininity and virtually becomes a man. Dr Reuben even describes menopausal women as living in the "world of intersex". This is an extraordinary view – think how angry men would be if their masculinity was measured by their testosterone production. This negative picture of the menopause painted by men is far from the truth. The real truth is that it can be a time of new opportunities and challenges that are potentially the best years of our lives.

The lifespan of the modern woman is nearly 80 years, and this means that you will be living a substantial part of your life beyond the menopause. Moreover, you carry the advantage of wisdom that only years of experience can give you. It is essential that you keep a positive outlook, and disregard the myths, misconceptions, and stereotypes perpetuated by society and the media.

A woman who may have devoted a third or a half of her life to raising a family can still have time to go back to college, start a new career, travel, write, learn new skills, and take care of her body so that she is fitter than she ever has been.

The end of fertile life doesn't have to imply new restrictions and physical decline; our options can increase rather than decrease. Try to remember the following positive statements:

- Being well informed and prepared for the menopause will help you deal effectively with symptoms.
- You deserve sympathy and understanding from your partner and family as much as you did at any other time of your life.
- The speed of ageing does not suddenly accelerate after the menopause.
- If you experience menopausal symptoms, talk about them. The menopause is not an unmentionable subject. The more open you are about it, the more you will help to break down taboos.
- You have the right to take control of this stage of your life, as much as any other stage. If you don't want to rely on doctors or medicines, you don't have to. There are plenty of relaxation and meditation techniques, as well as complementary and dietary approaches that can help you deal with symptoms effectively and successfully.
- You can take steps to maintain and even improve the quality of your sex life even though there is less oestrogen in your body. There is no reason why the menopause should be a time of sexual decline.
- There's no time like the present for developing a new hobby or project. You can even embark on a second career. (See the action plan on page 23).
- You should embark on financial planning for retirement as early as possible, to take advantage of what are potentially your most creative years. Financial planning is helpful if you have to simplify your life as you grow older.
- Femininity does not have to equal fertility. The menopause is not the beginning of the end; it's the beginning of the rest of your life.

THE MENOPAUSE TIMETABLE

To understand the changes that happen to us during the menopause, it is necessary to understand the terminology that doctors and others use. Most of the time we use the word "menopause" incorrectly. Strictly speaking, the menopause means the end of menstruation, and could hypothetically be a moment in time. The word "climacteric" more accurately describes the ongoing changes and symptoms, as it refers to a phase or transition period that may last 15–20 years. During this phase, ovarian function and hormonal production decline, and the body adjusts itself to these changes. The word climacteric comes from a Greek word that, literally translated, means "rung of a ladder".

It may help to think of the menopause as being the counterpart of the menarche, which was the time when your periods started. The climacteric can be compared with the years of adolescence or puberty when your ovaries began functioning and maturing. This makes the differences between the menopause and the climacteric clear.

Menopause
- Comparable to menarche.
- A single biological event.
- Cessation of periods.
- Occurs at any one time, usually between the ages of 48 and 52.

Climacteric
- Comparable to puberty.
- A series of hormonal changes.
- Transitional phase when ovarian function and hormones decline.
- Usually spans the ages of 40–60.

THE CLIMACTERIC

This can be divided into three stages: the pre-, peri-, and postmenopause. The menopause is a point in time that signals the end of the premenopause and the beginning of the postmenopause.

Premenopause This refers to the years when your menstrual cycle is regular; in other words, most of your fertile, reproductive life. However, "premenopause" is also sometimes used to refer to the early years of the climacteric, after the age of 40, when menstrual periods may become irregular or heavy. If your doctor ever tells you that you are premenopausal, you should ask for a precise definition of what he or she means.

Perimenopause This is the stage lasting several years on either side of your last menstrual period. This means that the perimenopause is, in part, a retrospective diagnosis, since it's only when your periods cease that you can measure backwards two years in time to when the perimenopause began. Vague symptoms that you may not have connected in your own mind can become significant when viewed as part of the perimenopause. It's during this time that you notice most physical changes, when your periods may become irregular, and when hot flushes may start.

Menopause This has a very precise meaning – the menopause is your final menstrual period. This is another date that can only be identified retrospectively, when you have not had a menstrual bleed for 12 months. In other words, it is impossible for a woman to know the exact moment in time that she is experiencing the menopause.

Postmenopause This overlaps with the end of the perimenopausal stage and will extend into the years that follow your last menstrual period until the end of your life.

Symptom Timetable
Some symptoms, such as hot flushes, are associated with the perimenopause, and will be present during the years immediately before and after the menopause. Other symptoms, such as dry skin, may be due to a long-term deficiency of oestrogen and will last for the entire postmenopause. The severity of your symptoms will depend on how much oestrogen is present in your body, and what self-help measures you adopt. Not all menopausal symptoms are inevitable, for instance many women never suffer from prolapse.

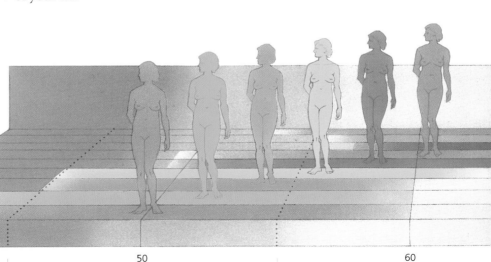

40 years   50   60

perimenopause

CAN I PREDICT MY LAST MENSTRUAL PERIOD?

Most women anticipate that they will experience their last menstrual period around the time that they reach 50, though the average age for the menopause in the UK is 51 years of age. This age has remained fairly constant over the centuries, even though the average age for the onset of menstruation has become earlier. Roughly half of all women will stop menstruating before they turn 51, and half will stop menstruating afterwards. Studies carried out on women in the United States show that 90 percent of women experience a natural menopause by the age of 54; and 100 percent of women have stopped menstruating by the age of 58.

There is no need to be alarmed if you stop menstruating before your 45th birthday. As has been shown by statistics, this happens to approximately a third of all women and is not necessarily a sign of any abnormality. At the other end of the scale, many women carry on menstruating into their early 50s, and a few into their mid-50s.

Although there is no way in which you can predict exactly when your menopause will occur, research has shown that there are several factors that may influence its timing. It is thought that the age you begin to menstruate may affect the age that you experience the menopause, but no studies have yet proved this. It is possible that the age at which your mother experienced the menopause will have some bearing on when you stop menstruating, but again this relationship has not been scientifically proven.

Studies have shown that two factors that definitely do not influence the time of your menopause are whether or not you took the oral contraceptive pill, or your age when you had your first and last child. We each have an individual biological clock that is probably programmed before birth to set off the hormonal events that trigger the beginning and the end of menstruation. The physical or behavioural factors overleaf, such as weight and smoking, are likely to influence the timing of the menopause by causing our internal clock to either slow down or speed up.

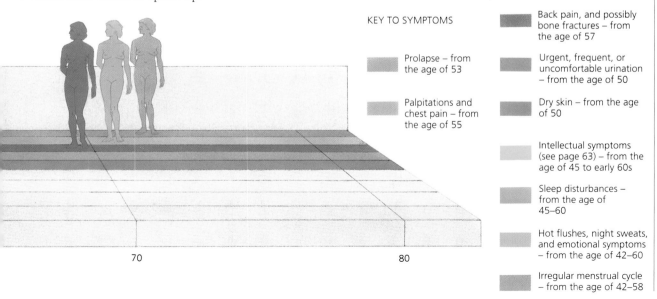

KEY TO SYMPTOMS

Prolapse – from the age of 53

Palpitations and chest pain – from the age of 55

Back pain, and possibly bone fractures – from the age of 57

Urgent, frequent, or uncomfortable urination – from the age of 50

Dry skin – from the age of 50

Intellectual symptoms (see page 63) – from the age of 45 to early 60s

Sleep disturbances – from the age of 45–60

Hot flushes, night sweats, and emotional symptoms – from the age of 42–60

Irregular menstrual cycle – from the age of 42–58

70   80

Diet Several studies have shown that nutrition is a significant factor in determining the age that a woman enters the climacteric. Under-nourished women start the menopause earlier than those who are well nourished (for instance, at 43 instead of 47). European women have a later menopause than American women, and healthier eating habits have been implicated.

Smoking As a group, smokers experience an earlier menopause than non-smokers, and there are two possible explanations for this phenomenon. First, smoking may decrease the secretion of oestrogen from the ovaries. Smokers have lower levels of oestrogen in their bloodstreams, and it's conceivable that nicotine, which acts on the central nervous system, may slow down the production of ovarian stimulating hormones. Second, nicotine may activate enzymes within the liver that metabolize our sex hormones, speeding up the rate at which they are removed from the body.

Body Weight Women who weigh more than 59 kg (130 lb) tend to experience the menopause later than women who weigh less than this. Oestrogen is manufactured in fat cells as well as in the ovaries, so the more fat a woman carries, the more oestrogen she creates, and the longer her menstrual cycle continues.

Medical Conditions Women who have fibroids or diabetes may experience a later-than-average menopause. Again, this is because they have higher levels of oestrogen than usual.

PREMATURE MENOPAUSE
Less than one percent of women experience the menopause before the age of 35. However, women who do have a premature menopause can suffer an early onset of symptoms and may need a higher than average dose of hormones in hormone replacement therapy (HRT; see chapter 6) to alleviate them. Premature menopause also means that the childbearing years are shortened. Research is now being conducted on methods to facilitate pregnancy in prematurely menopausal women. The most promising treatment at the moment is a combination therapy of natural oestrogen and progesterone applied as a skin patch. This simulates a natural menstrual cycle and makes an ovum (egg) donated by another woman more likely to be accepted by the recipient.

The Timing of the Menopause
Although it is impossible to predict when you will stop menstruating, there are certain factors that will make your menopause earlier or later. For example, smoking may cause an earlier than usual menopause, and obesity may cause a later than usual menopause.

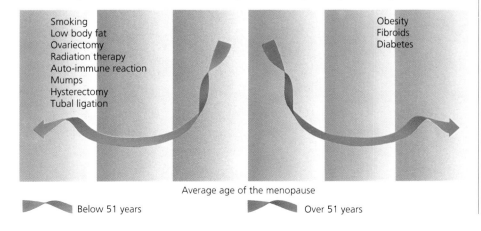

Smoking
Low body fat
Ovariectomy
Radiation therapy
Auto-immune reaction
Mumps
Hysterectomy
Tubal ligation

Obesity
Fibroids
Diabetes

Average age of the menopause

Below 51 years   Over 51 years

Surgical Removal Of The Ovaries This is by far the commonest cause of premature menopause. Both ovaries must be removed for the menopause to occur, since a single ovary, or even a portion of an ovary, can continue to produce ova (eggs) and hormones as efficiently as if both ovaries were still there. You should only have your ovaries removed if they have been destroyed by an ovarian tumour (see page 75), pelvic inflammatory disease, or cancer. Removal is often carried out unnecessarily during hysterectomy (see page 76). Before you agree to an oophorectomy (also called an ovariectomy), make sure that your doctor can give you a satisfactory reason for the removal of your ovaries. Doctors often argue that the ovaries should be removed to prevent the later development of ovarian cancer, to avoid the risk of ovarian failure due to the absence of the uterus (very rare, and unproven), or to prevent future surgery to remove ovarian cysts, should they occur. The counter argument is that none of these problems are actually present at the time of surgery and may never even develop; therefore surgery may be quite unnecessary.

Radiation Therapy The menopause may come early if the ovaries have received significant doses of radiation, for instance, during treatment for cancers of the abdomen and pelvis. This is why the ovaries should be protected by a lead apron when X-rays are taken.

Hysterectomy And Tubal Ligation After a hysterectomy in which the ovaries are left behind, women usually experience a loss of ovarian function five years earlier than they would do normally. Tubal ligation, a sterilization procedure, should not have the same effect. If it does, it is due to interference with the blood supply to the ovaries.

Mumps Very rarely, the ovaries can be damaged by the mumps virus, leading to a premature menopause. Mumps may cause irreparable damage to the ovaries, in the same way that it may damage a man's testes.

Auto-immune Reaction Auto-immune diseases, such as lupus erythematosus (a disease of the connective tissue), or rheumatoid arthritis (see page 86), may cause a woman's body to start producing antibodies that react against her ovaries as foreign tissue, and attack them. This process may destroy the supply of eggs in the ovaries and reduce the output of female hormones. This is another cause of an early (premature) menopause.

LATE MENOPAUSE
If you're still menstruating after the age of 55, you are considered to have a delayed or late menopause. For women who are overweight and producing extra amounts of oestrogen, regular periods continuing into the late 50s can be perfectly natural. However, you should talk to your doctor and have a precautionary check-up. There could be another cause for your late menopause, such as fibroids (see page 95).

You should also be aware of the health hazards associated with a late menopause. Because your fertile life is prolonged, your body is exposed to oestrogen for longer than usual, and this can slightly increase your risk of uterine and breast cancer. For this reason, you should make sure that you have an annual mammography, pelvic examination, and smear test.

SYMPTOM TIMETABLE
The cessation of female hormone production has an effect on every part of the body and can lead to a range of symptoms. The peri- and postmenopause are each associated with specific symptoms.

Early Symptoms These may be experienced when your periods become erratic and irregular. The first two are the classic symptoms.

- Hot flushes.
- Night sweats.
- Anxiety.
- Irritability.
- Loss of interest in sex.
- Itchiness of the skin.
- Insomnia.
- Mood changes.
- Loss of memory.
- Loss of confidence and self-esteem.
- Headaches.
- Dry vagina.
- Genital itching.
- Painful sex.

Intermediate Symptoms These symptoms mainly affect the bladder and genitals and they may not appear until your periods have stopped. They form part of the late perimenopause.

- Vaginal dryness.
- Pain on intercourse.
- Symptoms of vaginal thinning, such as genital itching.
- The need to pass urine urgently and frequently, perhaps accompanied by a burning sensation.
- Loss of bladder control.
- Generalized muscle aches and pains.
- Thinning skin and hair.

(A combination of the first five symptoms is known as urogenital ageing; see page 90.)

Late Symptoms Serious medical problems are most likely to occur during the postmenopause, due to low levels of oestrogen. Women who are over 60 are the most vulnerable.

- High blood pressure and angina that may indicate arterial and heart disease, and a risk of stroke related to atherosclerosis (see page 79).
- General aches and pains, backache, joint stiffness and swelling, spinal curvature, and bone fractures – all problems related to osteoporosis.

SEVERITY OF SYMPTOMS

Slightly more than three-quarters of all women will experience one or more symptoms during the climacteric. Only one in three women, however, will be distressed enough to seek medical help. These statistics beg the questions, what is meant by distress? And, how do we measure severity of symptoms? Some women may rightly argue that they don't wish to suffer any distress and that any symptom that interferes with normal life is severe. In my opinion, symptoms shouldn't have to be severe in order to go to a doctor, nor should they have to interfere significantly with day-to-day life to warrant treatment.

You can assess your menopausal distress level by completing the inventory opposite, known as the Kupperman Menopausal Index. In the column titled "severity", enter the number that most accurately reflects the severity of your current symptoms: 0 for no symptoms and 3 for severe symptoms. Then multiply your severity score by the number listed in the column titled "factor". Add up the figures for each symptom.

If your score is higher than 35, you have severe menopausal symptoms. If your score is less than 20, your symptoms are said to be mild. Even if you have mild symptoms, you shouldn't be deterred from asking your doctor for treatment or from finding remedies for yourself. If your doctor is not sympathetic, look around for one who is.

CALCULATING YOUR MENOPAUSAL DISTRESS

Symptom	Factor	x	Severity (0–3)	= Number
Hot flushes or night sweats	4	x		=
Genital burning or itching	2	x		=
Insomnia	2	x		=
Nervousness	2	x		=
Depression	1	x		=
Dizziness	1	x		=
Fatigue	1	x		=
Aches and pains	1	x		=
Headache	1	x		=
Palpitations	1	x		=
Formication	1	x		=
(itching and tingling) of skin				
			TOTAL	

WHY DO SOME WOMEN SUFFER MORE THAN OTHERS?

It's clear that changing ovarian physiology is only one of the factors that determine how severe menopausal symptoms are. Other factors include our initial genetic programming, upbringing, attitudes towards our bodies and ourselves, lifestyle, education, and diet. Although we don't know exactly how much these influence menopausal distress, we can generalize. Profile A (below) describes characteristics that are associated with low menopausal distress. Profile B (below) describes characteristics associated with high menopausal distress.

Profile A
- Unmarried.
- Had children after the age of 40 or never been pregnant.
- Started to menstruate at a relatively late age.
- Reasonably high income and relatively well educated.
- Above average amount of body fat.

Profile B
- Married.
- Mother.
- Has undergone premature menopause (natural or surgical).
- Suffered dysmenorrhoea (painful periods).
- Suffered severe PMS.
- Below average amount of body fat.

There are no hard and fast rules, however, and in addition to these characteristics there are other factors that may affect a woman's ability to adjust to climacteric changes. Some studies have tried to identify a personality type that is associated with a difficult climacteric, but I prefer to look at a woman's life events and the obstacles she has had to overcome.

In general, women with a history of emotional problems will have the hardest time. This includes women who have been sexually abused as children, women with chronic sexual difficulties, women whose sexual attractiveness forms a chief part of their identity, childless women facing the loss of fertility, women who are prone to depression, and married women who have invested a great deal in their children and feel that their meaningful years are over.

THE EMPTY NEST SYNDROME

The observation that women who react badly to the climacteric have a low opinion of themselves is not a new one. Particularly vulnerable are women who have defined their role in life in terms of pregnancy and motherhood. For such women the menopause can take away part of their identity, and in some cases can make them feel purposeless. If motherhood was the focal point of your life, it is easy to understand how the climacteric can bring a sense of loss. The same is true for women who have never had children, but have wanted to.

Many women, to varying degrees, suppress their own desires, talents, and personal growth, and invest all their energies into caring for their children, husbands, and families, so that they only express themselves through the activities and accomplishments of others. When their children leave home, they may undergo an emotional and intellectual trauma similar to bereavement. Such women have to find a new focus to their lives, and the climacteric can be a time of major reassessment. Being aware of this eventuality means that a woman can prepare herself, perhaps by taking up activities or hobbies, and making career moves.

Because Western culture celebrates youth, many women fear growing older, and this can affect the way they handle the climacteric. We all have to deal with ageing at some time in our lives and we may feel forced to do so around the time of the menopause. Difficulties can arise when we try to continue living life exactly as we did in our 30s. Women who accept the climacteric as a natural progression of life are much more likely to sail through it than women who see it as something complicated, mysterious, and negative. If you have interests outside of the home, a job you enjoy, intellectual and creative outlets, challenging responsibilities, and lots of mental stimulation, you will almost certainly have an easier time during the menopause. At the very least, you will have less time to think about your symptoms. Knowledge of the physiological details of the climacteric and familiarity with the workings of your own body will help to keep up your self-esteem.

MENSTRUAL PATTERNS

Our bodies dislike change. Given time we can adjust to anything, but sudden change nearly always causes physical distress. Therefore, the rate at which oestrogen levels drop is another variable that can influence the number and severity of climacteric symptoms we experience. No one can tell us how quickly or slowly our oestrogen levels are waning, but most of us experience one of three typical patterns.

Abrupt Ending This is the immediate cessation of menstruation when periods stop without any warning at all. It is quite unusual because the ovaries very rarely stop functioning suddenly. Ovarian activity more characteristically wanes slowly. If oestrogen supplies cease abruptly, the chance of your experiencing uncomfortable symptoms is therefore much greater (although this is not an absolute rule – some women who fall into this category have registered relatively few symptoms).

Gradual Ending This is a much more common way for women to experience the menopause and involves a progressive decline in both the amount and duration of the menstrual flow. Typically, periods become shorter, less frequent, or are even skipped, until finally they terminate altogether. You may not even be aware of the irregularity of your menstrual cycle until something alerts you to it. With this pattern, your symptoms may be insignificant or easy to deal with, since your ovaries continue to supply small amounts of oestrogen, and your body is given time to adjust.

Irregular Ending Relatively common is the irregular menstrual pattern in which flow becomes sporadic. It may become heavier, then lighter, or it may alternate. The number of days between periods may increase or decrease. Some women may go for months on end without a period, and then without warning start menstruating again. Many babies have been born to women who mistakenly thought they had experienced the menopause and were "safe". I would advise you to continue birth control (see page 121) for two years after your last menstrual period as a precaution.

TESTS THAT TELL YOU WHEN YOU ARE MENOPAUSAL

Simply measuring levels of oestrogen in the blood is not an effective way of diagnosing menopausal status because oestrogen levels fluctuate so greatly. However, blood levels of follicle-stimulating hormone (FSH), secreted by the pituitary gland, give a much more accurate picture. FSH levels tend to rise dramatically around the time of the menopause as a result of decreasing oestrogen levels (see page 198), and are an accurate reflection of what is happening in the ovaries. A doctor may be able to arrange this test for you.

A vaginal smear will reveal the state of the cells lining your vagina. These cells can be studied under a microscope to help determine whether you're near or past your menopause. When oestrogen production is normal, vaginal cells

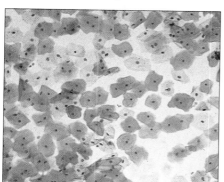
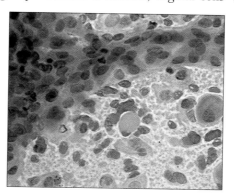

Vaginal Atrophy
Before the menopause, vaginal cells are large and flat with small nuclei (see far left). After the menopause, the cells become thin and dry, and appear clumped together, with large nuclei (see left). This may cause soreness, and an increase in the likelihood of vaginal infection.

are thick, numerous, and healthy, whereas when oestrogen levels fall, cells become thin, sparse, and look quite different under a microscope. Both cervical and vaginal smears are carried out in the same way, although the former is a more common procedure.

MONITORING YOUR PERIODS

It can be helpful to keep track of your periods as you approach the menopause – you can follow irregularities more closely and be alerted to signs of possible problems. Using a calendar, indicate with a star the first and last days of bleeding, and indicate with the letters "l", "m", or "h" whether your flow was light, moderate, or heavy on each day. Make a note of any spotting or bleeding that occurs at any other time of the month, particularly after sex. Also note any changes in your mood and any premenstrual symptoms that you experience.

Keeping this type of detailed menstrual diary will make you observe your body closely, and you should become more confident about how your body works. This will give you a feeling of control, and it will give you an early warning of any potential problems so that you can consult your doctor or gynaecologist. If you notice any of the following patterns, it is important to discuss them with your doctor, even though they may be temporary and perfectly normal signs of the menopause.

- Very heavy periods with clots.
- A particularly long period.
- Periods that occur more frequently than every 21 days (count from the first day of one period to the first day of your next period).
- Any bleeding whatsoever between periods.
- Severe menstrual cramps that you've never experienced before.
- Bleeding that begins after 12 period-free months.
- Bleeding after sexual intercourse.
- Any bleeding or pain that is particularly unusual for you.

DEVELOPING A POSITIVE ATTITUDE

The first step in developing a positive attitude towards the menopause is to look back and assess what we have already accomplished. This can reassure us and give us the impetus we need to make decisions about the future. If we forget to acknowledge what we've already done, we can make future goals seem much less attainable.

No matter how active we've been, or what contributions we have made to our work and our family, contemplation of the future can bring mixed emotions. We may find ourselves debating two alternatives: trying to continue living and working as we have always done; or starting to make changes, perhaps reducing our workload. You might justifiably say to yourself that you've been working all your life, so why should you feel guilty for not working now? It's important as we get older to learn how to enjoy leisure time and to find new and varied diversions.

Find out what excites and motivates you. Stop spending time on things that don't interest you, household chores for example. You have as much potential as when you were young, but now you are better equipped to harness it. Make a list of things you "must" do in the rest of your life. For example, Janet Lowe, chief executive of the Digital Equipment Corporation, at the age of 46, said,

"I still feel I have at least two more careers in me". She felt the desire, even after a crowded professional life, to go into industry and "manufacture something" – a task that she'd never attempted before. Another thing she'd always wanted to do was to "generate money", and even as the menopause approached, she decided to raise 20 million dollars to support her new career.

Some women break out of their usual lifestyle after many years as wife, mother, and family caretaker to indulge an entrepreneurial spirit and branch out entirely on their own, perhaps setting up a guest house, opening a shop, or running a small business. You may remember your mother in her 50s claiming that she was growing old. If you're still alive at 85, as my mother is, 35 years is a long time to be old, and an intolerable length of time to be inactive.

We have a responsibility to ourselves to make the most of each month, year, and decade. Repeat this to yourself every day, and if you feel you lack energy, heed the advice of Merlin Stone: the best technique is to get angry, particularly if you feel you've stifled your anger and held back in the past. Put yourself in touch with your anger, and use it as fuel. It's absolutely crucial to respect and to trust who you are. You need self-respect before you can respect others and understand them as individuals. Older women are perceptive, experienced, and wise about relationships and life. We can benefit even more from joining a group of women of a similar age to us and sharing our experiences.

Female Role Models

There are comparatively few older women who enjoy a high profile in society. This may in part be due to the process of "invisibility" that women undergo as they reach midlife. The women featured here have all been successful, not just in their youth, but during and after the menopause as well.

Vivienne Westwood
UK fashion designer

Tina Turner
US pop singer and celebrity

Margaret Thatcher
Former British Prime Minister

Brigitte Bardot
French actress and animal activist

Kiri Te Kanawa
New Zealand opera singer

Billie Jean King
US tennis player and coach

Lauren Hutton
US model and actress

Maya Angelou
US activist and writer

If you think your goals and visions seem impossible or idealistic, read about women who have accomplished things in the second halves of their lives – you'll find it inspirational and encouraging. At the age of 42, the ballerina Margot Fonteyn, partnered by Rudolph Nureyev (then aged 23), was aware that everyone would be judging the way they looked together. She responded by making sure that she was strong enough to keep up with him. She did this by filling her repertoire with her most difficult roles so that her stamina, strength, discipline, and most of all her courage would never drop below her already high standards.

Find yourself a role model for continuing a productive and creative life, forget about your weaknesses, list all your strengths, and then go out to make your ideas reality.

COMPILING A SKILLS PROFILE

We all have more skills, achievements, and resources than we imagine, and it's a very useful exercise to list them. Doing this is the antidote to feeling inadequate and jaded, and it gives us a firm basis on which to plan future programmes of self-development. You can set your own framework for doing this, or you can follow these guidelines; use the following questions I have suggested and adapt them to your needs.

WHAT ARE MY SKILLS?

In answer to this you should list a broad range of your personal strengths. You may be surprised just how many skills you can come up with; do not undervalue yourself. You could note qualities like "calm under pressure", "good at making decisions", "good listener". Also include physical strengths like "lots of stamina". Now list your experience. If you've raised a family and kept a home, you can do domestic jobs, budget and cater efficiently, and you can motivate and coordinate a group. Note down your job experience and any other experiences that you see as accomplishments. You will end up with a curriculum vitae of your life experience, including your education, jobs, hobbies, and achievements.

WHAT WOULD I LIKE TO DO?

Under this heading, note down everything that you have always wanted to do and haven't yet done. You may have wanted to paint, write, learn DIY, ride a horse, ski, or do voluntary work. Now is the ideal opportunity to realize those unfulfilled ambitions, so don't leave anything out. Make an exhaustive list – nothing is too silly to write down.

HOW CAN I IMPROVE MY SKILLS?

Ask yourself whether it is possible to take a refresher course in a skill that you previously learned, such as computer programming. Or are there any skills that you could train or retrain yourself in? Consider everything from languages and typing to abseiling and driving. Would you like to go back to college full time or part time? Would you choose vocational training like hairdressing or carpentry, a course that would result in extra qualifications, or something purely for your own pleasure? Think about enrolling for night classes as a trial, to see if you like a subject.

HOW CAN I APPLY MY SKILLS?

In order to evaluate how you might best use your skills – both actual and prospective – you need to consider exactly what kind of work you would like to do. Factors such as time available, transport, location, finance, and domestic responsibilities will obviously be relevant here. Does your life allow you to do voluntary work, full-time paid work, or part-time work? Could you work flexitime? Do you have financial requirements that need to be met? Could you work in the evenings or at night? Do you have to rely on public transport, and, if so, are you prepared to travel distances away from home? What openings would you consider? What would you definitely not consider? What would be the ideal way to spend your time? Imagine that the sky is the limit and write down every single opportunity that might be right for you. Don't dismiss anything at this stage.

ACTION PLAN

Review the profile that you have created from the previous four questions. What kind of work suggests itself? Show your notes to your partner and discuss them. Does he have any suggestions? Consult your friends as well. Type up a conventional CV from your profile and take it to an employment centre or agency and ask if they have any suitable openings. You may also find it useful to visit your local careers library in order to find out what options there are available to you. It may be possible to arrange a careers interview, where you may also receive help in compiling your CV.

If you decide to improve your skills with further training, consult your local college timetable and see if you can draw up a programme for the medium-term future, which includes a training course with a certain goal in mind. List every action that you are going to take and establish deadlines for yourself. Make sure your aims are practical and possible to achieve within a reasonable period of time to avoid becoming disheartened. When you are satisfied with your plans, it's a good idea to have some positive feedback from others, so discuss this action plan with your partner and friends – their support will act as encouragement and it will be the first step in putting your plans into action.

Back-To-Work Plan
Using your skills profile, develop a plan that is best suited to your needs and abilities.

THE MALE MENOPAUSE

If your life is disrupted by the perimenopause, then your partner is likely to suffer disruptions too. Unless you're both aware of this, and take mutual responsibility, the climacteric can be quite stormy. While there may not be a male equivalent of the menopause, middle-aged men sometimes behave unpredictably. They may stray from their wives towards younger women, they may suddenly buy an expensive car, or they may begin to dress and act flamboyantly. It's legitimate to ask whether men go through hormonal changes that create physical, emotional, and behavioural changes.

To date, there is no evidence to suggest that men do experience major hormonal or psychological changes in midlife. Minor chemical and hormonal changes do occur, but they are relatively insignificant. A study of male patients who claimed to be suffering from a male menopause found that there was no age-related increase in depression or tiredness. The symptoms that do increase in men with advancing age are disturbed sleep, failing memory, and a waning sex drive. Although these symptoms resemble female symptoms, there is a major difference: male symptoms are not clustered between the ages of 45–55; they simply increase slowly as a man ages.

If men don't have a menopause, what causes the changes in behaviour that some middle-aged men exhibit? The answer to this may stem from the fact that the 50s are a time when most of us are reminded of the deterioration of our physical and mental capacities. We all begin to have intimations of mortality and may feel forced to take stock of our lives.

If men feel that they have not achieved as much as they would have liked to, or that they are losing their grip at work because younger colleagues are snapping at their heels, they may be worried that time is running out, and feeling very anxious as a result. What you may perceive as odd behaviour could be an expression of your partner's need for recognition and reassurance. He needs to feel in control and worthwhile, and sometimes a new relationship or material possessions are a misdirected attempt to get rid of his feelings of inadequacy.

If your partner is well balanced, this time may be manageable and thought provoking. For others, it can be incredibly frightening and a time of emotional turmoil. It can be especially difficult if your partner experiences these problems at the same time as you are perimenopausal. When you feel that you most need your partner for support and reassurance, he may be feeling the need to prove himself outside of your relationship.

Many of us fear death and ageing, but, ironically, men may be the weaker sex in midlife, because they are more prone to heart disease. Men may also feel especially vulnerable if they witness one or more of their friends or colleagues suffering from heart disease, cancer, or a stroke.

SURVIVING A TURBULENT RELATIONSHIP

How you and your partner negotiate the potentially choppy waters of the middle years is largely to do with your view of each other. You may be suffering symptoms of the climacteric, and be living with a man who's feeling insecure, defensive, and possibly aggressive. Admitting that you both have a clash of interests at this time is the first step towards dealing with problems.

It's possible that part of your partner's awareness of the problems in his life are triggered by your perimenopausal symptoms and vice versa. If he seems unsympathetic, you may feel that this is an unfair and sad response to the years of commitment and loyalty that you've both shared. But your partner may be feeling a very deep desire to run away from confronting the fact of his own ageing. Women, it seems, are much better at accepting the changes of age both in themselves and in their partners. A man, on the other hand, may notice changes in your appearance, but because he feels young, may consider that he still looks youthful and fail to relate your ageing to his. Finally, when he is forced to confront his age, he gets an enormous shock that may precipitate changes in his behaviour. He tries to flee from reminders that he's getting older, whether it is your symptoms, the fact that you find sex painful, or that you have to change the bed linen because of your night sweats. Instead of helping you to cope, he may be plunged into despair. In extreme cases, men may experience a loss of sex drive or embark on an affair.

COMMUNICATING WITH YOUR PARTNER
All of the above problems can be dealt with by honest, open communication, and the last thing you should do is blame yourself. You can work through problems once you understand them, so try to get your partner to explain his feelings to you. Don't abandon the relationship to silence or infidelity. Encourage your partner to take the space and time to relax quietly and do some soul-searching about his feelings, his past accomplishments, and what he wants from the rest of his life. Remind him of a few achievements that he should feel proud of and help him to evaluate his current set of values. What does he think is important? Does he want to continue his working life at the present rate? How could he give himself more free time? Ask him about his emotional response to ageing. Is it making him feel resentful, or angry, or despondent? What about his attitude towards your ageing? Does he feel that the two of you are growing apart? Is it possible to build bridges? Could you come together again and build a new sense of companionship?

Explain to him that you recognize this time of life holds potential problems for you both. Tell him about your feelings and what you think is happening in both of your lives. Include your negative feelings, but also the options that you think are opening up for you, and for the two of you together. Tell him about your experience of the climacteric. Make him understand that you accept growing older and that you're going to concentrate on living and building a happy, active, and interesting future.

LESSONS FROM OTHER CULTURES
Western culture with its accent on youth, fashion, and sex necessarily labels middle-age as unfashionable and unsexy. It's hardly surprising that women become infected by negative attitudes towards ageing and the climacteric when they are surrounded by media images that perpetuate such a stereotypical view of femininity. In many non-Western cultures, however, less emphasis is placed on youth and glamour, and the menopause is a marker of increased social status, and therefore viewed very positively. Women in these cultures report comparatively few menopausal problems and depression is a rarity.

There are some cultures in which women do not appear to have menopausal symptoms. In one study, 500 Indian women reported that they were free of menopausal symptoms. Not a single woman mentioned hot flushes, or other signs or symptoms of menopausal distress. If hot flushes are culturally induced,

SELF-HELP STRATEGIES
- Try to talk rather than argue with each other.
- If your children are still living with you, explain to them, as honestly as you can, the problems you and your partner are having. Don't assume they won't notice.
- Seek help. Organizations such as Relate exist to counsel couples facing emotional problems (see page 219).
- Don't act as a prop for your partner. The sooner you discuss your problems, the sooner they can be resolved.
- Develop a sense of independence, so that you can be more objective about your relationship.

25

CULTURAL BELIEFS

Although the menopause is a universal biological phenomenon, it is perceived and experienced differently in other cultures from our own. In some traditional societies, where women live as part of an extended family alongside their children and their children's children, menopause can confer new status, power, and prestige. A woman may take on a new influential role in which she advises her children about childrearing and helps to look after and educate her grandchildren.

CANADA
After the menopause, the Cree women in Canada are entitled to exercise shamanic and healing powers.

AMERICA
In the US, the menopause may represent the start of the ageing process, which is perceived as negative. Black American women may pass more easily through the menopause, perhaps because they seem to associate age with sexual maturity.

MEXICO
Age is looked upon positively, and Mexican women are unlikely to seek medical help at the time of the menopause.

AFRICA
For some African women, the menopause signals a higher status when they can command the labour of their juniors. For the Kung women of Botswana, the postmenopause is a time of sexual liberation.

UNITED KINGDOM

Women in Western cultures are more inclined to perceive the menopause as a medical condition requiring treatment. Because of the emphasis on sexual attractiveness in the West, some women may see the menopause as the end of youth and femininity, and the beginning of sexual decline.

GREECE

A study of Greek women on the island of Evia found that they suffered from few symptoms that are conventionally associated with the menopause. They also held very few negative expectations of the menopause.

JAPAN

Japanese women complain of relatively few symptoms, but they do suffer from complaints such as headaches and stiff shoulders. Japanese culture may encourage women to repress symptoms.

CHINA

Studies show that Chinese women perceive the menopause as a natural event and are unlikely to consult their doctors about symptoms. HRT is rarely prescribed.

INDIA

In Rajasthan, women who are postmenopausal no longer have to wear a veil. Older women are treated with heightened respect, and play an important decision-making role in the family.

INDONESIA

Ageing and maturity are venerated, and women have fewer menopausal symptoms than women in the West.

it is an extraordinary and sad reflection of the influence of culture on women. However, I believe that this is not quite the true picture. It is much more likely that cultural influences affect women's ability to tolerate menopausal distress, not cause it. In a society where ageing is celebrated, a woman may be able to cope with distressing symptoms much more easily than she can in one where she feels devalued.

A recent study of menopausal Japanese women revealed some interesting cultural differences from menopausal Western women. More than a thousand women were studied – as well as their Japanese doctors – in order to investigate how Japanese women and the medical community view the menopause. The qualities of self-control and the ability to sustain a balanced outlook are considered important aspects of health among the Japanese. It is considered healthy to repress physical and psychological symptoms. Japanese women therefore tend not to complain when they do have symptoms.

Another difference was in the type of symptoms that were reported. Although one in ten women reported hot flushes, two other "Japanese" symptoms of the menopause occurred with greater frequency. These were stiff shoulders and headaches (more one in two women reported suffering from stiff shoulders, and nearly one in three suffered from headaches).

Chinese women living in Hong Kong are more likely to receive reassurance than medication for menopausal symptoms. One study found that less than a sixth of women had consulted their doctors about problems relating to the menopause and only two percent were offered HRT. The women who were not offered HRT were reassured that the menopause was natural. This attitude of doctors affects women's expectations of treatment and the degree to which they ask for medical help. The reluctance of some Western doctors to take the menopause seriously may have a detrimental effect on a woman's interpretation of the symptoms, encouraging her to blame herself.

In another study of Hong Kong's Chinese women, between 66–80 percent of women complained of menopausal symptoms, although hot flushes were only recorded in 10–24 percent of women (in contrast, over 85 percent of Western women suffer from hot flushes). Emotional symptoms, such as nervousness, irritability, depression and insomnia, were reported in as many as 70 percent.

THE MENOPAUSE AS A MEDICAL CONDITION

The process of medicalization of the menopause can be dangerous, as was found in a study of menopausal women in north-eastern Thailand. This study explored the different ways that the menopause was perceived by the village women and their health carers. Whereas the village women viewed the menopause as a natural biological event, their medical and health carers perceived it as a hormone deficiency disease. During the perimenopause, a number of women suffering from irregular periods and hot flushes consulted their health carers and were told that their symptoms could be "cured" with HRT. Thus the menopause became a condition requiring medication, rather than a natural occurrence.

What we should be trying to achieve is a balance between seeing the menopause as a natural life event and seeing it as a hormone deficiency state. Without question, the degree to which a woman suffers from symptoms will be affected by her feelings of self-worth and usefulness, prevailing cultural values, and the extent of her health and fitness.

2
WHAT HAPPENS DURING THE MENOPAUSE

As the supply of eggs in a woman's ovaries dwindles, the two hormones oestrogen and progesterone fluctuate and then begin to decline. This produces the hallmark of midlife – the end of menstrual periods – but it also has manifold effects on the rest of the body. Menopausal symptoms are felt largely because of the suddenness of oestrogen withdrawal; if this deficiency is counteracted with HRT, good diet, and proper exercise, bones will remain strong, hair and skin will stay healthy, and you will keep your shape, and positive attitudes to life.

MIDLIFE MENSTRUAL CHANGE

I would like to begin this chapter by saying what does *not* happen during the menopause – or rather, what *need* not happen during the menopause. Myths abound and they are rarely contradicted because, as Gail Sheehy explained in her book *The Silent Passage*, the menopause is not often talked about. The first myth I'd like to explode is that the menopause is a disease. Like pregnancy, which has also become medicalized in Western culture, the menopause should be monitored carefully so that problems are avoided, abnormalities are corrected, and complications are treated. Nor is the menopause a psychological crisis. It may be a change, but we cope with a series of changes in our lives without drama. And looking back, we would regard many changes as positive, particularly if they free us to focus on priorities. The menopause does not usher in old age – it is part of a continual life cycle. Postmenopausal women don't lose their femininity, nor do they stop being attractive. Far from it. As we get older we take on fresh allure and sex appeal, based on confidence and wisdom.

It is well known that the menopause can very occasionally occur in women in their teens and early twenties, but the average age in the Western world is 51 years. The climacteric – the interval between the beginning and the end of menopausal symptoms – can span seven or more years. During this time your menstrual cycle will become increasingly irregular and, ultimately, there is a complete cessation of menses and the menopause occurs.

Menstrual changes vary from woman to woman. Some women experience a shorter cycle – menstruation every 20 or so days is not uncommon – others find themselves menstruating less frequently, perhaps only once every six months. The flow pattern may also change; a woman may go on bleeding regularly but notice that the number of days of menstrual flow are fewer, or that the flow itself is diminished. On the other hand, flow may increase. You could have a shorter cycle with heavier bleeding, or fewer cycles with many days of very light flow. However, less bleeding, less often is the commonest pattern.

Ninety percent of women who don't menstruate for six months will not menstruate again. But some women may have intervals of no menses and then irregular menses for quite a number of years. It is important to understand that there is no fixed pattern of change.

EFFECTS OF FALLING HORMONE LEVELS

If you have a history of regular menstruation, your oestrogen and progesterone levels will have been changing daily in a predictable and orderly rhythm. As you become menopausal, your menstrual cycle is likely to change, reflecting the major upheavals in hormone secretion in your body. Oestrogen levels in the first two weeks of the cycle get lower and lower – this is because fewer egg follicles are stimulated to grow. In addition, ovulation becomes less likely since the supply of eggs is running out. If ovulation *does* occur, conception is less likely, since the quality of the eggs released is more likely to be substandard.

Without ovulation there is no corpus luteum to produce progesterone (see column). As a consequence, oestrogen stimulates the growth of the uterine lining in the first half of the month, which becomes unopposed by progesterone in the second half. Without progesterone the endometrium becomes thicker and thicker, and the result can be heavy bleeding (see page 94).

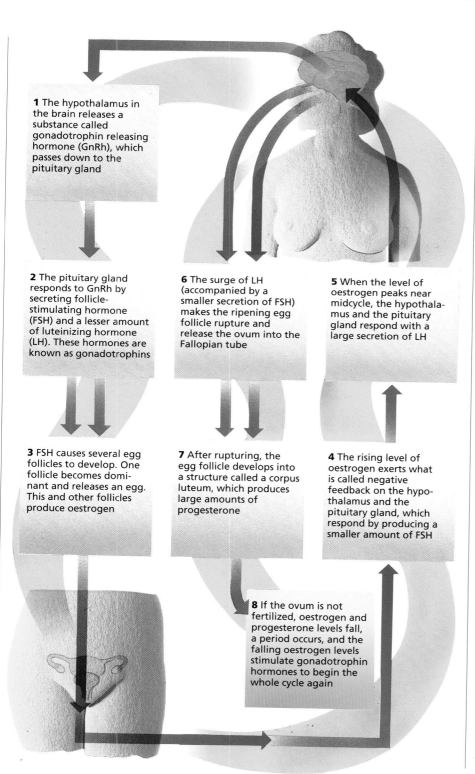

1 The hypothalamus in the brain releases a substance called gonadotrophin releasing hormone (GnRh), which passes down to the pituitary gland

2 The pituitary gland responds to GnRh by secreting follicle-stimulating hormone (FSH) and a lesser amount of luteinizing hormone (LH). These hormones are known as gonadotrophins

3 FSH causes several egg follicles to develop. One follicle becomes dominant and releases an egg. This and other follicles produce oestrogen

4 The rising level of oestrogen exerts what is called negative feedback on the hypothalamus and the pituitary gland, which respond by producing a smaller amount of FSH

5 When the level of oestrogen peaks near midcycle, the hypothalamus and the pituitary gland respond with a large secretion of LH

6 The surge of LH (accompanied by a smaller secretion of FSH) makes the ripening egg follicle rupture and release the ovum into the Fallopian tube

7 After rupturing, the egg follicle develops into a structure called a corpus luteum, which produces large amounts of progesterone

8 If the ovum is not fertilized, oestrogen and progesterone levels fall, a period occurs, and the falling oestrogen levels stimulate gonadotrophin hormones to begin the whole cycle again

The Hormonal Control Of Menstruation

The menstrual cycle is controlled by a sequence of hormones, which are produced in the hypothalamus, the pituitary gland, and the ovaries. When the level of one hormone rises, the levels of other hormones decrease. This relationship is known as a negative feedback mechanism.

THE MENSTRUAL CYCLE

At the beginning of the cycle, small quantities of oestrogen are produced by ripening egg follicles within the ovary. Oestrogen production gradually increases until it peaks just prior to ovulation, roughly 14 days before the first day of the next period. After the release of an egg into the Fallopian tube, the follicle changes into a structure called a corpus luteum, which secretes progesterone.

At the end of the cycle, there is a small surge of oestrogen that falls away with the progesterone levels just prior to menstruation. This hormone drop causes the uterus to shed its lining.

Oestrogen makes the lining of the uterus thick, and progesterone then encourages growth of blood vessels and glands so that the uterus is prepared to receive a fertilized ovum. Menstruation gets rid of the old uterine lining when fertilization does not occur, and it prepares the uterus for the beginning of a new cycle in case fertilization occurs the next month.

Menstruation is just one event in the monthly hormonal cycle. There are many effects on other organs in the body that are just as important and under the control of the hypothalamus, often described as the conductor of our hormonal orchestra.

From the age of about 35 the menstrual cycle becomes less consistent, and in the late 30s a woman may not ovulate in every menstrual cycle. Without eggs, oestrogen and progesterone are not secreted, and the symptoms of the menopause begin to appear (see page 46). When oestrogen levels fall too low to stimulate the uterine lining, menstruation ceases.

With the decline of oestrogen and progesterone, the negative feedback mechanism involving the hypothalamus and pituitary gland (see page 31) results in larger and larger quantities of follicle-stimulating hormone (FSH) and luteinizing hormone (LH) being secreted. The ovary cannot respond consistently despite the high hormone levels and women may experience normal menstrual cycles interspersed by cycles of troublesome oestrogen deficiency. High levels of FSH and LH alone can disturb many aspects of a woman's metabolism, including brain chemistry, mood, thyroid function, bone integrity, lipid metabolism, and blood sugar levels.

A HORMONE DEFICIENCY STATE?

Some doctors regard the menopause as natural, and interference with it unnatural and unnecessary. I disagree. While I believe that the menopause is a normal stage in the development of a woman's life, I also believe that it is a true hormone deficiency state. Just as a deficiency of the hormone insulin gives rise to diabetes, lack of oestrogen and progesterone can give rise to osteoporosis, heart disease, and stroke. There is no question as to whether or not the symptoms of diabetes should be treated, and I think women have the right to treatment for menopausal symptoms.

Women have two major oestrogens – oestradiol and its breakdown product, oestrone. The levels of both start to decline even before there are any symptoms of the menopause. As a consequence, the blood level of FSH starts to rise, and a blood test that shows this heralds the menopause. The menopause has three identifiable stages: premenopause, perimenopause, and

HORMONE LEVELS BEFORE, DURING, AND AFTER THE MENOPAUSE
Until the menopause, the hormones oestrogen and progesterone are produced in approximately a 28-day cycle. When the supply of eggs runs out in midlife, hormone production becomes erratic.

KEY

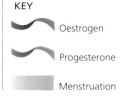

Oestrogen

Progesterone

Menstruation

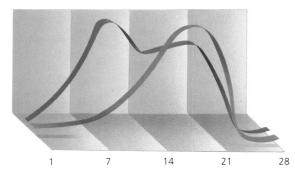

1   7   14   21   28

The Normal Menstrual Cycle
Oestrogen secreted by developing egg follicles in the ovary rises and peaks in the first half of the menstrual cycle. This is followed by ovulation, and the egg follicle that is left behind changes into a structure called a corpus luteum. This produces progesterone and smaller amounts of oestrogen. Bleeding occurs when the levels of progesterone and oestrogen drop.

postmenopause. The perimenopause refers to a span of time before and after the last period. The menopause is the point in time after which a woman no longer menstruates, and the postmenopause is the span of time after the last period. Women at any menopausal stage are eligible for hormone replacement therapy (HRT; see chapter six). At the very least, they should be given hormone supplements to smooth out the dramatic fall-off of female sex hormones, and serious consideration must also be given to long-term hormone supplements to stave off life-threatening diseases, such as osteoporosis.

Every organ in a woman's body is, in some way, affected by oestrogen and progesterone. There are at least 400 actions of oestrogen at a cellular level alone. Practically every important body tissue contains oestrogen receptors that keep the body normal and stimulate its function. When the secretion of oestrogen and progesterone varies, the health and well-being of our organs reflects these changes. For example, in each premenstrual week, the decline in hormones can result in mood changes and fluid retention. If your menstrual cycle is roughly lunar (28 days long), you will experience relative oestrogen and progesterone deficiency 13 times a year. This is equivalent to a tiny menopause each month and probably explains why women have premenstrual tension.

Normally, we are largely unaware of bodily changes related to hormone levels and we think about them only when our health is affected and symptoms such as muscle fatigue, bone pain, and joint stiffness appear. As part of our female inheritance, we grow up with, and take for granted, a variety of symptoms that are due to fluctuating hormone levels.

During the normal menstrual cycle, oestradiol is the major oestrogen and it is synthesized by the developing follicle in the ovary. After the menopause, oestrone takes over as the major oestrogen, but rather than being produced in the ovaries, it is made by a secondary process in fat cells and muscles. Oestrone is synthesized from the male sex hormone androstenedione, which continues to be secreted by the postmenopausal ovaries and the adrenal glands. Because oestrone is not produced cyclically after the menopause, the rate of its

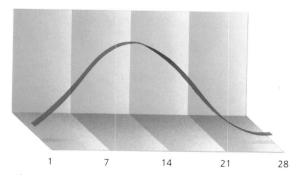

1   7   14   21   28

The Menopausal Phase

Oestrogen is produced by eggs in the ovary, but sometimes no single maturing egg becomes dominant, and so ovulation does not occur. This means that progesterone is not secreted in every cycle, and a menstrual bleed may occur in some cycles and not others. Because hormone levels can fluctuate dramatically at this time, women may experience menopausal symptoms.

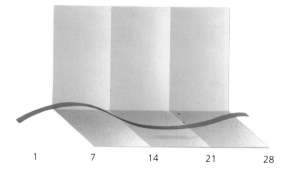

1   7   14   21   28

The Postmenopausal Phase

Oestrogen is present in small amounts after ovulation and menstruation have ceased – it is mainly converted by the fat cells from the male sex hormone androstenedione. Because ovulation no longer takes place, there is no corpus luteum, and progesterone is absent. Unless you take HRT, any bleeding after the menopause should be considered abnormal.

EFFECTS OF FLUCTUATING HORMONE LEVELS	
Uterine muscle	*dysmenorrhoea (menstrual cramps)*
Uterine lining	*menorrhagia (heavy bleeding), pelvic pain*
Breasts	*lumpiness prior to menstruation, mastalgia (tenderness and soreness prior to menstruation)*
Muscles	*tiredness, backache, reduction in strength, loss of muscular coordination*
Water balance	*fluid retention leading to weight gain, increased blood pressure, increased pressure inside the eyes, swollen ankles, swollen face*
Brain	*mood changes, irritability, depression, increased alcohol intake, cravings for carbohydrates, and bingeing*
Bladder	*tendency to cystitis*
Intestine	*lowered intestinal motility, leading to constipation and bloatedness*
Blood vessels in the skin	*increased sensitivity to heat, leading to blushing and facial rashes*
Skin	*acne, pimples, and pustules prior to menstruation*
Lungs	*asthma in the premenstrual week*
Head	*migraine and other forms of headache can get worse premenstrually*
Joints	*loss of mobility, stiffness, and premenstrual pain*

formation does not fluctuate in the way that it did premenopausally. Oestrone is also biologically much less active than oestradiol, and this can manifest itself as a relative excess of male hormones. This means that our overall hormonal profile begins to move nearer to that of men. The most visible signs of this shift are the appearance of facial hair, male-pattern baldness, and the tendency to put on weight around the waist and the abdomen (in the premenopausal years fat is laid down on the hips rather than the waist). However, the most dangerous change is one that is invisible: cardiovascular health deteriorates, bringing the rate of female heart disease into line with the rate of male heart disease. The chances of these changes occurring may be lessened by supplementing your natural oestrogen with HRT.

HOW THE BODY CHANGES
Some women find the menopause particularly disconcerting because they feel that their bodies are changing, even letting them down, and they really can't understand why or how. You will be better prepared to cope with the following changes if you have an understanding of why they are taking place or what you can do to prevent them.

UROGENITAL TISSUE
The cells of the urethra and the vagina contain oestrogen receptors that bind with oestrogen (see page 90), keeping the tissues healthy. When oestrogen levels start to fall at the menopause, the results include a decrease in blood supply to the tissues and a lowering of cellular starch (energy). The latter leads to a change in the pH of the vagina so that it becomes more alkaline. This encourages vaginal soreness, itching, and infections. Similar cellular changes are seen in the lining of the urethra, giving rise to urgent, frequent, or

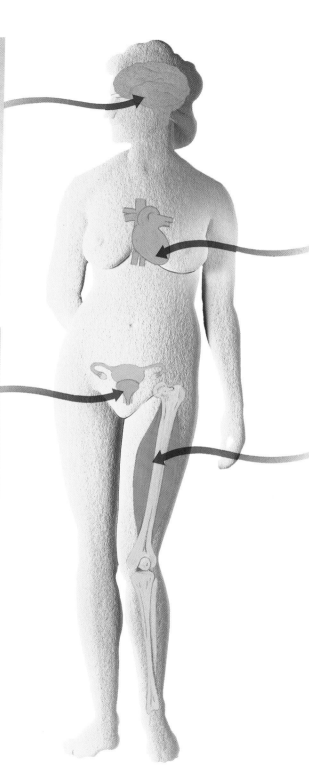

Fluctuating oestrogen levels may cause emotional symptoms, such as mood swings, anxiety, irritability, depressed mood, nervousness, and tearfulness

The hippocampus functions less well, making us more forgetful

Brain control of movement changes so that we are less dextrous

Brain control of balance and coordination may be impaired

Cognitive functions such as conceptual thinking may be more difficult

The vulval and vaginal lips become thinner and flatter

The vagina shrinks and the walls become thin and dry

The bladder walls become thin and the sphincter muscle, which controls urine flow, may become weak

The uterus shrinks and its lining thins. The cervix has fewer nerve endings

The rectum, bladder, and other pelvic organs are less well supported and are more likely to sag

Ovaries stop releasing eggs and the outer shell of the ovaries becomes thinner and wrinkled. The inner part continues to secrete hormones – mostly the male hormones testosterone and androstenedione

The Body's Response To Hormone Decline

Many changes that occur as a result of low oestrogen levels become apparent in the post-menopause. Although changes to the heart and bones can be severely detrimental to health, many changes are minor and are not life-threatening.

The heart may be less efficient and more vulnerable to disease. Blood pressure may rise, leading to hypertension

The blood vessels under the skin may respond to fluctuating oestrogen levels by suddenly and rapidly dilating, leading to hot flushes and night sweats

Bones lose their density and may be prone to fracture

Joints become less mobile

Muscles lose their strength and become slack

Collagen is lost, making ligaments weaker

uncomfortable urination. A local application of oestrogen cream will reverse these changes and relieve symptoms. Urogenital problems will also respond to other forms of HRT.

UTERUS

This is a smooth muscle with an inner lining, known as the endometrium, which contains glands and blood vessels. The endometrium builds up and breaks down each month throughout a woman's fertile life, unless she is pregnant. In about half of all menopausal women the endometrium begins to thin out, becoming atrophic endometrium. The endometrial thickness depends on how much oestrogen is present in a woman's body, whether manufactured by conversion from adrenal androgens (male sex hormones) or introduced to the body in the form of HRT.

The cervix is the neck of the uterus that dips into the upper part of the vagina. During fertile life there are sensitive nerves in the cervix that, when stimulated during sexual intercourse, give between 30 percent and 50 percent of women a deeply satisfying feeling. As the cervix ages, these nerves gradually disappear and the sensitivity of the cervix to deep penile thrusting can begin to wane. However, the cervix does not become completely insensitive and can still contribute to orgasm.

FALLOPIAN TUBES

During the fertile years, waves of contraction can be seen to pass down the Fallopian tubes. Such movements help to transport your ovum to the cavity of the uterus, and sperm towards their rendezvous with the waiting egg. After the menopause, when oestrogen levels decline, not only does the internal cellular structure of the tubes begin to regress, but the tubes become immobile. Fortunately, these internal changes have no detrimental effect on your general well-being and fitness.

OVARIES

As women approach the menopause, the declining number of eggs in the ovaries means that ovulation will not necessarily take place in every 28-day cycle. This in turn means that the secretion of oestrogen becomes erratic and women may experience menopausal symptoms, such as hot flushes and night sweats. After the menopause, the egg follicles in the ovary no longer grow and mature each month. Ovulation does not occur, and this means that there is no ruptured egg follicle (corpus luteum), which means that no progesterone is produced.

The outer shell of the ovary, which produced oestrogen and progesterone during your fertile life, becomes thinner and wrinkled, and the entire ovary shrinks. However, during the postmenopause the inner part of the ovary, called the stroma, continues to actively secrete hormones, chiefly the male hormones, androstenedione and testosterone. The latter is important in keeping up your energy and enthusiasm for life. Unfortunately, it also promotes changes

Ovulation
Every 28 days an egg is released from one of the ovaries. However, as the menopause approaches ovulation is less likely to occur.

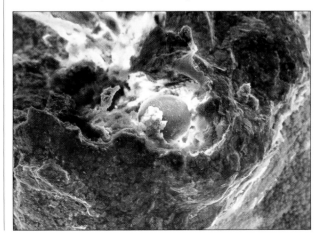

in your fat metabolism that increase your risk of suffering from conditions such as heart disease and stroke. Androstenedione is converted in small quantities to the weak female hormone, oestrone, which helps to maintain the integrity of the pelvic organs, the skin, the hair, and the vagina. If you have your ovaries surgically removed (see page 76), you lose an important source of postmenopausal oestrogen and it is important to take HRT.

VAGINA

When oestrogen levels drop, the vagina begins to atrophy (becomes thin and dry). While not all women lose oestrogenic stimulation of vaginal tissue as they get older, the activity of the glands in the vagina do begin to wane for many women. Healthy mucus is no longer secreted to keep the vagina lubricated, and it becomes more prone to infection and abrasions, which can lead to pain and bleeding during intercourse. Such vaginal discomfort is a primary reason for a loss of sex drive in postmenopausal women, and you may find that you need to use a lubricant to enable penetration. If you go to your doctor, he or she may prescribe oestrogen pessaries or cream to restore the vaginal lining to its premenopausal state. Research shows that women who remain sexually active after the menopause suffer less from vaginal atrophy than women who do not masturbate or have sexual intercourse.

VULVA AND PERINEUM

All structures of the vulva and perineum (the area between the vagina and anus) become less plump. The labia minora and majora become thin and flat, and the urethral opening becomes slack and wider. The skin of the perineum becomes thinner and dryer. All of these changes can lead to itchiness and, in the extreme form, a condition called pruritus vulvae (see page 92), infections, and slow healing. The use of oestrogen cream can completely reverse these changes, so that itchiness vanishes and healing occurs more rapidly.

PELVIC FLOOR

The muscles of the pelvic floor are called the pubococcygeal muscles, and they give support to all the pelvic organs, including the rectum, bladder, and uterus. Without adequate levels of oestrogen, the whole pelvic support structure loses its tension, elasticity, and strength during and after the menopause. This means that pelvic organs, particularly the uterus, are no longer well supported by the pelvic floor muscles and inclined to sag or prolapse. The vagina may also be affected, resulting in a loss of sensation during sexual intercourse. This can be combated by doing pelvic floor exercises, known as Kegel exercises (see page 50).

When the vaginal walls are thin and stretched, the rectum, bladder, and urethra can prolapse down through the front or back of the vagina (see page 93). This may be avoided if HRT is taken to keep the pelvic support structure strong and elastic (unless prolapse is due to trauma during childbirth). Local HRT such as oestrogen cream, will keep the pelvic organs healthy, while avoiding side-effects.

The Pelvic Floor Muscles
The muscles that support the pelvic organs may become weak after the menopause leading to symptoms such as poor bladder control. Exercising these muscles by repeatedly contracting and relaxing them can prevent this.

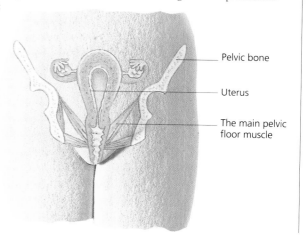

Pelvic bone

Uterus

The main pelvic floor muscle

BREASTS

As we get older the breasts tend to sag and flatten – the larger the breasts, the flatter they may become. With the menopause there is a reduction of oestrogen stimulation on all tissues in the body, including the breast tissues, and as a result, they lose their earlier fullness. There is also a reduction in the glandular tissue of the breast and an increase in fat cells. Women who take HRT will find that breast fullness is restored to a large degree and this will remain for as long as hormones are taken. Breast cancer is a risk after the menopause, and the later the menopause, the higher the risk. If you have breast cancer you should seek advice from a doctor or gynaecologist about HRT (see page 136).

Some women suffer from breast tenderness or mastalgia (see page 58) at the time of the menopause. Mastalgia is not a contraindication to HRT, in fact HRT often brings relief.

ABDOMEN

If you exercise regularly, you should not experience any sudden changes in the size and shape of your abdomen. However, if you stop having periods and notice that your abdomen suddenly increases in size, you should consult your doctor, because a sudden enlargement of the abdomen is sometimes the only sign of an ovarian tumour (see page 75).

Alternatively, if you feel bloated or distended and your waist size has grown, you may be eating a diet that is too low in fibre, or taking insufficient exercise. If you don't do much exercise, you will experience a gradual loss of abdominal wall tone. You will find that you simply cannot pull in your tummy the way you used to. Healthy abdominal muscles support the internal organs. Regular muscle exercise makes a huge difference not only to the shape of your abdomen, but also to your self-image – and you're never too old to start a fitness programme. Wearing a girdle will actually promote the development of lazy musculature, leading to an increase in abdominal bulging.

CONNECTIVE TISSUE

The body consists of a skeleton, muscles, and organs, surrounded by skin and supported by connective tissue, such as that found in ligaments. The major component of connective tissue is collagen, which is affected by the blood levels of sex hormones. Oestrogen receptors have been identified on the skin cells that manufacture collagen. After the menopause the body loses collagen, and connective tissue becomes weaker. Bones and skin, which also contain collagen, become thinner and less resistant to trauma.

SKIN

Decline of oestrogen during the menopause is one of the things that accelerates skin ageing, and you should really take special care of your skin after the age of 40. As you get older, the following skin changes occur:
- Its ability to spring back into shape is lost.
- It is less easily compressed and loses its mobility.
- Water-filled cells lose their turgidity.
- There is a decrease in total skin collagen, which is one of the main supporting proteins in your skin. The structure of the skin starts to collapse and wrinkles appear. Ultraviolet light is largely responsible for the break-up of collagen fibres in the skin.

● There is a continual loss of cells called melanocytes, which manufacture the pigment melanin. Melanin causes your skin to become tanned in the sun, so as you grow older its loss means you are more prone to sunburn, and in turn collagen destruction and cancer. It is crucial that you guard your skin from the damaging rays of the sun. Use sunscreens, wear a hat to shield your face, and, when possible, limit your exposure to the sun.

The cells on the surface of your skin are similar to those that line the urinary tract and the vagina, so when you begin to notice changes in your skin, such as wrinkling, sagging, loss of elasticity, dryness, and flaking, very similar changes may be happening to the cells lining the inside of your vagina, urethra, and bladder. The dryness and flakiness of your skin is made worse by the declining activity of the sebaceous glands. Because they no longer secrete sebum, your skin is no longer so well lubricated. All these menopausal changes can be reversed by HRT. Skin may also be preserved to some extent by regularly using a cream or moisturiser.

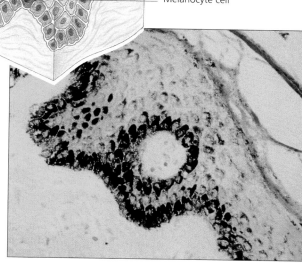

Melanocyte Cells
These are cells in the epidermis (opposite) that cause the skin to become tanned. With the menopausal decline of oestrogen, melanocyte cells (below) are lost, and skin becomes more vulnerable to sunburn.

Epidermal cells

Melanocyte cell

HAIR

There are oestrogen receptors in hair follicles that maintain the growth and rest cycle, and the health of each hair. When oestrogen levels are low, hair growth is disturbed. For this reason, hair growth patterns change at the time of menopause and beyond. Women may notice that their hair loses its body and thickness, and becomes thinner, finer, and more difficult to style. This must be distinguished from alopecia, where patches of complete hair loss occur, or from male pattern baldness, which may occur in women who have a substantial excess of androgens (male sex hormones). The average age of hormonally related hair loss is about 40. At present there is no known cure.

The other major change in hair growth is hirsutism, the growth of excess body hair. Fortunately, this is a problem that plagues only a few peri- and postmenopausal women. Men and women have two kinds of hair; the fine unpigmented hair that usually covers most of the body, and the darker, thicker hair that is responsive to sex hormones. These hormone-responsive hairs are located on the pubic and genital areas, and under the arms in both men and women, and on the back, face, chest, and lower abdomen in men. At the menopause, the ratio of male to female sex hormones increases due to the decline in oestrogen. Male sex hormones circulating in the bloodstream may promote the conversion of fine, unpigmented hair to dark, thick hair. This means that a few women may experience hair growth on the face, chest, arms, abdomen, and legs. Fortunately, this can be counteracted by oestrogen in the form of HRT. If you take female hormones, even in small quantities, you should have few problems with unwanted hair.

Unfortunately, facial hirsutism usually gets worse with age. If you suffer from facial hirsutism, your doctor must identify the cause before any attempt at treatment is made.

BONES

Despite its solid appearance, bone is actually porous and becomes more porous with age. There are two types of cells that actively influence bone health. Osteoblasts are responsible for building up bone, and osteoclasts are responsible for the removal or resorption of bone. At the time of the menopause the activity of the osteoclasts becomes greater than the activity of the osteoblasts. In other words, more bone is removed than is created, and bone mass and density are lost. The decline of oestrogen is responsible for this.

While a woman is still menstruating, the presence of oestrogen in her body allows her to fully utilize other hormones, such as calcitonin and parathyroid, and vitamins, such as vitamin D, all of which influence bone health. Parathyroid hormone and calcitonin keep the amount of calcium in the body at a constant level (parathyroid hormone prevents too much calcium from being lost from the urine by acting on the kidneys and by increasing calcium absorption from food). Insufficient oestrogen in a woman's body during and after the menopause means that calcium is lost from the body, making bones weaker and prone to osteoporosis (see page 66).

Although hip fractures are common in women with osteoporosis, they tend to affect older women in their 70s. Women who are recently postmenopausal and have osteoporosis are more likely to suffer from Colles' fracture (see page 89), or vertebral fracture. Women who are diagnosed as being at risk of osteoporosis can prevent their bones from deteriorating by taking HRT.

MUSCLES AND JOINTS

With advancing age and a decline in oestrogen and progesterone production, the muscular system loses its strength, bulk, and stamina. The average elderly person has little muscle mass left and is at risk from a variety of problems. Weak muscles mean that many elderly people have poor coordination, and if they trip and fall, serious damage may be more likely – particularly if osteoporosis has made their bones brittle and vulnerable to fracture. Diminished muscle strength can be debilitating. Just getting out of an armchair and climbing the stairs is difficult. Without exercise, life can quickly become sedentary.

With deficient collagen synthesis at the time of the menopause, joints may become stiff and painful, particularly on waking. Some studies have shown that two out of three women attending clinics for menopausal symptoms experience some joint discomfort (arthralgia) or pain with limitation of movement. HRT can virtually eliminate these symptoms and regular exercise will ensure that joints stay mobile.

VASOMOTOR SYSTEM

This is the system of tiny blood vessels under the skin. Dilation occurs when blood vessels relax and fill with blood, and constriction occurs when blood vessels narrow and empty. A woman experiencing a hot flush will have fully dilated blood vessels, which will cause the skin to become swollen, red, and warm. Constricted blood vessels will cause the skin to become thin, pale, and cold.

Hot flushes and night sweats result from aberrations in the way that the vasomotor system works. Both are harmless, but women often find them uncomfortable and distressing. Eighty-five percent of women going through the menopause experience hot flushes, although there is a wide variation in their frequency and severity. For some women, only a few mild flushes occur in a week. For others – a quarter to half of all women – flushes can be very troublesome with up to 50 a day, even ten years after their last period. In very severe cases, hot flushes may come as often as six or seven times in an hour, and this pattern can go on for many years.

For two-thirds of all women, hot flushes start well before their last menstrual period. Then flushes tend to become worse in frequency and duration at the time of the menopause, and continue to occur, with occasional flush-free months, for about the next five years. When you first begin to experience hot flushes they are usually infrequent and are on the face and neck only. Once they start, they tend to get worse before they get better.

Why does a hot flush come when it does, and what causes it? The explanations are complex, but the onset of a flush may correspond with an increase in the level of the pituitary hormone, luteinizing hormone (LH). Significant changes in levels of LH secretion are common as the menopause approaches (see page 198) and appear to be a response to the shrinking of the ovaries and decreased oestrogen secretion.

Other internal secretions also surge during a hot flush. For example, there is a significant rise in the blood level of some of the adrenal hormones. Hot flushes and night sweats often cause insomnia and a reduction in rapid eye movement (dream) sleep so that sleep is not as refreshing, contributing to fatigue.

HEART AND BLOOD VESSELS

The exact effect the menopause has on the heart and blood vessels is not fully understood. What is known is that, irrespective of age, women with functioning ovaries are less prone to heart disease than women who have gone through the menopause either naturally or after surgical removal of the ovaries. For example, women who experience a surgically induced menopause before the age of 35 have a two to seven times greater risk of a heart attack than premenopausal women with intact ovaries.

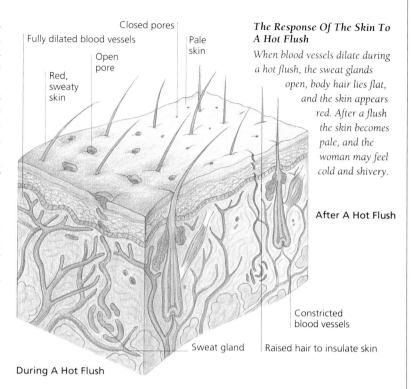

Closed pores

Fully dilated blood vessels

Pale skin

Open pore

Red, sweaty skin

The Response Of The Skin To A Hot Flush

When blood vessels dilate during a hot flush, the sweat glands open, body hair lies flat, and the skin appears red. After a flush the skin becomes pale, and the woman may feel cold and shivery.

After A Hot Flush

Constricted blood vessels

Sweat gland

Raised hair to insulate skin

During A Hot Flush

In the United States, close to half a million women a year die of a cardiovascular disease – nearly all of them postmenopausal. This is eight times higher than the combined death rate for all reproductive system cancers. Until oestrogen declines at the menopause, cardiovascular disease is almost never a cause of death in women.

Each year over one million postmenopausal American women experience a malfunction of the cardiovascular system. The heart may not pump adequately, the blood vessels may tear and form scar tissue, or dangerous fats travelling in the blood may clog and narrow the arteries – all of these affect blood circulation and compromise the pumping capacity of the heart, which can be fatal.

Cholesterol levels normally increase in women as they grow older. However, the levels increase at an even faster rate in women who have had their ovaries removed. Loss of ovarian function leads to an increase in the dangerous low-density type of cholesterol (LDL), and a reduction in the cardioprotective high-density cholesterol (HDL). These changes lead to heart disease, but may be controlled in women taking HRT. Recently, oestrogen receptors have been found in the muscle layer of arteries. Loss of oestrogen causes the muscles to tighten, which constricts the blood vessels and increases blood pressure. Reduction of blood pressure can occur within a few weeks of starting HRT.

CALCIUM METABOLISM
This is specifically linked to bone health, which declines with the menopause. Oestrogen plays an important role in keeping blood calcium levels normal by aiding the absorption of calcium from food. It also promotes absorption of calcium from the blood into the bone, facilitating the renewal and repair activity of osteoblasts (see page 40). When oestrogen levels in the body fall, calcium absorption is less efficient and uptake of calcium into the bone slows down so that the bones may become brittle.

TEMPERATURE-REGULATING MECHANISM
Keeping the body at a regular temperature is a complex process, but one of the body's most efficient cooling mechanisms is the production of sweat. When the body becomes hotter than normal, the sweat glands secrete sweat, and when sweat evaporates it cools down any heated blood near the surface. At the menopause, the sweat glands seem to work less effectively than before because lack of oestrogen changes the way in which they're programmed. Not only do the sweat glands not cool as efficiently as before, but there also appears to be a change in brain chemistry that affects the temperature control centre in the hypothalamus. The temperature set-point for the body core is lower than normal and this triggers a dilation of blood vessels in the skin and sweating as the body attempts to reset its thermostat. These adjustments are never smooth and often the body overcompensates, which may be one reason why women have hot flushes.

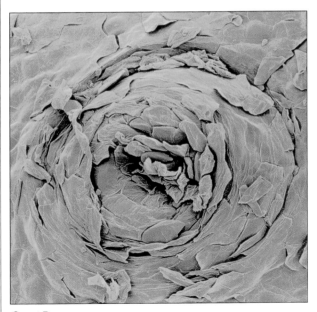

Sweat Pore
Glands deep in the dermis of the skin produce sweat, which leaves the body via sweat pores. Sweat glands become less efficient around the time of the menopause.

FAT DISTRIBUTION

One of the first changes in girls approaching adolescence is the appearance of fat on the hips, breasts, upper arms, and upper thighs. Throughout fertile life, oestrogen and progesterone are responsible for maintaining the female shape, with its narrow waist and rounded hips. We now know that these proportions are more than simply an expression of the female gender. They have a much greater significance for both health and longevity.

The narrow waist and rounded hips pattern of fat distribution is closely and unequivocally related to coronary health. The usual ratio of the waist to hip measurement is less than one and this is associated with a low risk of a heart attack. If your waist to hip ratio creeps above 0.8, you are much more at risk (see page 60).

After the menopause, when levels of oestrogen and progesterone are low or absent, one of the first things that a woman may notice is a thickening of the waist and the appearance of "middle-age spread". She may also notice abdominal swelling because of increased fat on the front of her abdomen. Her shape comes to resemble a more masculine outline, and her risk of having a heart attack increases in relation to this increased fat distribution.

CARBOHYDRATE METABOLISM

Women who are approaching the menopause may not be secreting progesterone in the second half of the menstrual cycle (see page 30). This changes their tolerance to sugar and raises the level of the baseline at which they suffer symptoms of low blood sugar. As a result, the blood sugar level does not have so far to fall before the effects of hunger are felt. Women who could go for five or even six hours without food during most of their fertile life, find that fasting for the same length of time once they become menopausal can lead to acute cravings, particularly for carbohydrates. This can result in frequent bingeing and possible weight gain.

Like other symptoms of the menopause, there are a number of things you can do to prevent these changes from affecting your life. Increase your intake of healthy carbohydrates, such as oats (porridge), thick homemade vegetable soup, and wholegrains. All of these should quell cravings if eaten two or three times a day and they are not so fattening as sugary foods. You could also try eating small amounts of food at frequent intervals instead of three meals a day.

BRAIN CONTROL OF EMOTIONS AND BEHAVIOUR

There are many sites in the brain where oestrogen receptors are found in high concentration. Oestradiol, our most active oestrogen, has at least 50 actions in the brain alone. Oestrogen receptors control function in the part of the brain, the hippocampus, that is responsible for memory, and this may explain why some women experience forgetfulness and memory loss before the other symptoms of the menopause.

New research into the effects of oestrogen on receptors in the brain is very revealing and provides great insight into intellectual and emotional changes in menopausal women. The hippocampus oversees a complex system of information storage. Even during the menstrual cycle, its ability to store data changes noticeably. Oestrogen controls cognitive functions, such as conceptual thinking and perceptions, and qualities such as possessing a flexible attitude to change. During the menopause these functions and qualities may become impaired.

PREMENOPAUSAL FAT DISTRIBUTION

POSTMENOPAUSAL FAT DISTRIBUTION

Changes in Body Shape
Before the menopause, fat tends to be laid down on the hips, thighs, and bottom (top). After the menopause, fat is more concentrated around the waist, abdomen, and breasts (above).

Perhaps the most important finding is that oestrogen prevents anxiety, which may explain why anxiety is such a dominant symptom of the menopause. Some of the effects of oestrogen are as therapeutic as those of tranquillizers, and in a way, menopausal women are suffering from "natural tranquillizer withdrawal". The range of oestrogenic activity in combating anxiety, tension, and depression is wide, even encompassing the ability to make a smooth transition from lightness to darkness, finding a way through a strange environment, interacting with a stranger, and taking criticism.

In contrast, progesterone receptors in the brain can bring on negative moods – in one study, depression occurred within hours of taking progestogen. This may account for the black moods that some women suffer during the progestogenic days of HRT and during the week before menstruation.

The amygdala is a centre in the brain responsible for psychological well-being and sexuality, and it contains hundreds of oestrogen receptors that maintain its ability to respond to stimuli. Loss of oestrogen reduces the amygdala's excitability, resulting in a lowered sense of well-being and sex drive. Women taking HRT experience increased arousal and more sexual fantasies than previously. Low oestrogen levels also affect our ability to learn new facts and skills, and recall recently-read material. HRT improves these skills.

BRAIN CONTROL OF MUSCLES, JOINTS, AND MOVEMENT

Oestrogen appears to increase cellular metabolism in the brain where there are no specific oestrogen receptors. This "tonic" effect is very apparent in the areas of the brain controlling our ability to make fine movements. The cerebellum controls balance and coordination, and recent research has shown that taking oestrogen can bring about a threefold increase in cerebellar function within three minutes, which is not reversible within nine hours. All kinds of muscular activities are improved by oestrogen stimulation, including manual dexterity. Without oestrogen our abilities to perform intricate movements, such as playing the violin or guitar may be impaired.

There is a centre in the brain, the olive, that acts as a timing device, synchronizing movements to actions. For instance, without correctly timed responses we can trip over a curb. The olive helps by sending out rhythmic electrical discharges that tell the cerebellum when to move muscles so that our movements are synchronized. After taking oestrogen, synchronicity of muscle movement improves markedly, and progesterone enhances this oestrogen effect. Studies also show that the olive is 30 percent more sensitive to errors when oestrogen levels are high.

Areas Of The Brain Affected By Oestrogen

Many sites in the brain contain oestrogen receptors. When oestrogen levels are low these areas may be affected, resulting in symptoms such as anxiety, depression, and forgetfulness.

The amygdala – controls psychological well-being

The hippocampus – controls memory

The olive – synchronizes movements

The cerebellum – controls balance and coordination

3
SYMPTOMS
OF THE
MENOPAUSE

*Some women experience no menopausal symptoms, or
slight discomfort, while other women may be incapacitated
by symptoms that affect them not only physically, but also
emotionally and intellectually. Although the two symptoms
classically associated with the menopause are hot flushes
and night sweats, there are other symptoms that you
should be prepared for.*

THE RANGE OF SYMPTOMS

The list of symptoms associated with the menopause is long, and at first glance may be daunting. Fortunately, no woman experiences the whole range of symptoms – you will probably only have a few and many women have none. The list shown below is long simply because it's helpful to know the array of disparate symptoms, especially if you need to discuss your treatment with a doctor. The physical effects of the menopause are so diverse, it is sometimes hard to connect them to a single cause. There are some classic symptoms, such as hot flushes and mood swings, that women may readily associate with the menopause, but others, such as poor bladder control or back pain, often appear to be just incidental. All the symptoms below are directly or indirectly related to a drop in oestrogen levels.

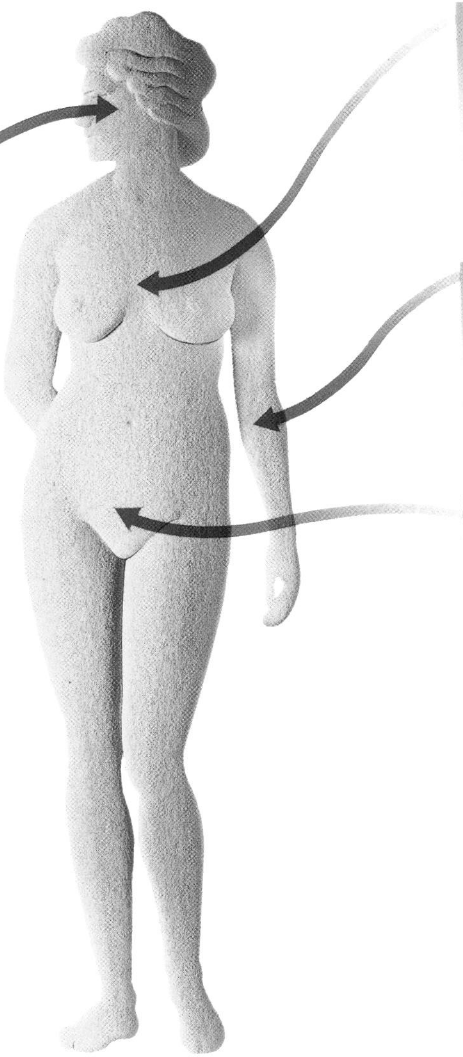

Back pain
Breast soreness
Chest pain
Itchy skin
Night sweats
Palpitations

Anxiety and low self-esteem
Depressed mood
Dry hair, eyes, and mouth, and dry, wrinkled skin
Feelings of pessimism
Forgetfulness
Headaches
Hot flushes
Inability to concentrate or make decisions
Increase in facial hair
Insomnia
Irritability and tearfulness
Lowering of the voice
Mood swings and PMS
Thin hair
Tiredness and lethargy

Aches and pains
Brittle nails
Muscle soreness
Pins and needles
Swollen or stiff joints

Bloated abdomen
Constipation
Dry vagina
Heavy/irregular periods
Itchy vulva
Loss of bladder control
Loss of libido and painful sex
Slower sexual arousal and lubrication
Urgent or frequent urination

Signs Of The Menopause

The early symptoms associated with the menopause, such as mood swings, are different from the later symptoms, which include dry skin and slower sexual arousal. This reflects the body's response to fluctuating oestrogen levels, and then to permanently lowered oestrogen levels.

HOT FLUSHES

These are experienced by more than 85 percent of menopausal women, although their frequency and severity varies greatly from woman to woman. During a hot flush, a woman can perspire so profusely that perspiration runs down her face, neck, and back; her skin will rise in temperature, her heart will beat faster, and she may experience palpitations. Very occasionally, a woman may faint during a hot flush, but this is rare.

Hot flushes occur because the brain decides that the body is overheated. We now know that this is because the natural temperature set-point (above which the brain considers the body is too hot, and below which the brain considers the body too cold) becomes lowered. This means that even under normal conditions, the brain may think that the body's temperature is too high, and respond by increasing the blood flow through the skin. The heated skin reddens and begins to perspire. When the sweat starts to evaporate, the body temperature cools down again.

Even though a hot flush may feel most severe in the head, face, and neck, the rise in temperature occurs throughout the body. Even the finger and toe temperatures rise sharply at the beginning of a flush.

In a Danish study of menopausal women, a third of those interviewed continued to have hot flushes for ten years after their last period. In the most severe cases, women had hot flushes six or seven times every hour – a pattern that could continue for years. Two out of three women suffered hot flushes well before their last menstrual period, but for most of these women the frequency went on to increase dramatically at the menopause, and continued for about the next five years.

The discomfort from a hot flush is unique – it's not the same as simply being overheated. In one study, investigators tried to induce hot flushes in menopausal women using hot water bottles and blankets. They found that applying external heat does not produce the same dramatic changes in heart rate and blood pressure that a menopausal flush does. However, hot flushes can be aggravated by hot weather.

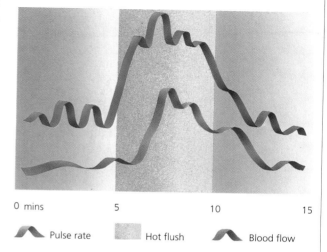

0 mins   5   10   15

Pulse rate   Hot flush   Blood flow

The Sensation Of A Hot Flush
Before you experience a flush, your blood flow (shown here as blood flow to the hand over a period of 15 minutes) increases dramatically, and your pulse rate becomes faster. The sensation of a hot flush usually lasts for about three to five minutes.

SELF-HELP

- Keep a record of your flushes and you may see a pattern developing. You may find that you have flushes at a particular time of day or in a particular situation. If the former applies, try to avoid activities at those times of day; if the latter is the case, work at avoiding the recurrence of the situation.
- Choose your clothes very carefully. Try not to wear synthetic fabrics, such as polyester and nylon, which trap perspiration, and avoid clothes with high necks and long sleeves, which can intensify feelings of suffocation. Instead, wear loose clothing with short sleeves and round or v-necks, or clothes that can be unbuttoned at the neck.
- Discover ways of cooling down: keep a thermos flask of iced water near you, take a cold shower, or use a battery-operated fan. Turn your central heating down and keep your rooms well ventilated.

- Give up smoking. Smoking affects the circulation and intensifies hot flushes and night sweats.
- Limit food and drinks that trigger hot flushes. These include sugary, salty, or spicy dishes, chocolate, alcohol, coffee, tea, and cola drinks. Hot soups and drinks or large meals can also trigger a hot flush. Eat plenty of citrus fruits, such as oranges and grapefruit; these contain bioflavonoids, which have a weak oestrogenic effect on the body.
- Bearing in mind that there is no proof of its effectiveness, you could try taking vitamin E, which may help the proper functioning of blood and aid the production of sex hormones. A thousand international units a day is recommended and you should not exceed that dose. Vitamin E appears to work more effectively when it is taken with vitamins B and C (see page 144 for sources). It is also absorbed better in the presence of fats, so vitamin E supplements should be taken at the end of meals. Avoid vitamin E if you suffer from hypertension, diabetes, or heart problems.
- Take regular physical exercise; women who exercise tend to have fewer hot flushes than those who don't. Exercise vastly improves circulation, and it can make your body more tolerant of temperature extremes and better able to cool down quickly. Exercise also helps to increase the amount of oestrogen and endorphins (chemicals that have a morphine-like effect) circulating in the blood. The more oestrogen that you have, the less chance there is of your having a hot flush.
- Learn to relax. It's not always easy, but relaxing during a hot flush can diminish its intensity. If possible, find a cool, peaceful place where you can sit or lie quietly. Breathe deeply and slowly, and practise mental imagery and calming thoughts (see page 156).

COMPLEMENTARY THERAPY

The following herbs and plant products are most frequently suggested by herbalists and homeopaths for hot flushes. You can find these remedies in health food shops and at natural pharmacies, or you can consult a qualified homeopath or herbalist (see page 219).

- Lachesis
- Pulsatilla
- Ginseng
- Dong quai
- Black cohosh
- Fo-ti-tieng
- Goldenseal
- Wild yam root
- Soya beans
- Sage

Ginseng, dong quai (the female root of ginseng), and black cohosh all contain oestrogen-like substances. The mild oestrogenic effect they exert on the body may help to compensate for declining levels of natural hormone.

Acupuncture relieves hot flushes and increases the production of endorphins. Both electro-stimulated acupuncture (ESA) and superficial needles position acupuncture (SNPA) decreased the number of hot flushes by almost a half in a sample of menopausal women in Stockholm. This change persisted for three months after the treatment.

MEDICAL TREATMENT

Hormone replacement therapy (HRT; see chapter six) has a 98 percent success rate at relieving hot flushes. The drugs clonidine, propranolol (for the treatment of high blood pressure), and sedative drugs may also be helpful.

NIGHT SWEATS

The night-time equivalent of the hot flush is the night sweat, in which you wake up hot and drenched in perspiration. Most women who experience night sweats also have hot flushes during the daytime, but the reverse isn't always so. Night sweats can very occasionally be a symptom of stress, or a disease that is unrelated to the menopause – if you consult your doctor, he or she will be able to make a diagnosis.

Sleeplessness in menopausal women is nearly always linked to night sweats. Women describe waking up, throwing off their bed covers to relieve the intensity of a night sweat, and being so drenched in sweat that they have to get up to change their nightclothes and bed linen. In the most severe cases, this can happen several times a night.

We know that a night sweat is a physiological process involving a fever that lasts a minute or two and then disappears. The heart rhythm goes wild, the body temperature rises, and the woman is left with a sweaty face and chest, followed by a feeling of being chilled. Some women with severe night sweats become very depressed. Furthermore, their depression doesn't go away until the night sweats are controlled.

SELF-HELP
- Keep your bedroom temperature fairly cool. Leave a window open if possible and try to create a draft through the room.
- Avoid nightclothes and bed linen that are made of nylon or polyester; they can act like sheets of plastic, holding the sweat next to your body. Cotton fabrics will be more comfortable.
- Keep a battery-operated fan, a bowl of tepid water, and a sponge on your bedside table so that you can cool yourself down quickly and easily. Never use cold water as it can cause you to overheat after you have applied it. Allow the tepid water to evaporate on your skin – as it evaporates it will take the heat from your skin, which will make you feel cooler and bring the feeling of fever to a more rapid end.

COMPLEMENTARY THERAPY
Relaxation is particularly therapeutic because it calms the mind and body, which in turn normalizes body chemistry and makes the skin sweat less. Try some of the exercises that are shown on page 118. Meditation slows down your metabolism, and can slow your brain waves from the fast beta waves that are characteristic of the normal working day to a slower alpha or theta wave. This is the wave pattern that occurs just before sleeping – if you can achieve this state it can be as restful as sleep. There are also herbal remedies that may alleviate insomnia (see page 112).

MEDICAL TREATMENT
As with hot flushes, any form of HRT will treat night sweats. The exceptions to this are oestrogen creams or pessaries, which contain hormone levels that are too low to have a generalized effect on the body.

Relief From Night Sweats
Wearing cotton nightclothes and cooling yourself with a fan and some tepid water will help ease the discomfort of a night sweat.

Hand-held fan

Lavender water

Bowl of water

Flannel   Sponge

Cotton bed linen

Cotton nightshirt

VAGINAL AND URINARY SYMPTOMS

Urogenital problems are very common during the menopause, yet only four in ten women consult their doctor about them. Anatomically, the vagina and the lower urinary tract lie very close, separated by just a few layers of cells. They both respond to a lack of oestrogen by becoming thin and dry.

Urinary symptoms typically include discomfort in passing urine, and frequent and urgent urination, even when there is very little urine in the bladder. There may also be some dribbling because the sphincter muscle guarding the exit from the bladder becomes weak due to low oestrogen levels. Sometimes urine escapes from the bladder on laughing, coughing, or carrying a heavy weight. This is called stress incontinence and it is due to increased pressure inside the abdomen squeezing urine from the bladder. With any or all of these symptoms you may have genital dryness and itching. Vaginal soreness, particularly during or after intercourse because the vagina fails to lubricate, is also common among menopausal and postmenopausal women.

SELF-HELP
- For urinary symptoms of any kind, it is extremely important to keep the bladder flushed out. Try and drink a minimum of two litres (approximately four pints) of fluid a day, especially if you are prone to cystitis (see page 90).
- Keep your urine alkaline as this discourages infections. There are many proprietary products on sale in pharmacies that will alkalinize your urine, or you can drink milk, or take antacids.
- A vaginal moisturizing gel, known as aqueous gel, is available over the counter and will greatly relieve vaginal dryness, soreness, itchiness, or pain during intercourse. It has adhesive properties that make it stick to the vaginal walls. Moisturizing the vagina also helps to discourage vaginal infections. One application of aqueous gel may last up to four days, and it can be used twice a week.
- Exercise such as swimming and cycling causes a vigorous pumping action of the muscles and brings blood, oxygen, and nutrients to the pelvic area, and keeps tissues healthy. Regular sex or masturbation can do the same thing – loving caresses and erotic massage can also improve circulation to the pelvic area and encourage vaginal lubrication.
- A set of exercises developed by Dr Arnold Kegel in the 1940s will strengthen all the pelvic muscles, but particularly those of the urethra, vagina, and anus. The exercises will not only help to combat urinary incontinence but they will also make sex more pleasurable and give women more acute vaginal sensations. You can locate the muscles that you use in Kegel exercises by stopping the flow of urine midstream when you're emptying your bladder. Kegel exercises can be done at any time and in any place: all you have to do is draw up the vaginal muscles, hold for a count of five, and then relax. Repeat this process five times. You should do the whole routine at least ten times a day.
- Wearing loose cotton underwear should help prevent irritation of the urogenital tract. You should also avoid using perfumed additives in your bath.

COMPLEMENTARY THERAPY
Herbs that may relieve urinary symptoms include wintergreen, blackberry root, and coleus, which has anti-spasmodic properties. Golden seal may have some anti-infective properties and uva ursi is said to improve urine flow.

MEDICAL TREATMENT

Treatment consists almost entirely of HRT, whether in the form of tablets, skin patches, or locally applied creams. A vaginal cream is an excellent way of treating vaginal thinness and dryness, stress incontinence, and urgent, frequent urination. It works by rapidly diffusing through the walls of the vagina to reach the lower urinary tract. Recent research has shown that HRT also reduces the frequency of cystitis recurring.

MUSCLE AND JOINT SYMPTOMS

Collagen is a protein that provides the scaffolding for every tissue in the body, and when it begins to disintegrate at the menopause, muscles lose their bulk, strength, and coordination, and joints become stiff. Muscles become more prone to soreness and stiffness after exercise, and joints may swell so that their mobility becomes restricted. If you retain fluid, you may get pins and needles or numbness in the hands. These are symptoms of carpal tunnel syndrome (see page 89) caused by tissues bloated with water pressing on the nerve to the hand and the fingers.

Osteoporosis causes aches and pains all over the body, especially in the upper back due to the thinning of vertebral bones.

General fatigue at the menopause may be profound. Besides underused muscles and joints there are other causes of chronic fatigue, such as low blood sugar, anaemia, and an underactive thyroid gland. Ask your doctor to check all of these if you experience disabling fatigue.

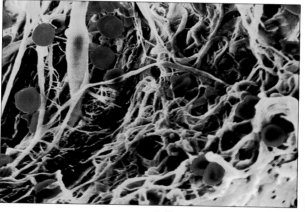

SELF-HELP

- If you keep your muscles strong with exercise you will be more agile and, if you do trip up, muscle strength and coordination will help you to fall with less impact.
- If you are suffering from rheumatoid arthritis or osteoarthritis (see page 86), your doctor will advise you about self-help aids for use in the home.

COMPLEMENTARY THERAPY

If you are suffering from stiff and swollen joints, a poultice made with cayenne pepper may be helpful. Other herbal remedies include alfalfa, sarsaparilla, feverfew, and white willow. Camomile, rosemary, and lavender essential oils may relieve pain when diluted with a base oil and used in a local massage or compress (see page 109).

MEDICAL TREATMENT

HRT rapidly relieves the joint stiffness caused by oestrogen deficiency and it maintains muscle strength and the integrity of ligaments. Although HRT will not reverse the wear and tear in joints, which we call osteoarthritis, it does appear to be beneficial in treating rheumatoid arthritis, in which collagen is lost. Osteoporosis is such an important subject that it is given special prominence elsewhere in this book (see page 66).

Collagen Fibres

The fibres that provide strength to connective tissue appear under the microscope as an irregular mass of yellow strands, interspersed by red blood cells. Where strength and elasticity are required (in ligaments, for example), collagen fibres are very densely packed.

PREMENSTRUAL SYMPTOMS

If you have suffered from premenstrual syndrome (PMS) all your life, you are more likely to experience intensified symptoms as you become menopausal. The symptoms of PMS usually include fatigue, anxiety, irritability, tearfulness, breast soreness, water retention, skin problems such as mild acne, sugar cravings, and insomnia. If you suspect that your mood swings are PMS-related, you can confirm this by charting your menstrual cycle for three months and recording your symptoms on a day-to-day basis.

SELF-HELP

- Avoid sugar cravings by eating several small meals a day – you will find that your cravings lessen if your blood sugar level is stable.
- Eat less salt as it increases water retention and bloating.
- Avoid alcohol and caffeine because they aggravate many of the emotional symptoms of PMS.
- Make sure you are getting enough calcium, magnesium, vitamin B6, and vitamin E, as these may reduce emotional symptoms.
- Get plenty of exercise; it's a great mood-lifter and can help you to work off tension and anxiety.

COMPLEMENTARY THERAPY

The standard remedy for PMS is evening primrose oil, which is available in health food shops and most chemists. Aromatherapists recommend the oils of ylang-ylang, lavender, and lemon grass, which you can use in a warm bath.

MEDICAL TREATMENT

Premenstrual symptoms should disappear along with your periods. If you suffer from water retention, a diuretic may help, and HRT will treat emotional symptoms such as irritability. If PMS returns during the progestogen phase of HRT, it can be controlled by modifying the dose and type of progestogen.

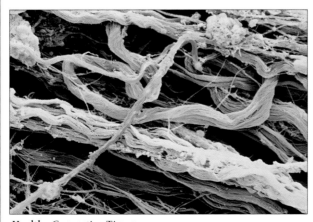

Healthy Connective Tissue
Bundles of collagen and elastic fibres provide support for tissues and organs throughout the body. After the menopause, collagen fibres start to disintegrate and elastic fibres become weaker.

SKIN, HAIR, EYE, MOUTH, AND NAIL SYMPTOMS

The lowered oestrogen levels that occur at the menopause cause changes in the skin, hair, nails, eyes, mouth, and gums. These changes are in part due to the disintegration of collagen fibres and the weakening of the protein, elastin, which gives connective tissue its strength and suppleness. Lack of collagen leads to a decrease in skin thickness and suppleness, dry hair, brittle nails, sore eyes, mouth dryness, gum shrinkage, and an increase in joint stiffness. One of the most noticeable changes is the appearance of wrinkles in the facial skin. The reduction in blood flow in the skin and the subcutaneous tissues contributes to the loss of skin firmness, as does shrinkage of underlying muscles. Deterioration of nerve endings in the ageing skin can lead to itchiness and a condition called formication. This is an

CHANGES DUE TO COLLAGEN DEFICIENCY

Skin	Dryness or oiliness, wrinkles, flaking, bruises easily, wounds heal slowly, patches of brown pigmentation, prominent veins
Nails	Brittleness, white spots, splinter haemorrhages appear
Eyes	Dryness, dark circles under eyes, small yellow lumps of fat on the white part of the eyes, night vision deteriorates, red blood vessels around the corners of the eyes
Gums	Bleeding and sponginess, recession leaving tooth roots exposed, infection and periodontal disease
Hair	Dullness, dryness, oiliness, split ends, poor growth, thin patches, dermatitis of the scalp, hair loss, dandruff
Mouth	Bad breath, cracks on the corners of the lips, mouth ulcers that are slow to heal
Tongue	Thick white spots may appear, the sides may become scalloped

intense tingling that some women describe as a feeling that insects are crawling across their skin. The word is derived from the Latin word for ant, *"formica"*. Formication is a classic symptom of menopausal distress. In a study of 5000 women, one in five suffered from formication within 12–24 months after their last menstrual period. About one in ten women continue to suffer from formication for more than 12 years after the menopause. Although it disappears eventually, its precise cause is still not completely understood.

SELF-HELP
- Moisturizing the skin is important as you grow older. Avoid soap, which strips skin of its natural oils, and use special cleansing creams and lotions. Beauty treatments may temporarily rejuvenate the skin (see page 170).
- Toenails and fingernails need special care, so give yourself a manicure and a pedicure (see page 215) at least every six to eight weeks.
- Ulcers in the mouth and on the tongue should be treated immediately. Rinse your mouth with salty water, or use a proprietary ointment. If rough edges on your teeth are causing ulcers, have them filed down.
- Guard your skin from the sun. As the years pass, you will be less protected from exposure to sunlight – the number of melanocyte cells in your skin decreases by 10–15 percent over each decade. Melanocytes form the substance melanin, which is responsible for giving you a tan. Avoid direct sun at all times, and when you go out in sunny weather, wear a sun block. If possible, limit your exposure to the early and late parts of the day.
- The health of the skin, nails, hair, and eyes is largely dependent on a diet rich in vitamins, minerals, and trace elements. The list is extremely long but it is essential that you have a sufficient intake of the vitamins A, B, C, and E, as well as potassium, zinc, magnesium, bioflavonoids, iron, calcium, and essential fatty acids. Particular attention should be paid to the B vitamins, especially B1, 2, 3, 6, 12, and folic acid.

MEDICAL TREATMENT
The skin responds quickly to HRT by becoming thicker and better toned. The more aged the skin when hormones are taken, the greater the degree of collagen increase. Most women report a change in their skin tone within a few weeks of taking HRT.

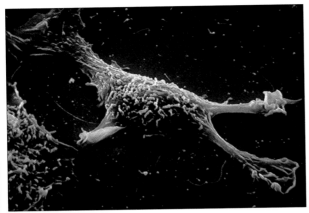

Fibroblast Cell

These cells are responsible for the secretion and synthesis of collagen and elastin, which keep skin and connective tissue strong and elastic. Oestrogen receptors are present in fibroblast cells, so when oestrogen levels decline, the activity of fibroblast cells is diminished.

HRT also provides relief from formication, and restores hair to its former health. Thinning and baldness will be halted and hair will regain its spring and bounce (although if hair follicles have been lost, oestrogen cannot stimulate the growth of new ones). Dry eyes, tongue soreness, and mouth dryness also benefit from HRT; shrunken gums may fill out, nails become less brittle, the tendency to bruise lessens, and cuts and wounds will heal faster.

SEXUAL SYMPTOMS

A common myth about the menopause is that it marks the beginning of a woman's sexual decline. Nothing could be further from the truth. The majority of women can continue to experience sexual pleasure well into old age, indeed as long as their health remains good. Some women even report that their sexual enjoyment starts to increase after the menopause. This may be due to a higher testosterone to oestrogen ratio than before (see page 34). Most menopausal women, however, notice some changes in the way their bodies respond during arousal and sex. This is often due to physical changes in the urogenital tract rather than a decreased psychological desire for sex. Research on sexual pleasure by Alfred Kinsey some decades ago has shown that women who have an enjoyable sex life before the menopause are likely to continue to enjoy sex after it. On the other hand, for women who have not enjoyed sex throughout their lives, the menopause is more likely to be associated with a decrease in all kinds of sexual activity.

One of the most common sexual problems after the menopause is lack of lubrication. The vaginal lining may actually crack and bleed and this makes penetration painful, and sometimes impossible.

In youth, blood flow out of the genitals is slow during arousal, causing swelling and sensitivity to touch. After the menopause, there is less engorgement of the clitoris, the vagina, and the vulva, leading to subdued arousal.

The breasts also increase in size during sexual arousal in young women – by as much as a quarter in some cases. The rush of blood to the tiny veins of the breasts that causes this does not occur so often after the level of oestrogen has declined. As a result your breasts may no longer be so sensitive to touching and stroking. Another part of the sexual response that disappears is the "sex flush" – the rash that may appear on a woman's chest and other parts of the body just before orgasm. This does not affect sexual enjoyment, but it does show that your body responds to sexual arousal differently from the way it used to.

In a young woman, the vagina expands during sexual arousal to allow easy penetration. After the menopause, the vagina does not expand so much, but it still remains large enough to accommodate an erect penis (as long as you allow time to achieve proper lubrication).

Healthy adrenal glands are also critical to sex drive. Long-term stress, such as bereavement, divorce, moving house, and family problems can adversely affect glandular activity. Internal "stress", such as too much sugar, fat, coffee, or alcohol, can have the same effect. Finding ways of handling stress and eating a healthy diet are conducive to a good sex life.

Sexual desire can also be diminished by certain drugs, such as tranquillizers, muscle relaxants, antidepressants, amphetamines, diuretics, antihypertensives, and hormones. Alcohol, smoking, coffee, overwork, tension, and depression have the same effect.

Women who have had a hysterectomy or surgical removal of the ovaries may also experience a diminished enjoyment of sex and a reduced ability to reach orgasm (see page 76).

SELF-HELP

- Before sex, put some sterile, water-soluble jelly on your vaginal entrance. You may want to put a small amount inside your vagina and on your partner's penis or fingers. Water-based jellies are better than oil-based ones because they are less likely to promote bacterial growth and infections, and they will not cause the rubber of a condom to perish.
- Avoid douches, talcum powder, perfumed toilet papers, and any fragranced bath oils and foams, which can irritate the vagina.
- Avoid washing the inside of your labia with soap as it will dry the skin.
- Avoid remedies for genital itchiness containing an antihistamine or perfume.
- Spend longer on foreplay to give your body more time to produce its own lubrication. Gentle massage of the breasts, belly, thighs, and genitals can be extremely erotic and aid lubrication. Menopausal women can usually lubricate as well as younger women; it simply takes them longer.
- Research shows that regular sex or masturbation may help to keep the vagina lubricated. This may be because sexual activity stimulates the adrenal glands that in turn help to keep the vagina lubricated. The muscle contractions that occur during orgasm, and the increased blood flow during sex, also seem to exercise the vagina, helping it retain its premenopausal state.
- Women who have low histamine levels may find it difficult to reach orgasm, whereas women with high histamine levels achieve orgasm easily. Women who take antihistamines regularly need to be aware of the possibility of decreased sexual desire and delayed orgasm.
- Zinc is a mineral associated with histamine production, and deficiency can be common in women who suffer from heavy bleeding or women who diet a lot. You can increase your zinc intake by taking a supplement, or you can include more zinc-rich foods in your diet, such as sardines and wheatgerm. Niacin, one of the B vitamins, is another nutrient that may be associated with histamine production, and may also stimulate mucus formation in response to sexual arousal.
- Practising Kegel exercises (see page 50) will make you more aware of your vagina and will increase your sexual enjoyment, as better toned muscles will enable you to grip your partner's penis more tightly.

COMPLEMENTARY THERAPY

Throughout history herbs have been used to treat low sex drive. Many plants, such as ginseng, are used for their aphrodisiac properties. However, some herbs such as nutmeg have been found to irritate the urogenital system, and these should be avoided. Traditional Indian medicine uses the saffron crocus as an aphrodisiac, and an African tree, yohimbine, is the source of several drugs used to treat impotence.

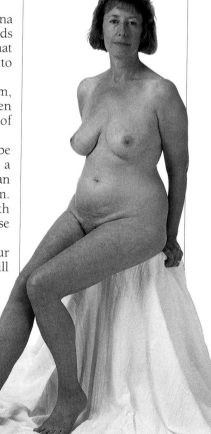

The Sexual Woman
Despite changes, the female body remains capable of responding to sexual stimuli throughout the menopause and beyond. Ideally, the menopause should be a time when we become more open and uninhibited about our bodies.

MEDICAL TREATMENT

All forms of HRT should relieve vaginal dryness and soreness if an adequate dose of oestrogen is given. If vaginal symptoms are your only menopausal problem, you could ask your doctor for a local vaginal oestrogen cream or pessary. It takes about four weeks of oestrogen treatment before the physical symptoms affecting the vagina begin to improve. A low-dose testosterone product can be used to increase sex drive.

Hypothyroidism becomes more common in the menopausal years, and this may be another cause of low sexual desire. Conversely, an overactive thyroid that speeds up the body's basal metabolism can greatly increase sexual desire – people who take thyroid hormones may also report an unusually strong interest in sex. A number of minerals, such as iodine, copper, zinc, and the amino acid tyrosine can help activate the thyroid gland, whereas foods such as turnips, kale, cabbage, and soya beans contain an anti-thyroid substance. Treatment for hypothyroidism may restore sex drive and you should seek medical advice if you suspect that you suffer from this condition (see page 97).

INSOMNIA

If you are feeling depressed or anxious, or you are suffering from night sweats it can become difficult to get to sleep, and common to wake early in the morning. Eventually, a good night's rest can become a rarity.

Laboratory studies have shown that women who have normal levels of oestrogen, or who take HRT, fall asleep faster than women who don't. Women who have adequate levels of oestrogen also spend more time in the deepest (dream) stage of sleep, and they feel more refreshed when they awake. Dreaming seems to be particularly important for the feeling of rest and renewal that comes from sleeping. Without oestrogen, we can sleep for a whole night but still feel tired on waking.

SELF-HELP
- In order to sleep undisturbed your first priority should be to rid yourself of night sweats or bring them under control (see page 49).
- Take a long walk or some other form of aerobic exercise an hour before bedtime, the quality of your sleep should improve noticeably.
- Warm milk at bedtime works for many insomniacs. This may be due to the action of calcium on the nerves.

COMPLEMENTARY THERAPY

Valerian root has been used for centuries as a sleep-inducing herb. It is widely used in Europe as a treatment for insomnia and its sedative effect can be very therapeutic during the menopause. Insomnia can also be helped by passion flower, peppermint, catnip, camomile, and hops.

MEDICAL TREATMENT

Before deciding on an appropriate medication, you and your doctor should make a correct diagnosis of your insomnia. If menopausal symptoms such as night sweats or anxiety are preventing you from sleeping, then HRT will cure your insomnia. If your sleeplessness is caused by a medical complaint or emotional problem unrelated to the menopause you may be prescribed sleeping tablets. Although these are sometimes useful to help you through a traumatic. life event, such as bereavement, you may suffer from withdrawal effects, particularly if you take sleeping tablets over a long period of time. Even though nowadays most doctors prescribe short-acting benzodiazepines, which are quickly eliminated by the body, you should be wary of taking sleeping pills unless it is absolutely necessary.

STOMACH AND BOWEL SYMPTOMS

Bloating with abdominal distension may be a problem during the menopausal years. It is usually due to gas in the large intestine, produced by fermentation in the bowel. As we age, small pockets of tissue may balloon out from the bowel, giving rise to the condition called diverticulitis. Within these small pockets (diverticula) food may lodge, become stale, ferment, and produce large amounts of gas. The intestine may end up coated with food remnants that form small centres of fermentation. It is quite common for the sufferer to wake in the morning with a flat stomach and for the abdomen to swell as the day progresses, so that by bedtime the swelling resembles a six-month pregnancy! During the night, lack of food and sugar in the intestine allows fermentation to abate. After a breakfast that contains sugars and yeasts, fermentation in the bowel flares up again. Alternatively, bloating may be a side-effect of taking HRT.

Constipation is another frequent symptom at the menopause because intestinal motility (movement) is affected by the sex hormones. We know that progesterone reduces bowel movements so that the motions become infrequent, dry, and pebble-like. Oestrogen, on the other hand, speeds up bowel movements and the stools revert to a normal consistency and frequency.

SELF-HELP
- A high-fibre diet, plenty of fluids, and frequent exercise will keep the bowels normal. Cutting down on sugar, dairy products, and alcohol will also help.
- Eat foods that cause fermentation, such as foods containing yeast (e.g., yeast extract) and sugar, only in the early part of the day.
- A fast effective remedy for constipation is to eat lots of prunes and figs, fruits that are both high in fibre.

COMPLEMENTARY THERAPY
There are several homeopathic and herbal remedies available in health food shops, such as the Bach Flower Remedies. Gentle "scouring" herbs and foods, such as sunflower seeds, may help, and senna has a gentle purgative action. Some people recommend specialist treatments, such as colonic irrigation, in which the lower part of the intestine is flushed out with water.

MEDICAL TREATMENT
If necessary, you can take laxatives to cure constipation, but these should not be relied upon for a long time. If you are taking HRT and you are suffering from fluid retention and bloating throughout your HRT cycle, it may indicate too high a dose of oestrogen. This can be solved by lowering the dose or switching from oral HRT to transdermal therapy (the patch). If constipation is due to HRT, it is usually in the progestogen phase and may be helped by modification of the type or dose of progestogen.

Diverticulitis
As women grow older, the gut is more inclined to balloon out into small pockets (below). Food may lodge here and ferment, giving rise to bloating and gas.

BREAST SYMPTOMS

Most women experience breast discomfort in the week before they menstruate, due to fluid retention in the breast tissue and a consequent increase in breast tension. As women reach their early 40s, this discomfort may develop into a more severe pain called mastalgia. The breasts become hard, tender, and extremely painful. An attack of mastalgia can last for up to ten days.

In severe cases, the breasts can be so painful that you cannot bear anything to touch them. The pain is especially intense in the nipples, and may keep you awake at night. Even turning over in bed can be agony.

It is estimated that 70 percent of women in Britain suffer from breast pain at some time in their lives, but particularly in the pre- and perimenopausal years. It is one of the most common symptoms in women attending a breast clinic and the most frequent reason for breast-related visits to the doctor. Sadly, some GPs can be unsympathetic, and reluctant to treat breast pain, perceiving it as non-pathological or part of a "woman's lot".

Mastalgia is often cyclical, fluctuating with the menstrual cycle and usually becoming worse immediately before menstruation. But non-cyclical mastalgia can occur at any time of the month and is most common in women over 40 years of age. The causes are not completely understood, but mastalgia may stem from abnormal sensitivity of breast tissue to the fluctuation of the female hormones at the menopause. Diet can make this problem worse. Women who suffer from breast pain tend to have low levels of essential fatty acids and high levels of saturated fat in their blood – this appears to exaggerate the effects of female hormones on breast tissue. Cyclical pain may be a side-effect of oral contraceptives or HRT if the doses of hormone are too high.

If you are suffering from severe mastalgia, you may find that your life is extremely compromised. You may be anxious and depressed, and you may be frightened that the pain is due to breast cancer. In the majority of cases, mastalgia is a benign condition. Your doctor will be able to allay your fears and carry out a breast examination to exclude malignancy. You can also request a mammogram (see page 194).

SELF-HELP
- Wear a good supportive bra; if necessary, go to a specialist bra fitter. Wearing a bra in bed may relieve pain during the night.
- Cut down on the amount of saturated fat you eat.

COMPLEMENTARY THERAPY
One of the essential fatty acids, gamolenic acid, which is found in evening primrose oil, significantly reduces breast pain in up to 70 percent of women and has not been found to have any side-effects.

MEDICAL TREATMENT
The very least you deserve from your doctor is a sympathetic hearing and physical examination. In a survey that was undertaken in a Cardiff breast clinic, it was found that 85 percent of women were satisfied by reassurance and an explanation of mastalgia. If mastalgia is very severe it may be treated by drugs such as danazol and bromocriptine, which alter hormone balance. Both drugs may have side-effects, including nausea, weight gain, and sometimes hirsutism (see page 39) and lowering of the voice.

WEIGHT GAIN

Some postmenopausal women strive to maintain their premenopausal weight. Medically this is quite unsound: the weight that you may gain at the menopause is due to a slower metabolism – something that affects both men and women as they grow older – and a decline in oestrogen levels, which affects the way that fat is distributed.

It is important to have a realistic outlook and be aware that changes in body shape happen to all postmenopausal women. Excessive or faddy dieting is unhealthy, and it may mean that you fail to meet your daily calcium requirements. Try using exercise as a means of maintaining muscle tone instead.

We know from actuarial records that middle-aged women who are underweight live shorter lives than those who are overweight. I don't wish to encourage any woman to become obese, but I do wish to free her from the constraints of having to be thin.

SELF-HELP

● How do you know whether you are too fat or too thin? Health experts agree that people are taller now than they were 30 years ago, and that "normal" weight ranges have changed greatly. Furthermore, we now know that there should be no difference between acceptable weights for men and women. The only variables are age and height. Check your weight against the chart on page 154.

● Consider your body shape. Do you carry more weight around your stomach and waist or more round your hips and thighs? The former is more likely to predispose you to heart disease.
– Measure your waist at its narrowest point while you stand relaxed.
– Measure your hips at their widest point.
– Divide your waist measurement by your hip measurement to obtain your waist-to-hip ratio.
Ratios above 0.8 (for women) are linked to a greater risk of diabetes, heart disease, high blood pressure, osteoporosis, and arthritis. If you fall into this category, discuss your weight and how it affects your health with your doctor.

● If your weight is within the range of the table on page 154, your waist-to-hip ratio is not in the high risk category, and you have no serious medical problems related to body mass, then there is no health advantage in reducing your weight. By eating a variety of healthy foods and by exercising regularly, you can let your body settle down to its natural weight.

● If your weight is over the recommended weight for your height and age, the following tips may help you to lose weight:
– Drink half a pint of water before you start to eat. This will make you feel more satiated at the end of a meal.
– Put your food on a small plate. This controls the amount you can reasonably eat at one sitting.
– The more time you take eating food, the more satisfied you're likely to feel. People who over-eat usually eat quickly, they don't taste the food, and have to eat more in order to feel satisfied.
– Taking exercise an hour or so before a meal is a potent appetite suppressant.
– Eat your largest meal early in the day, when you have most time to burn up the calories you've eaten. Avoid eating large meals late in the evening – sleeping during the night does not burn off many calories.

Body Shape and Heart Disease
Before the menopause, the waist to hip ratio is less than 0.8 and there is a correspondingly low risk of heart disease. After the menopause, fat distribution changes and the risk of heart disease increases. You can assess your risk by dividing your waist measurement by your hip measurement. If the resulting figure is over 0.8 you fall into a higher risk group for heart disease.
For example:
74 ÷ 99cm = 0.74 (low risk)
81 ÷ 99cm = 0.82 (higher risk)

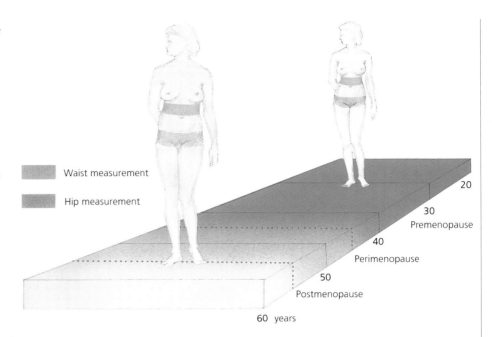

Waist measurement

Hip measurement

20 — Premenopause
30
40 — Perimenopause
50
60 years — Postmenopause

MEDICAL TREATMENT
Unless you are so overweight that your health is being affected, weight gain requires no medical treatment. But if your weight is posing a threat to your health, and you have other risk factors for heart disease, such as high blood pressure and smoking, it is a good idea to ask your doctor to recommend a diet and to supervise your weight loss programme. Some women resort to surgical techniques such as liposuction in an attempt to lose weight, but this should be regarded as an extreme measure.

LOWERING OF THE VOICE
There are two reasons for the voice deepening after the menopause. First, there is a relative increase in the amount of male hormones, or androgens, circulating in the blood. Long after the ovaries have stopped secreting oestrogen, they continue to secrete androgens. This relative excess of male hormone has a masculinizing effect on various organs of the body, including the larynx, causing a deepening of the voice.

The second cause can be an underactive thyroid or hypothyroidism (see page 97). The voice becomes deep, gruff, and slightly hoarse, and there are other accompanying symptoms, such as thick, dry skin, hair loss, a tendency to feel the cold, weight gain, and mental and physical fatigue.

MEDICAL TREATMENT
If you are suffering from hypothyroidism, your voice will return to normal when you start to take thyroid supplements. If the change is due to a relative excess of male hormones, the process is harder to reverse, even with HRT. If you feel that medical treatment is necessary, you should consult your doctor as soon as you notice your voice deepening so that HRT can halt the process.

HEART SYMPTOMS

The earliest symptom of postmenopausal heart disease (heart problems are rare in premenopausal women because of the presence of oestrogen) is nearly always angina. This is a crushing pain in the middle of the chest brought on by effort, and alleviated by rest. Without rest, the pain can worsen and radiate up into the neck, teeth, and down the arm (usually the left arm but occasionally the right). Eventually the pain will become so bad that you are forced to stop what you are doing. Angina is a warning sign that insufficient oxygen is reaching your heart muscle. You should take any chest pain seriously and go to your doctor for a cardiac check-up.

Other symptoms relating to heart health are palpitations and shortness of breath on exertion. You may find that normal exercise leaves you unusually breathless and climbing several flights of stairs gives you a pumping, fluttery feeling in your chest.

If you are suffering from other symptoms, such as dizziness, headaches, or blurred vision, you should have your blood pressure checked, as you may have hypertension (see page 83).

SELF-HELP

- Try to avoid risk factors such as smoking and obesity. Try to lose weight if you are more than a few kilograms or pounds over your ideal weight.
- Try to limit the amount of salt you eat from all sources, including processed food. You can drop your blood pressure several points by eliminating salt.
- Recent research seems to confirm that garlic improves cardiovascular health, although many doctors remain sceptical. You can eat garlic in meals or take garlic pearls, which are odourless.
- Regular exercise is the only way to strengthen a weak heart, and it will help reduce high blood pressure. However, if you have heart problems, you should consult your doctor before you start exercising to ensure that you do not go beyond your physical capabilities.
- Knowing how to keep yourself calm during times of stress is important. Try to practise breathing and relaxation techniques.

MEDICAL TREATMENT

There is a wide range of drugs to treat heart conditions, including hypotensives, betablockers, diuretics, cardiac stimulants, and coronary vasodilators. Angina can be controlled by taking a coronary vasodilator drug whenever you have an attack. The tablet is placed underneath the tongue and rapidly dissolves into the bloodstream, giving almost immediate relief. You can even take one of these tablets before exercising to prevent angina in the first place.

If you have high cholesterol, your doctor will probably prescribe drugs to lower it and reduce the possibility of serious heart complications. If you do suffer from heart disease, treatments include an artificial pacemaker, a coronary bypass operation (see page 81), or balloon angioplasty (see page 82).

However, prevention is better than cure, and oestrogen can play an important role in maintaining your cardiovascular health. If you come from a family with a history of serious heart disease, you should start taking HRT pre- or perimenopausally. HRT is also appropriate if you have had early symptoms of heart disease or even a heart attack. There is much research to show that oestrogen decreases the risk of a heart attack by up to 50 percent.

EMOTIONAL SYMPTOMS

Feelings such as tension, anxiety, depression, listlessness, irritability, tearfulness, and mood swings can occur at any age, but they rarely occur together, or as frequently as they do during the menopause. If you are experiencing several negative feelings simultaneously, it may be helpful to know that the menopause is the reason.

For many women, menopausal mood changes resemble a roller coaster ride. Women describe subtle sensations such as trembling, fluttering, unease, and discomfort. More severe feelings of anxiety or panic can arise with little provocation. Tasks that you used to be able to tackle can leave you in total disarray. Mood swings from elation to despondency are common. Your patience is easily exhausted. The future may look hopeless, your loss of self-esteem is precipitous, and you may feel truly depressed.

The centres in the brain (see page 44) that control a sense of well-being, a positive state of mind, and a feeling of control and tranquillity are affected by the absence of oestrogen. Taking oestrogen supplements in the form of HRT can cause a dramatic return to normality.

For some women, the emotional troubles they experience around the menopause may mainly be due to the fact that their sleep is being interrupted by night sweats. People who are tired are often irritable and anxious. If you're experiencing this problem, try the self-help tips on page 217.

A major depression, although rare, can descend upon you during your menopausal years, and this is distinct from other emotional symptoms that you may experience, such as tearfulness and anxiety. The following are possible predictors of depression during the menopause:

- A past or recent history of stressful events, such as divorce or bereavement.
- A surgically induced menopause.
- Having negative expectations of the menopause.
- Severe hot flushes and night sweats.
- A family history of depressive illness.

Depression can be a debilitating illness that can last for weeks, months, or even years if left untreated. It affects your body, your mood, your thoughts, and severely interferes with normal life. As a woman, you're more likely to experience a depression than a man is. Consult your doctor if you have experienced four of these symptoms for at least two weeks.

- Any extreme eating patterns, such as bingeing or periods of starvation.
- Unusual sleeping patterns, such as sleeping all the time or insomnia.
- Being exceptionally lethargic or restless.
- An inability to enjoy a once pleasurable activity; including a loss of sex drive.
- Debilitating fatigue or loss of energy.
- Feelings of worthlessness and self-reproach.
- Difficulty concentrating, remembering, and making decisions.
- Thoughts of death or suicide, or suicide attempts (seek help straight away).

SELF-HELP

- Severe mood swings and irritability can distance you from your partner and, occasionally, can jeopardize a relationship. However, if you share your feelings you may find your partner is very supportive. Several studies show that partners are keen to understand menopausal symptoms and would prefer to have insight into potential problems before the onset of the menopause.

- Women who go to self-help groups may be better able to deal with depression. Think about joining such a group, or starting one yourself.
- Twenty to 30 minutes of strenuous exercise results in the release of endorphins, which are brain opioids similar to morphine. This can lift the mood and produce an "exercise high" that lasts up to eight hours. Exercise can also benefit hot flushes and night sweats, which is helpful if this is the root cause of your depression.
- Yoga, relaxation techniques, and meditation all promote tranquillity and combat anxiety and tension (see page 156).

COMPLEMENTARY THERAPY

Herbs that may have a calming effect are passion flower and valerian root, taken as a tea or a tincture. Passion flower helps insomnia, and elevates the levels of serotonin in the blood, which creates a feeling of well-being. A bath made from an infusion of your favourite herbs can also be therapeutic.

Menopausal depression and stress may be alleviated by ginger, cayenne pepper, dandelion root, and Siberian ginseng. These may work because they contain essential nutrients, for instance, dandelion root contains magnesium, potassium, and vitamin E; and cayenne pepper contains a high level of magnesium and bioflavonoids. Ginseng contains oestrogenic compounds, and Siberian ginseng and liquorice root have been important medicines in the Far East for thousands of years and are said to combat lassitude and depression.

MEDICAL TREATMENT

The mainstay of treatment for emotional symptoms is HRT. Studies from all over the world show that after a short period (between two weeks and two months), HRT can bring about a significant decline in anxiety and depression. Oestrogen even lifts the mood in non-depressed, healthy young women. It acts through several well-known antidepressive mechanisms in the brain, on which other antidepressant drugs act. The tranquillizing effect of oestrogen is at least the equivalent of tranquillizers such as diazepam and chlorodiazepoxide, and oestrogen is a great deal healthier to take.

INTELLECTUAL SYMPTOMS

Forgetfulness is one of the most common symptoms that menopausal women complain of, and they may experience it long before they actually stop menstruating. You may forget where you put something, you may miss appointments, and things that used to be easy to remember can suddenly require enormous effort. The ability to concentrate can also become difficult. These problems combined can make it hard to carry out work that involves complex assessments and major decision-making. Even minor decisions can sometimes be quite paralyzing.

SELF-HELP

- Any sort of work or studying will go a long way to preserve your intellectual ability. It's never too late to get a job, although many women in their menopausal years express fear about how to go about finding one. Many universities, colleges, and evening classes offer courses in a range of subjects, including employment retraining.

SOOTHING BATH HERBS

Choose plants and herbs that have a calming effect

Immerse bag in boiling water

Infusing The Herbs
Place the dried herbs in a calico or muslin bag and leave to infuse in a basin of boiling water. Then put the infusion and bag into the bath.

VITAMINS AND MINERALS TO ALLEVIATE EMOTIONAL AND INTELLECTUAL SYMPTOMS	
Vitamin B3 (niacin)	Insomnia, nervousness, irritability, confusion, depression
Vitamin B1 (thiamine)	Loss of appetite, depression, irritability, memory loss, sensitivity to noise, inability to concentrate
Calcium	Fatigue, sleeplessness, tension
Pantothenic Acid	Depression, inability to tolerate stress
Vitamin B12	Poor concentration, forgetfulness
Potassium	Nervousness, irritability, disorientation

DIETARY THERAPY

Relatively little research has been conducted on the effects that nutrients have on intellectual processes, but there is some evidence that the above vitamins and minerals may contribute to brain health. Bear in mind, however, that most vitamins need to be taken in conjunction with other vitamins and minerals in order to be absorbed by the body. A shortage of one vital element can cause the others to be less effective.

MEDICAL TREATMENT

Most intellectual skills improve as soon as you start to take HRT. You feel more self-confident about making decisions, more assertive, better able to concentrate, and you are less forgetful.

We know from very sophisticated research that normal oestrogen levels are responsible for memory. Oestrogen exerts an extremely subtle effect on the memory process. It improves our verbal memory and the way we store information; it affects the way we relate our past experiences to present situations by helping us to have realistic expectations; it helps our working memory; and it helps us to process information efficiently, in fact to put two and two together and make four. It also allows us to use information flexibly so that we respond reasonably and rationally to situations instead of being rigid, inflexible, and impatient.

4

MENOPAUSAL MEDICAL COMPLAINTS

The falling level of oestrogen during the menopause combined with the natural ageing process in the post-menopausal years means that women can become increasingly susceptible to illness. One of the most painful conditions is osteoporosis, but there are also more minor conditions, which can be overcome with a combination of medical and self-help measures.

OSTEOPOROSIS

A painful, crippling, and life-threatening condition, osteoporosis is the single most important health hazard for women past the menopause – it is more common than heart disease, stroke, diabetes, or breast cancer. In its early stages, osteoporosis has no obvious symptoms, so many women may be unaware that they have it. Because of its life-threatening nature, it is vital that every woman be told the facts about this disease; women must become vigilant and take measures to prevent osteoporosis from destroying their lives.

The word "osteoporosis" is derived from the Greek and means "bone that has many holes". A clinical definition of osteoporosis is "a condition where there is less normal bone than expected for a woman's age, with an increased risk of fracture". However, some experts restrict the term "osteoporosis" to describe low bone density where fractures have already occurred, and use the term "osteopenia" to describe women who have bones with low density, but have not suffered fractures.

WHY IT HAPPENS

As oestrogen and progesterone levels fall, bones begin to lose mass by 0.5–3 percent a year. By the time a woman is 80, she can easily have lost 40 percent of the bone mass in her body.

From the outside, bone seems convincingly hard and solid. However, the strong and smooth surface of bone is porous, and encloses an inner, spongy matrix of honeycomb-like appearance.

Healthy bone has blood vessels and nerves and a very efficient repair and maintenance system. There are special cells that cause bone breakdown, and others, called osteoblasts, that renew, repair, and lay down new bone. The activity of these cells is controlled mainly by hormones, including oestrogen, which is thought to increase the repair and renewal rate of bone. If oestrogen levels fall, bone is not replaced as efficiently.

Oestrogen also facilitates the uptake of calcium from the blood into the bone and inhibits its loss. A fall in oestrogen levels, therefore, leads to bone disintegration.

The formation of tiny holes within the bone results in two things. First, the overall structure and supporting tissue of the bone is thinned out, and, second, there is less bone matrix in which calcium can be deposited. Eventually the tiny craters in bone increase to look like holes in Swiss cheese. Bones lose their thickness and density and become brittle and break comparatively easily. For a woman with severe osteoporosis of the spine, minor knocks, jolts, or falls can cause the spinal bones to fracture.

RISK FACTORS

Ageing is the main cause of osteoporosis, but it can also be the result of malignant disease, chronic liver disorder, or rheumatoid arthritis. Black women, who have greater bone density, have a lower risk of osteoporosis than white women. Certain conditions, situations, and habits, as outlined below, are also contributory factors. The most significant of these is impaired peak bone density.

LOW BONE DENSITY

From infancy, your bones grow in size until peak bone mass or density is achieved between ages 25 and 35. After this point bone mass no longer increases. The amount of bone in your skeleton as you approach the menopause will depend on the peak level of bone mass you achieved, the time at which your bone loss begins, and the rate at which bone loss proceeds. If your peak bone mass is low to begin with, you have a much greater chance of developing severe osteoporosis after the menopause.

AMENORRHOEA

Osteoporosis occurs in some women with premenopausal amenorrhoea (lack of menstrual periods), and is related to low oestrogen levels. Two examples of high risk categories are young women with anorexia nervosa, who eat a near-starvation diet, and young sportswomen, who exercise excessively while living on restricted diets. When the body receives so little food that the fat-to-muscle ratio drops, it responds by switching off oestrogen production in the ovaries, presumably to prevent the undernourished woman from becoming pregnant.

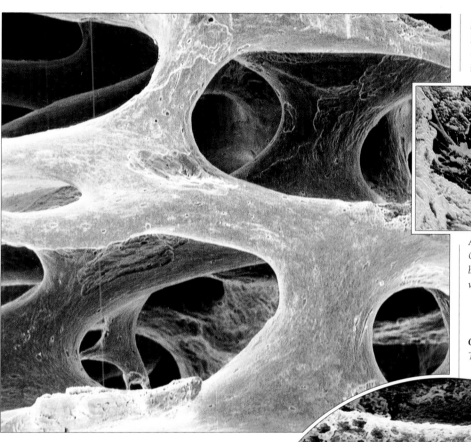

Healthy Bone
Bone that is rich in calcium has a resilient internal structure, which makes it resistant to fracture.

An Osteoblast
Osteoblasts renew and repair bone, but their activity declines when oestrogen levels drop.

Osteoporotic Bone
The bone is brittle, has holes, and is prone to fracture easily on minor impact.

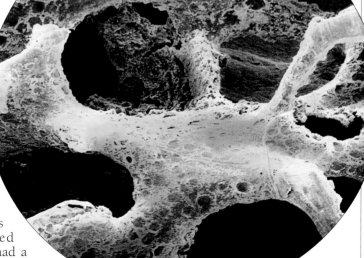

HYPERTHYROIDISM

Women who have an overactive thyroid gland or who take high doses of thyroxine for thyroid deficiency are at risk of developing osteoporosis. Women overtreated with thyroxine may lose bone mass at seven times the normal rate. If you are taking thyroxine, ask your doctor to check your thyroid function and dosage requirements periodically, and ask about a bone density test.

PREMATURE MENOPAUSE

The earlier the age of the menopause, with its depletion of oestrogen, the greater the risk of osteoporosis. The National Osteoporosis Society (see page 219) reports that a very high number of women aged between 60 and 69 who have osteoporosis had a premature menopause. While most doctors would

FACTORS AFFECTING PEAK BONE MASS

How much tissue your bones contain when they are at their most dense is the best determinant of how much will be present when you're older. Bone density is affected by the following:

● *Adequate amounts of calcium and vitamin D are essential.*

● *Little or no exercise in your 20s will lower peak bone mass; too much exercise, causing amenorrhoea, is also unhealthy.*

● *Bone mass is affected positively by the early onset of menstrual periods, a late menopause, taking hormonal contraceptives, and multiple pregnancies.*

● *Traits inherited from parents – if your parents have thick or heavy bones, generally you will have a similar bone structure.*

offer hormone replacement therapy (HRT; see chapter six) to treat the more obvious and immediate menopausal symptoms, such as hot flushes and night sweats, they often neglect prescribing it for the full length of time needed to protect against osteoporosis.

HYSTERECTOMY AND SURGICAL REMOVAL OF THE OVARIES

The ovaries are a woman's main source of oestrogen, so it is not surprising that their removal leads to loss of bone mass. Most women show early signs of osteoporosis within four years of removal of the ovaries if HRT is not given. Even women who have had hysterectomies without having the ovaries removed are more prone to bone loss than women who retain their uterus.

The National Osteoporosis Society produced statistics showing that only two women out of 100 who had undergone hysterectomies and removal of the ovaries had been offered HRT.

SMOKING

The menopause may start up to five years early in heavy smokers. Smoking severely reduces the benefits of HRT to bone health, and limits the amount of oxygen your body can take in. When oxygen consumption is low, bones tend to be weak. Passive smokers are also at risk. Blood tests have shown that a passive smoker inhales one fifteenth of the nicotine that is inhaled by a smoker in the same room. Female passive smokers, on average, reach the menopause about three years earlier than women in non-smoking households. The golden rules are to stop smoking well before the menopause, or never to start in the first place, and to avoid spending time in a smoke-filled environment.

CORTICOSTEROIDS

Some of the most dangerous drugs that cause bones to become osteoporotic are steroids, such as cortisone or prednisone. These drugs treat a number of conditions, including severe cases of rheumatoid arthritis. When prescribed over long periods of time in high doses, corticosteroid usage can lead to osteoporosis. If you are taking these drugs, ask your doctor to prescribe the lowest effective dose, in order to minimize bone damage.

DIAGNOSING OSTEOPOROSIS

Successful treatment and possible prevention of osteoporosis depend on early detection of bone changes. Both sufferers and potential sufferers need to be identified. Your mobility and self-esteem may be severely affected if you allow osteoporosis to progress to the point where it causes severe medical problems, particularly spinal and hip fractures (see page 69) – a third of women over 65 will suffer a fracture of the spine, and by the age of 90, one third of women will have had a hip fracture. Both can be extremely painful and can make you housebound. These physical problems may be compounded by feelings of awkwardness or a loss in confidence. Take matters into your own hands and make sure you are given the treatments you need to keep your bones strong and healthy.

If you are 50 or over, any curvature of the spine (kyphosis) and loss of height deserve particular attention. Other symptoms of osteoporosis include pain, breathlessness, indigestion, acid reflux, and incontinence. If you suddenly begin to suffer low-back pain, you should ask your doctor to carry out a test for spinal osteoporosis, and consider the possibility of spinal fracture. No one can tell with complete certainty whether you will develop osteoporosis, although bone density tests can provide the most accurate predictions.

BONE DENSITY TESTS

There are several ways of assessing bone density, and a scan is considered the best predictor of fracture. Bone density tests (see page 197) measure the density of the spine, wrist, and other high-risk areas. A decrease in bone mineral density (BMD) measured in the spine or hip may indicate a 200 percent increase in the chance of any fracture, and a staggering 300 percent increase in the chance of a hip fracture.

FRACTURES

Osteoporosis usually remains undetected in the early stages, and most osteoporotic fractures caused by minor trauma are still not diagnosed as being due to osteoporosis. The working rule is that if you sustain a fracture after minor trauma, osteoporosis is present. Therefore, if you are over 40 and you fracture your wrist or hip after a minor fall, you are likely to have osteoporosis. Fractures of the wrist are known as Colles' fractures and usually result from attempting to break a fall with the hand. Hip fractures are one of the most serious types of fracture, since they are very painful and can severely impair mobility. Compression fractures of the vertebrae are also common, and if you don't receive treatment, you may experience further fractures. Don't leave it too late: 30 percent of your bone mass may have been lost by the time you have a hip fracture.

BACKACHE

Constant pain in the lower back should be taken as a sign for you to seek treatment from a menopause clinic, doctor or gynaecologist. On average, women who develop spinal osteoporosis begin to notice an increase in the incidence of severe backache about nine to ten years after their last menstrual period, or sooner, if they have had a surgically induced menopause (as a result of hysterectomy or surgical removal of the ovaries).

MEDICAL TREATMENT

The aim of prescription drugs is to halt bone loss, prevent further fractures, and replace or repair bone whenever possible. Once fractures occur, at least a third of bone mass has already been lost; in some cases as much as 60 percent is gone.

Over two million people in the UK have already suffered osteoporotic fractures, and although there are some treatments that can reverse osteoporosis, broken joints or bones

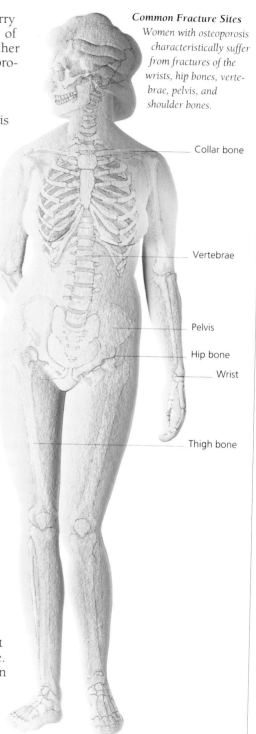

Common Fracture Sites
Women with osteoporosis characteristically suffer from fractures of the wrists, hip bones, vertebrae, pelvis, and shoulder bones.

Collar bone

Vertebrae

Pelvis

Hip bone

Wrist

Thigh bone

"DOWAGER'S HUMP"

This condition has the following characteristics: loss of height, hunched posture, a protruding abdomen, and a shuffling gait.

As the bones of the spine gradually lose density, the collapse of the vertebrae causes the ribcage to tilt downwards towards the hips. A curvature in the upper spine creates a second curve in the lower spinal column, pushing the internal organs outwards. Because of the compressed spinal column, up to 20 cm (8 in) in height can be lost. Internal functions are impaired as the compressed organs shift position and obstruct other organs and systems. Constipation can be a problem; breathing may become laboured; and aches and pains in the lower back and throughout the body may arise from pressure on the nerves emanating from the collapsed vertebrae. Day-to-day life can become increasingly difficult.

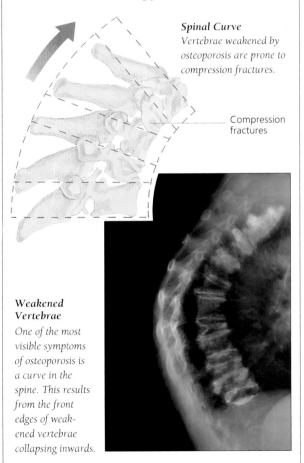

Spinal Curve
Vertebrae weakened by osteoporosis are prone to compression fractures.

Compression fractures

Weakened Vertebrae

One of the most visible symptoms of osteoporosis is a curve in the spine. This results from the front edges of weakened vertebrae collapsing inwards.

that have been severely damaged are not likely to respond to treatment. Fortunately, there are several methods that can be effective in halting bone loss – the most potent treatment being HRT.

HORMONE REPLACEMENT THERAPY (HRT)

If you have low bone mass, it is highly recommended that you take HRT. Even if you have high bone mass, your future risk of fracture will be reduced. Calcium loss can be reduced by very low doses of oestrogen, and several studies have suggested that when progestogen (the synthetic version of progesterone) is taken with oestrogen, bone metabolism responds favourably. The progestogen appears to stimulate a small amount of bone formation, while the oestrogen halts further loss of bone.

Studies have also demonstrated that oestrogen therapy helps bone to maintain its mineral strength and mass. The oestrogen effect here appears to be dose-dependent. With high dosage, oestrogen can increase bone mass in the spine, but a low dose merely slows down the natural ageing loss. It is interesting to note that menopausal women who used oral contraceptives (containing oestrogen) for long periods of time have been found to have heavier and stronger bones than women who have never taken oral contraceptives.

NON-HORMONAL TREATMENT

The first line of defence against osteoporosis is increasing calcium intake through diet. Eat plenty of calcium-rich foods, including dairy products and canned fish with bones, such as sardines, and ask your doctor about calcium supplements. To maximize benefits, calcium should be taken with other treatments, such as HRT.

A drug called etidronate has been shown to effectively treat established spinal osteoporosis. It works by inhibiting the bone-resorbing cells, the osteoclasts, and allowing the bone-rebuilding cells, the osteoblasts, to work more efficiently. This results in a small net gain in the amount of bone in the vertebrae. However, research studies have not yet given us conclusive evidence of etidronate's effectiveness against hip fractures.

Sodium fluoride can stimulate bone formation and may be given to women with severe vertebral osteoporosis. It is available only at specialist treatment centres and is not on prescription. Sodium fluoride is given in daily doses and must be taken with calcium supplements. A low, controlled dosage can increase bone density and may reduce fracture rate. However, in higher doses, it can be associated with an increase in hip fractures. Careful monitoring is required when taking sodium fluoride because there may be side-effects of indigestion and nausea.

PHYSIOTHERAPY

Increased muscle strength, improved spinal power and posture, maintenance of bone strength, relief of pain, and toning of pelvic floor muscles to cope with stress incontinence are all benefits of physiotherapy. Special exercises can also help with breathing difficulties that are exacerbated if the head falls forward, causing compression of the chest. Physiotherapy is often overlooked, but it should be an important part of your treatment for osteoporosis. A home exercise programme can be established to continue the treatment.

One of the most basic lessons taught by physiotherapists is how to breathe correctly. You don't need to go to a class to learn, but it is helpful initially to have a teacher's supervision to make certain you are learning the techniques correctly. People who keep themselves supple with exercise and special physiotherapy regimes are less likely to fall over, and they do less damage when they do fall than people who don't take regular exercise.

Hydrotherapy involves exercising in a pool of water at body temperature, 37°C (98°F), allowing you to move easily while the water supports you. The warmth relaxes the muscles and joints, relieves pain, and increases mobility. Buoyancy makes exercise easier, while the water resistance strengthens muscles.

PAIN RELIEF

Women with vertebral osteoporosis can suffer intense back pain, especially after a new fracture. If pain is very acute, a strong pain-reliever, such as morphine, will be prescribed. This produces rapid relief and may make a journey to hospital more comfortable. Curvature of the spine (kyphosis) produces ongoing muscular and ligament pain, but this can be treated with painkillers, such as paracetamol or codeine. Paracetamol is a safe, non-addictive drug, although you should not exceed the recommended dose or frequency of use; codeine may cause constipation.

Physiotherapists may also use various forms of electrotherapy or ultrasound to help relieve pain. Some now also use complementary techniques such as acupuncture, and recommend the use of heat pads, hot-water bottles, or ice packs at home. TENS (Transcutaneous Electrical Nerve Stimulation) machines are available in most treatment centres for pain relief.

If you have back pain, an occupational therapist can advise you on how to organize your home and work environment. You should sit in chairs with high backs that give support to the whole spine, and your bed should be firm, but not so hard that it cannot accommodate the altered shape of your spine.

Sufferer may feel housebound

Lack of exercise and vitamin D

Painful vertebral fractures

Pain on movement

Fear of being pushed in crowds

Immobility leads to further bone loss and fractures

Clothes don't fit properly

Loss of self-esteem

The Vicious Circle Of Vertebral Collapse

Women who suffer from osteoporosis can find themselves trapped in a vicious circle that erodes both their health and their sense of self-esteem.

PREVENTING OSTEOPOROSIS

Since all of us are at risk of developing osteoporosis, it is important that we adopt self-help measures in order to build up our natural resistance. Fortunately, there are a number of ways in which we can change our lifestyles to help maintain healthy bones.

SELF-HELP

As the greatest danger of osteoporosis is fracture, it is vital that you help yourself prevent its occurrence. Regular exercise, a balanced diet, and mental alertness can help to maintain overall fitness, and you should also have regular health checks with your doctor. As women get older, falls can be related to poor coordination and blackouts, so you should ask your doctor to check your heart and blood pressure. It is also important to maintain good vision by having your eyes tested regularly, particularly for a condition known as glaucoma (see page 200), which becomes more common with age. Avoid sedatives and other drugs that might reduce your alertness, such as antihistamines, and try to limit your alcohol intake.

Where possible, reduce the hazards in your home by removing any trailing electrical flexes and loose carpets. Make sure that there is always a firm handrail on stairs and be particularly on guard when walking on slippery or uneven surfaces.

Many women with painful spinal fractures suffer severe loss of confidence and self-esteem. This may be exacerbated because they become very conscious of their curved spine. Some women avoid going out and, as a result, may suffer from lack of exercise and vitamin D (through lack of exposure to the sun). This may make their osteoporosis worse. Loss of self-esteem in some women may cause problems that are as serious as their physical discomfort.

Counselling, emotional support, and talking to other menopausal women with similar problems can do much to give a woman a more positive attitude to life and help her become more outgoing and confident.

TAKE REGULAR EXERCISE

Investigators studying the relationship between bone density, prevention of bone fractures, and exercise found that the amount of weight-bearing exercise, such as jogging, relates directly to increased bone mass. Women who take exercise twice a week have denser bones than those who take exercise once a week, who, in turn, have denser bones than those who never take exercise at all. It is never too late to improve your body. Bones can be strengthened to resist the effect of oestrogen depletion during the postmenopausal years.

If you are not physically active, ask your doctor about the best exercise programme for your level of fitness. Brisk walking will help to strengthen your bones. Try to exercise daily for 20–30 minutes, enough to moderately accelerate your pulse rate.

EAT A CALCIUM-RICH DIET

The most important dietary advice for the early prevention of osteoporosis is to eat calcium-rich foods. Calcium is lost from the body in sweat, urine, and faeces, and maintenance of the correct amount is dependent on our dietary intake of calcium, combined with the presence of oestrogen and vitamin D. The bone deterioration that ends in osteoporosis begins a long time before the first fractures and the longer you wait to take action, the smaller your chances of recovery. Good nutrition is one of the best measures to slow down demineralization of bone. In brief, to prevent your bones from becoming brittle, you need calcium for bone mass, vitamin D to absorb the calcium into your body, and oestrogen to maintain the calcium inside your bones.

CONSIDER HRT

I would suggest that a sensible way of preventing osteoporosis would be to start a regular exercise routine from 35 onwards, and, once you are menopausal, to take enough oestrogen to maintain bone mass, and sufficient progestogen to stimulate bone formation. Oestrogen taken continuously in combination with progestogen taken for 10–13 days per month seems to optimize bone health, and prevent the incidence of life-threatening fractures. Ideally, you should have a bone density test to assess your bone health before HRT is prescribed.

BREAST CANCER

This is the most common type of cancer in women, and the leading cause of death in women aged between 35 and 50. In the UK, women have a one in 12 chance of developing breast cancer.

Despite great advances in the technology used to treat breast cancer, the mortality rate has hardly changed this century. We do know, however, that the cure rate for breast cancer depends on the stage at which it is detected, and whether it has spread. The earlier any abnormality is discovered, the more likely it is to be cured.

Although there is no equivalent of the cervical smear test (see page 195), which detects precancerous changes, an X-ray procedure called mammography exists (see page 194), which is able to detect very small breast tumours that cannot be felt manually. However, sometimes early and curable breast tumours can be found by routine monthly examination, and all women should learn how to examine their breasts (see page 193).

RISK FACTORS

Certain dietary habits can put you in a higher risk group than average. There is a documented link between breast cancer and a high intake of animal protein, saturated animal fats, and dairy products. Other risk factors are listed as follows.

MEDIUM TO HIGH RISK

Having a family history of breast cancer (especially close female relatives)
Early onset of menstruation and a late menopause
Being over the age of 40
Having children later than average
Being white
Obesity or a diet high in animal dairy fat

LOW RISK

Having several children
Breast feeding
Being short and thin
Late onset of menstruation and an early menopause

At one time, women taking oral contraceptives were thought to be at greater risk of breast cancer than women who did not take the pill. However, recent studies now suggest that there is no correlation.

SYMPTOMS

A small tumour may be detected during a routine self-examination of the breasts. The most common site for a malignant breast tumour is on the upper and outer part of the breast, where a lump can usually be felt rather than seen. A tumour is rarely

TYPES OF COMMON BREAST SURGERY

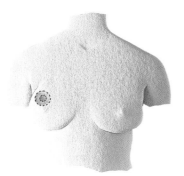

Lumpectomy
The whole lump and a small area of surrounding tissue is removed. Surgery is usually followed by radiotherapy.

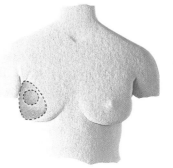

Partial Mastectomy
This is the removal of a substantial area of the breast tissue. The nipple is also removed in a partial mastectomy.

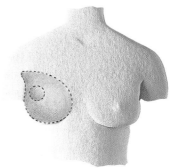

Extended Mastectomy
All of the breast is removed as well as some of the lymph nodes from the armpit, and sometimes part of the chest muscle.

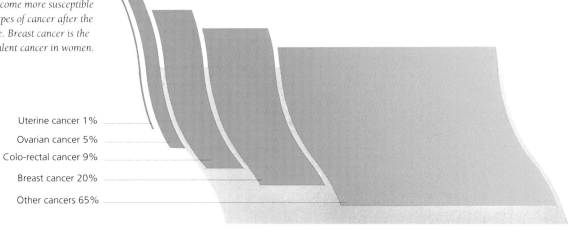

Comparative Death Rates From Common Cancers

Women become more susceptible to many types of cancer after the menopause. Breast cancer is the most prevalent cancer in women.

Uterine cancer 1%
Ovarian cancer 5%
Colo-rectal cancer 9%
Breast cancer 20%
Other cancers 65%

painful. Signs to look out for include a discharge from the nipple, a nipple that becomes inverted for the first time, lumps or swellings in the breasts, armpits, or along the collar bone, and a puckered or dimpled appearance of the breast.`

DIAGNOSIS
Most doctors will refer a woman with a breast lump to a hospital so that further tests can be made. If you have a cyst, the fluid can be removed and examined, and a clear-cut diagnosis made. This procedure is called a needle biopsy and it is a painless technique in which, under anaesthetic, a fine needle is inserted into the lump and some of the cells are drawn out. In 85 percent of cancerous tumours, malignant cells will be detected by a needle biopsy.

If a lump is small and shallow it is possible to have an outpatient lumpectomy. The lump is removed with some surrounding tissue and examined in the laboratory. If cancer is discovered, blood tests, X-rays, and bone scans will be carried out to help decide upon the right treatment.

MEDICAL TREATMENT
Radical treatments, such as mastectomy, do not necessarily improve survival rates. Many surgeons now recommend lumpectomy combined with radiotherapy or anti-cancer drugs (chemotherapy).

Sometimes, before you undergo breast surgery, you may be asked to sign a form that will allow your surgeon to carry out treatment during an

exploratory operation. Think carefully about this – you should always be an active participant in all decisions regarding your treatment.

If there are signs that a tumour has spread to the lymph nodes in the armpit, you will need more extensive treatment in order to prevent any further spread. If your tumour is sensitive to hormones, an anti-oestrogen drug may be prescribed.

Tamoxifen is a drug used in the treatment of certain types of breast cancer. It works by blocking the oestrogen hormone receptors in the breast cells and has fewer adverse effects than other anti-cancer drugs. Side-effects may include hot flushes, nausea, vomiting, swollen ankles, and irregular vaginal bleeding. Women at high risk of developing breast cancer may be prescribed tamoxifen to help prevent any cancer from developing (see page 8).

BREAST CANCER AND HRT
The use of HRT in women with breast cancer (past or present), as well as other female cancers, is controversial. Although many doctors regard cancer as a contraindication (see page 136) to HRT, some doctors will still prescribe it. Where appropriate, I have tried to reflect current medical thinking on HRT, but ultimately your doctor should decide your eligibility.

OUTLOOK
If a very small tumour is treated early, a complete cure is likely. All women who have had breast cancer will be asked to attend regular check-ups to detect

any recurrence of the cancer or spread to the rest of the body. It is very important that regular breast self-examinations and yearly mammograms are carried out. Even if the cancer recurs, it can be controlled for many years with surgery, drugs, and radiotherapy.

OVARIAN CANCER
Malignant ovarian growths are most common after the age of 50. There are about 5,000 cases of ovarian cancer diagnosed each year in the UK. Ovarian cancer is three times more common in women who have never had children, but less common in those who have taken the contraceptive pill. After breast, lung, colon, and stomach cancer, ovarian cancer is the fifth leading cause of death among women.

SYMPTOMS
In nearly all cases, ovarian cancer causes no symptoms until it spreads elsewhere, causing blockage of the bowel or pain by pressing on a nerve. The abdomen can hold surprisingly large masses without appearing swollen; however, generalized discomfort or bloating in the abdomen may be one of the first symptoms. Digestive symptoms, such as nausea and occasional vomiting are quite common. If the tumour spreads, fluid may collect in the abdomen, causing extreme swelling. Ovarian tumours very rarely cause vaginal bleeding unless they produce oestrogen. If an ovarian tumour is in the form of a cyst growing on a stalk, you may feel pain if the stalk twists, if there is a haemorrhage into the cyst, or if a large cyst ruptures.

If an ovarian cyst becomes extremely large, it can put pressure on the bladder, causing frequent urination. The veins of the legs may also be affected, resulting in varicose veins or swelling of the ankles. If a cyst puts pressure on the gut, it may cause discomfort, as well as intestinal and digestive problems. You may experience breathlessness if the tumour puts pressure on the diaphragm.

DIAGNOSIS
To determine whether a tumour is malignant or benign a laparoscopy will be carried out. This is an examination of the abdominal cavity through a fine fibre-optic viewing instrument. It is done through a tiny incision in the abdominal wall under general anaesthetic. If the tumour is very large, you may need an exploratory operation.

MEDICAL TREATMENT
All tumours will be surgically removed, and examination of the cells will identify malignancy. As much of the cancerous growth as possible will be removed, which may mean taking away part of the bowel, the Fallopian tube, the ovary, and the uterus. Surgery is usually followed by radiotherapy and anti-cancer drugs.

OUTLOOK
If the growth is confined to the ovary, two-thirds of patients will probably survive for more than five years. If the growth has spread, only one in five women will survive for more than five years. New techniques (see page 200) and drugs for detecting and treating ovarian cancer are improving survival rates. However, an annual pelvic examination by your doctor is the most important detection tool.

UTERINE CANCER
Unlike cervical cancer, which is most common in young women (see page 195), uterine or endometrial cancer is most common in older women – three-quarters of all sufferers are over the age of 50, and very few are under 40. Between the ages of 55 and 65, the incidence of uterine cancer more than doubles. As the proportion of older women in the population increases, this upward trend is likely to continue. In the UK, there are nearly 3,500 new cases every year.

Although it is the third most common cancer of the female reproductive organs, cancer of the uterus has a better survival rate than cancer of the ovary.

RISK FACTORS
Uterine cancer is more likely to occur among women who have never had children, and women of low fertility. There is also thought to be an association between uterine cancer and oestrogen replacement therapy when it is taken without progestogen (see page 126). However, nowadays HRT is prescribed in its combined form and this may actually protect against uterine cancer.

Women who are obese (which results in high blood levels of oestrogen), have a family history of uterine cancer, suffer from high blood pressure, diabetes, fibroids, or disturbed menstrual patterns with long intervals between periods, are all at a higher risk of developing uterine cancer.

SYMPTOMS

The earliest, most common sign of uterine cancer is abnormal vaginal bleeding, especially if you are postmenopausal. If you are still menstruating, any bleeding between periods, slight spotting, heavy and prolonged bleeding, or bleeding after intercourse are all symptoms that should be investigated. Advanced cancers may give rise to menstrual cramps, pelvic bloating and distension, with pressure in the lower abdomen. Symptoms affecting the bladder include frequent and urgent urination.

DIAGNOSIS

Occasionally, abnormal uterine cells are found in a routine cervical smear test, but this can be unreliable. A firm diagnosis is nearly always made after dilatation and curettage (D&C) of the uterine lining, when malignant cells are detectable on microscopic examination of endometrial tissue.

MEDICAL TREATMENT

A complete hysterectomy, with removal of the ovaries, Fallopian tubes, and uterus, is the usual treatment. In nearly all parts of the world this procedure, combined with radiotherapy in selected cases, before or after the operation, has vastly improved cure rates.

Occasionally, an extended total hysterectomy to remove the cervix and top of the vagina is carried out. All parts of the pelvis are carefully examined and all traces of tumour are removed. Afterwards, you will be given radiotherapy to the pelvis, which may last four to six weeks. If the tumour is widespread, and has spread to other parts of the body, however, neither surgery nor radiotherapy will be employed. Various combinations of anti-cancer drugs will be given, and large doses of progestogen are successful in removing or limiting the spread of the primary cancer and secondary deposits elsewhere in the body.

OUTLOOK

The overall cure rate is as high as 90 percent when the cancer is localized to the lining of the uterus. After five years, if the cancer has not spread beyond the muscles of the uterus, four out of five women survive. If the cancer is embedded deeper than this, or it has spread, the survival rate falls to 40 percent. This means that it is absolutely crucial to have irregular bleeding checked by your doctor.

HYSTERECTOMY

This is the surgical removal of the uterus with or without other reproductive organs. In the Western world it is one of the most commonly performed operations, second only to episiotomy (surgical enlargement of the vagina during childbirth) in frequency. You should always question your doctor's reasons for wanting to perform a hysterectomy.

WHY IS IT DONE?

- To remove cancer in the vagina, cervix, uterus, Fallopian tubes, or ovaries.
- To treat severe and uncontrollable pelvic infection.
- To stop acute haemorrhage.
- When certain life-threatening conditions affect the organs close to the uterus, and it is technically impossible to deal with the primary problem without removing the uterus.
- To treat extensive and very painful endometriosis.
- To remove large or multiple fibroids.
- After injury to the pelvic musculature during childbirth, which is severe enough to interfere with bowel or bladder function.
- To treat heavy vaginal bleeding that doesn't respond to treatment and results in anaemia.

Although these conditions are all debilitating, there are some serious but poorly publicized side-effects associated with having a hysterectomy. Loss of sexual desire is quite common even if your ovaries are intact. A significant number of women experience a decline in their sexual desire after having their uterus removed, and taking HRT doesn't seem to help. Indeed, several studies show that HRT eliminates a dry vagina and pain on intercourse, but it does not influence sex drive.

There is also data from Scandinavia that suggests sexual activity is greater, and the incidence of painful intercourse lower, in women who do not have their cervix removed. Some women who had had a complete hysterectomy (involving the removal of the cervix) claimed there was a significant loss in their capacity for orgasm, and they experienced orgasm in intercourse less than one in four times. The presence of sensitive nerve endings in the cervix may play a crucial role in your post-operative ability to have an orgasm.

We know that the ovaries, even after they stop secreting oestrogen, continue to secrete androgens, and these hormones are very important in maintaining libido in women. Removing the ovaries during a

TYPES OF HYSTERECTOMY

Surgical removal of the uterus can involve the removal of other pelvic organs, such as the ovaries and Fallopian tubes. Simple types of hysterectomy, in which the ovaries remain intact, prevent a sudden decline in oestrogen levels.

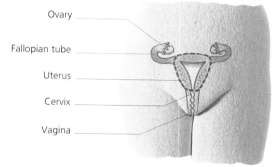

Ovary

Fallopian tube

Uterus

Cervix

Vagina

Vaginal Hysterectomy
The uterus and cervix are removed through an incision inside the vagina. The Fallopian tubes and ovaries are left intact.

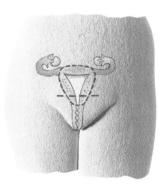

Total Abdominal Hysterectomy
The uterus and cervix are removed through an incision in the abdomen.

Bilateral Salpingo-oophorectomy
The uterus, cervix, Fallopian tubes, and ovaries are removed through a transverse incision in the lower abdomen.

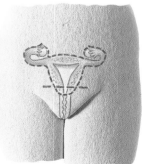

hysterectomy denies a woman this sexual stimulant. However, if testosterone therapy is taken after the operation, some women notice that their sex drive returns to normal.

There are other important health reasons for retaining the ovaries. They are our main source of oestrogen, and we know that oestrogen deprivation results in an earlier onset of heart disease (see page 79) and osteoporosis (see page 66).

These are indisputable reasons for discussing with your doctor exactly which reproductive organs will be removed. Do not make a decision without such discussion and ensure you have the power to make the final decision. Your partner will almost certainly support you in your decision. Make sure that he is involved in all discussions about treatment.

RECOMMENDATIONS

In theory, a hysterectomy should be a comparatively rare operation. However, 30 percent of all women aged 50 and over in the United States have had hysterectomies, often when it was not absolutely necessary. The removal of small fibroids, for instance, hardly warrants such a radical operation. Some doctors even advocate routine hysterectomy once childbearing is over. They argue that a hysterectomy forestalls the risk of cancers. Fortunately, this view is not widespread. You should make certain that you and your partner are fully informed of the consequences of a hysterectomy, and have no reservations about such an irrevocable step. Remember, it is you who decides whether or not you wish to spend the rest of your life without your uterus. Most medical conditions will respond to treatment without surgery, if a doctor is determined and positive. I personally would never have a hysterectomy without obtaining a second opinion, regardless of persuasive arguments.

If your ovaries are removed as well as your uterus, you will experience menopausal symptoms after the operation. These can, and should, be alleviated by long-term HRT.

OUTLOOK

Many women are concerned that they will gain weight after a hysterectomy. Fortunately, this is a myth. A diet rich in fresh vegetables, fruit, fish, and poultry will help you regain your strength and give you sufficient energy to start exercising and restore tone to flabby muscles.

Some women experience a psychological reaction after a hysterectomy. The following statistics have been compiled from various studies:

- Women who have their ovaries removed may blame the operation for hot flushes, lethargy, and other menopausal symptoms.
- Women who have had hysterectomies are four times more likely to become depressed in the three years after surgery than other women.
- Depressed women who have had hysterectomies are likely to remain depressed for twice as long – on average two years – as women who have not.
- Women who have had hysterectomies are five times more likely to seek psychiatric help for the first time than women who have not.
- The majority of women who seek psychiatric help following a hysterectomy are those who were not suffering from a life-threatening condition. This suggests that if a woman believes her hysterectomy was performed unnecessarily, she may become depressed as a result.
- Women grow more dissatisfied with the effects of their hysterectomies as time passes.

CANCER OF THE COLON

(Colo-rectal Cancer)

The colon in the large intestine is a very common cancer site: about 25,000 cases of colonic or rectal cancer occur in the UK each year. About two-thirds of these are cancers of the colon, accounting for 20 percent of all cancer deaths in the UK.

RISK FACTORS

The precise cause of colonic cancer is unknown, but there is thought to be a hereditary factor, and a Western diet is almost certainly a contributory cause. Nearly half a century ago, the connection between colonic cancer and low fibre in the diet was established, and it is probable that a diet that is high in meat and fat, and low in fibre encourages the production and concentration of carcinogens – chemical substances that promote the development of cancer. It is important to eat lots of fresh fruit and vegetables and high fibre foods in your diet.

SYMPTOMS

The most common symptom of colonic cancer is a sudden, inexplicable change in bowel movements in a woman who has always had regular, normal stools. Usually, she experiences constipation or diarrhoea, which may last more than a week and then return to normal. Another important warning sign is blood mixed in with the faeces. Blood from haemorrhoids usually coats the surface of the faeces, whereas blood from higher up in the colon has had a chance to mix in with the faeces. If the cancer is high up in the colon, the blood can only be detected with special chemical tests.

Because the colon and the abdomen can hold fairly large masses, there are sometimes no symptoms until the cancer is big enough to block the bowel, leading to symptoms such as profound abdominal pain, colic, or even vomiting.

DIAGNOSIS

Sometimes a cancer in the rectum can be felt by a doctor during a manual examination. More often, examination with a colonoscope or a sigmoidoscope, which can be passed up to 46 cm (18 in) into the bowel, will be necessary to view the surface of the intestine directly. This examination is often carried out in an outpatients' department, but it may be necessary to perform a barium enema, followed by special X-ray examinations, in order to detect the exact site of the tumour.

MEDICAL TREATMENT

Treatment depends on the extent of the cancer, but, in most cases, part of the colon is removed. The tumour, any diseased tissue, and a small amount of surrounding normal tissue are taken away, and the cut ends of the intestine are sewn together, restoring a channel for the passage of stools. If the cancer has spread, surgery may not be possible. If you have a complete blockage, you may need to wear a colostomy bag. This allows undigested food to be collected outside the body via an opening in the abdomen.

OUTLOOK

If the cancer is detected early, the outlook is generally good, and over half of all patients survive more than five years after surgery. Non-surgical treatments, such as chemotherapy and deep X-ray therapy, arrest the growth and spread of the cancer, but are not usually curative. As with all cancers, the earlier the tumour is detected, the greater the chances of a full recovery. This is why anyone over the age of 50 who experiences a sudden change in bowel habits should consult a doctor immediately .

ATHEROSCLEROSIS

This is a disease of the arterial wall in which the inner layer thickens, causing narrowing of the channel, reduced blood flow, and increased blood pressure (hypertension).

The thickening is due to the development of raised patches called plaques inside the artery. These plaques consist of a fatty substance known as atheroma, and they tend to form in regions of turbulent blood flow, such as the junction of two arteries.

Atheroma worsens with age, causing irregularities in the smooth lining of the blood vessels and encouraging thrombus (abnormal blood clot) formation. Sometimes, a fragment of thrombus breaks off and forms an embolus, which travels in the bloodstream and blocks smaller blood vessels.

Atherosclerosis is a leading cause of death in the UK and atherosclerotic heart disease of the coronary arteries is the single most common cause of death. Strokes resulting from interference in the blood supply to the brain are the third most common cause of death (cancer is the second most common).

Atherosclerosis can also cause serious illness by impeding blood flow in other major arteries, such as those that supply the kidneys, legs, and intestines.

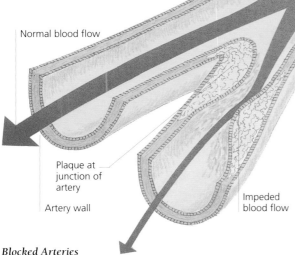

Normal blood flow

Plaque at junction of artery

Artery wall

Impeded blood flow

Blocked Arteries
Fatty patches known as plaques build up in the arteries, especially at junctions, impeding blood flow and encouraging the formation of clots.

Prior to the menopause, women are protected from atherosclerosis, so it tends to affect men and post-menopausal women. As most of the research on atherosclerosis and heart disease has been carried out on men, all statistics I have quoted relate to men, not women, unless otherwise stated.

RISK FACTORS

Your chances of suffering from atherosclerosis are increased by obesity, smoking, high blood pressure, being menopausal and postmenopausal, lack of

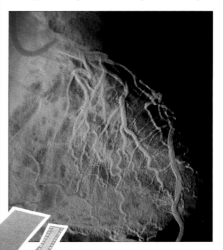

Arteriogram
Narrowing of the left coronary artery has occurred, causing reduced blood flow (see the constricted vessels at the top right of the photograph). Normal blood vessels appear as continuous pink ribbons.

exercise, a high cholesterol level, poorly controlled diabetes, and a family history of arterial disease. A personality type known as type A, characterized by aggression and competitiveness, may also be a risk factor.

Atherosclerosis incidence increases with age, probably because it takes time for plaques to develop. In the 35–44 age group, coronary artery disease kills six times as many men as women. In the 55–70 age group, death due to atherosclerosis is nearly equal in men and women, due almost entirely to the decline of oestrogen during the menopause.

Women who develop heart disease after the menopause are more likely to have been hirsute (see page 39) when they were younger (hirsute women have high levels of testosterone). They should pay particular attention to the cardiovascular risk factors that are under their control, such as smoking, diet, and stress levels. They should also discuss with their doctors the possibility of taking oestrogen in HRT to balance testosterone production.

SYMPTOMS

Until the damage to the arteries is severe enough to restrict blood flow, atherosclerosis is symptomless. When blood flow becomes impeded – generally after a number of years – you may experience angina, which is pain in the chest on exertion, or intermittent claudication, which is leg pain brought on by walking, and alleviated by rest. If blood flow is restricted in the arteries supplying the brain, you may experience temporary stroke symptoms, dizziness, and fainting attacks. Kidney failure is also possible if the renal artery becomes narrowed.

DIAGNOSIS

Atherosclerosis can be diagnosed by angiography, in which a radio-opaque substance is injected into the blood vessels, enabling X-rays to show up the blood flow in an artery. Other techniques include Doppler ultrasound scanning, or plethysmography, which produces a tracing of the pulse pattern.

MEDICAL TREATMENT

Treating atherosclerosis with drugs is difficult, since by the time symptoms appear, the damage to the arteries has already been done. Although anticoagulant drugs can be used to stop further damage by preventing secondary clotting and embolus formation, they do not provide a cure. Vasodilator drugs will open up the arteries of the legs, and help to relieve symptoms.

People who don't respond to treatment or who are likely to suffer complications, may need surgery. A common surgical technique used to treat atherosclerosis is balloon angioplasty (see page 82). This opens up narrowed blood vessels and restores blood flow. Coronary artery bypass surgery (see page 81) can restore blood flow to the heart, and there is a technique called endarterectomy, which can replace diseased blood vessels with woven plastic tubes.

PREVENTION

Lowering risk factors, especially in early adulthood and midlife, can help prevent atherosclerosis developing. You should try to give up smoking, have your blood pressure checked regularly, and get high blood pressure treated. Keep your diet low in saturated fats, and if your cholesterol levels still remain high, you may need medication. Meticulous control of diabetes mellitus is important, and regular exercise is essential.

HRT may prevent coronary heart disease in that oestrogen has a beneficial effect on fat deposits in the blood, blood coagulation, blood glucose and insulin levels, and blood pressure. Women receiving HRT have half the risk of heart disease of non-users. This may be because they have higher levels of the healthy HDL cholesterol and lower levels of the dangerous LDL cholesterol (see page 42) that leads to hardening of the arteries.

Other new findings show that when oestrogen and progestogen are combined in HRT, blood glucose and insulin are lower and healthier in users than in non-users. Although high blood pressure is sometimes regarded as a contraindication for HRT, studies carried out in 1993 showed no rise in blood pressure in women taking HRT.

There is also a lower level of fibrinogen (a coagulation factor) in the blood of HRT users. This means that the blood is thinner and the likelihood of forming clots that might lead to a heart attack or a stroke is diminished.

SYNDROME X

This relatively new medical condition (first described in 1971 and investigated at the Brompton Hospital in London in 1990–91) reveals a lot about the cardiac effects of oestrogen deficiency.

The syndrome has the following characteristics: anginal chest pain and an abnormal electrocardiogram on exercising, but normal coronary arteriograms. In one study, 107 women suffering from Syndrome X were tested and 89 percent were found to be menopausal, as indicated by low oestrogen levels. Forty-five patients had had a hysterectomy, and the onset of anginal chest pain in these women had been an average of eight years after the operation. However, the younger the woman at the time of the hysterectomy, the sooner the anginal chest pain had started.

The high prevalence of Syndrome X in women, especially menopausal women, suggests a relationship with oestrogen. Many women reported that hot flushes and headaches coincided with chest pain. Also, perimenopausal women stated that chest pain was most frequent in the second half of their cycle, when oestrogen is at its lowest.

Exactly why oestrogen deficiency may trigger chest pain is still a matter for speculation, but one theory is that a lack of oestrogen makes the lining of the arteries sensitive, causing transient spasm.

CORONARY ARTERY DISEASE

This disease is very prevalent in the UK and accounts for one-third of all deaths between the ages of 45 and 64. Whereas many developed countries have seen a decrease in deaths from coronary artery disease over the past two decades, the death rate in the UK, particularly in Scotland and Northern Ireland, remains very high.

Coronary artery disease damages the heart because the blood supply becomes limited or blocked. The two most common symptoms of coronary artery disease are angina pectoris (chest pain) and acute myocardial infarction (heart attack). Both of these are caused by the inability of the narrowed coronary arteries to supply the heart with sufficient blood (and oxygen).

As oestrogen levels fall during the menopause, we lose our cardioprotective umbrella and become as subject to coronary artery disease and heart attacks as men. In the 55–65 age group, the rate of heart attacks in men and women is almost equal.

ANGINA

The pain of angina is typically brought on by exertion such as running up a flight of stairs, and it is relieved by rest. Being angry or upset can also cause an attack. Sufferers describe the sensation as a profound tightening in the middle of the chest, and pain spreading up to the neck and down the arm (usually the left arm). Alternatively, some people experience pain in the arm, neck, or even teeth, without any chest pain, although this is unusual.

Medical treatment Angina can usually be helped by drugs that work by improving blood flow to the coronary arteries, thereby reducing the workload on the heart during exercise. These include nitrate drugs, such as glycerol trinitrate, betablockers, calcium channel blockers, and vasodilator drugs. Abnormal heartbeats are commonly treated with drugs such as betablockers, calcium channel blockers, and specific antiarrhythmic drugs.

If the heart's pumping action is weak, it may sometimes be improved by vasodilators or digoxin, which work by controlling muscle contractions in the blood vessels. If the symptoms are not improved by treatment with drugs, or if the pulmonary arteries are found to be considerably narrowed, a coronary artery bypass operation may be carried out to improve blood flow.

COMPARISON OF MALE AND FEMALE DEATH RATES FROM HEART DISEASE

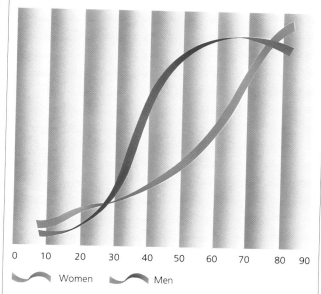

| | | | | | | | | | |
|0|10|20|30|40|50|60|70|80|90|

Women　　Men

Oestrogen exerts a protective effect on the heart, and women rarely die from heart disease until after the menopause when oestrogen levels drop. In contrast, the incidence of fatal heart disease in men rises steeply from the early 20s. After the menopause women have a greater amount of male hormones in their bloodstream, and this brings their death rate from heart disease into line with that of men's.

CORONARY ARTERY BYPASS

After a technique called angiography is carried out to detect the exact location of the blockage, the narrow, blocked segments of an artery can be successfully bypassed using a vein from the leg (or sometimes a mammary artery). One end of the vein is attached to the aorta and the other end to a point below the blockage.

Coronary artery bypass surgery may be carried out on a single coronary artery, and is usually employed when drug treatment, or self-help measures such as eating a low-fat diet, losing weight, or giving up smoking, have not had any significant impact on symptoms.

After the patient is given a general anaesthetic, the heart is temporarily stopped and a heart/lung machine takes over the circulation and oxygenation of blood. The duration of the operation can be up to five hours. A coronary artery bypass is usually performed by two surgeons.

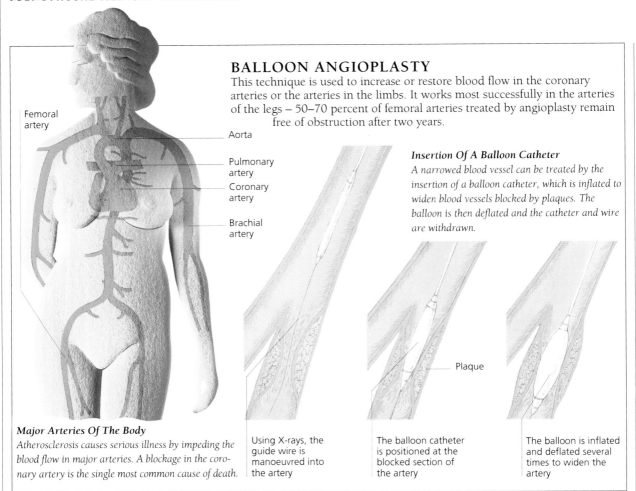

BALLOON ANGIOPLASTY

This technique is used to increase or restore blood flow in the coronary arteries or the arteries in the limbs. It works most successfully in the arteries of the legs – 50–70 percent of femoral arteries treated by angioplasty remain free of obstruction after two years.

Femoral artery

Aorta

Pulmonary artery

Coronary artery

Brachial artery

Insertion Of A Balloon Catheter
A narrowed blood vessel can be treated by the insertion of a balloon catheter, which is inflated to widen blood vessels blocked by plaques. The balloon is then deflated and the catheter and wire are withdrawn.

Plaque

Major Arteries Of The Body
Atherosclerosis causes serious illness by impeding the blood flow in major arteries. A blockage in the coronary artery is the single most common cause of death.

Using X-rays, the guide wire is manoeuvred into the artery

The balloon catheter is positioned at the blocked section of the artery

The balloon is inflated and deflated several times to widen the artery

MYOCARDIAL INFARCTION (Heart attack)

When the blood supply to part of the heart is cut off completely by a blood clot blocking one of the coronary arteries (coronary thrombosis), the result is an acute heart attack.

Symptoms The main symptom of a heart attack is intense chest pain similar to angina, but unrelieved by rest, and not necessarily brought on by physical effort. The sufferer may feel cold, sweat profusely, be weak and nauseated, and even lose consciousness as the pumping action of the heart is weakened.

During a heart attack the electrical conducting system of the heart may be disturbed. This results in heartbeat abnormalities, such as misplaced beats, rapid beats, and ineffective fluttering. The latter causes a rapid loss of consciousness and can be fatal if it is not treated within minutes.

Diagnosis A heart attack may be so sudden and dramatic that there is no doubt of the diagnosis, but it can be confirmed by taking an ECG (electrocardiogram), and by measuring the level of cardiac enzymes, which are released into the blood by the damaged muscle. ECGs, taken at rest and during exercise, are also used to assess the condition of patients who suffer from attacks of angina.

Medical treatment Initial treatment takes place in a hospital coronary care unit. Anticoagulants may be given to dissolve the clot in the coronary artery, or the affected artery may be widened by angioplasty or bypassed surgically. Balloon angioplasty is a procedure in which the narrowed segment of artery is widened by inflating it. This is recommended for cases that do not respond to drug treatment. Early mobilization of the patient is essential.

HYPERTENSION (High Blood Pressure)

Hypertension means having a blood pressure that is higher than normal. Although factors such as age, stress, and physical activity tend to increase blood pressure, a person with hypertension has high blood pressure for their age, even at rest. Measurements for blood pressure are expressed as two figures: 120/80, for example. Each figure represents millimetres of mercury (mmHg) – that is, the column of mercury the pressure will support – so 120 means the blood pressure will hold up 120 mmHg. The higher figure, or systolic value, represents the pressure when the blood surges into the aorta, the main artery from the heart. The lower figure, or diastolic value, is the pressure when the ventricles, the larger of the chambers of the heart, relax between beats.

Although there is no strict dividing line between normal and high blood pressure, a useful definition is that given by the World Health Organization, which defines hypertension as a blood pressure that is consistently above 160 mmHg systolic and 95 mmHg diastolic. A younger person with a systolic value of 140–160 mmHg might be regarded as having mild or borderline hypertension, but these values would be considered normal in an elderly person, since blood pressure increases with age. In the UK, 10–20 percent of the adult population suffer from high blood pressure. The condition is found more often in men than in women, and it is most common in middle-aged and elderly people.

A rise in blood pressure occurs when there is resistance in the blood vessels to the flow of blood. Resistance increases in the large vessels because of increased rigidity due to age, and occurs in the small vessels when they become constricted due to nerve or chemical control.

Risk factors Apart from being post-menopausal, risk factors for essential hypertension include smoking, obesity, excessive alcohol intake, a family history of high blood pressure, a sedentary lifestyle, stress, and old age. About 90 percent of sufferers have essential hypertension, which means that there is no obvious cause for their elevated blood pressure. The other 10 percent of sufferers have secondary hypertension, where there is an identifiable cause, such as a disorder of the kidneys or the adrenal glands,

coarctation of the aorta (a type of congenital heart defect), and use of certain drugs. Women taking the combined contraceptive pill also appear to be at greater risk of mild hypertension.

Symptoms High blood pressure usually causes few or no symptoms and it may only be discovered by a doctor during a routine physical examination. In very severe cases, however, the sufferer may experience headaches, a shortness of breath, giddiness, visual disturbances, confusion, and even seizures. Severe hypertension will also cause strain on the heart and blood vessels, and will increase the risk of stroke and heart failure. If it is left untreated, hypertension may cause damage to the kidneys and the retina.

Diagnosis Because high blood pressure can lead to serious health problems such as heart disease, every peri- and postmenopausal woman should make sure that she has her blood pressure checked at least once a year, and more frequently than this if the reading becomes high or borderline. Middle-aged and elderly people should have their blood

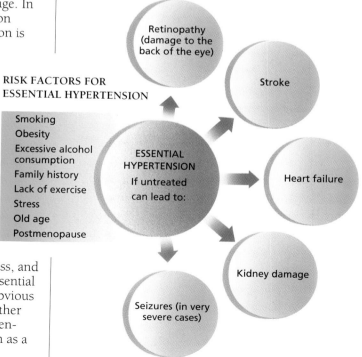

RISK FACTORS FOR
ESSENTIAL HYPERTENSION

Smoking
Obesity
Excessive alcohol consumption
Family history
Lack of exercise
Stress
Old age
Postmenopause

ESSENTIAL HYPERTENSION
If untreated can lead to:

Retinopathy (damage to the back of the eye)

Stroke

Heart failure

Kidney damage

Seizures (in very severe cases)

pressure checked every time they visit their doctor; a good general practitioner will offer to do this as a matter of course.

A doctor will not make a firm diagnosis of hypertension until a patient's blood pressure at rest is found to be raised on three separate occasions. However, hypertension can be diagnosed on the first reading if you are suffering from one of the complications of hypertension, such as retinopathy (disease of the retina at the back of the eye), or if your blood pressure is extremely high.

Self-help High blood pressure can often be reduced by making changes to your lifestyle. If you smoke, you should give up, or at the very least cut down, and you should assess your alcohol intake. If you are a heavy drinker you should cut down drastically or try and stop drinking altogether. If you are overweight, you should try to lose weight and take more exercise. Dietary measures include cutting down on your salt intake and eating less fatty food.

Biofeedback training can be helpful to some patients in reducing blood pressure. This involves learning breathing and relaxation techniques. During a biofeedback session your blood pressure is continuously monitored and you learn to respond immediately to any increase in blood pressure by practising relaxation techniques.

Medical treatment In severe cases of high blood pressure, your doctor may prescribe antihypertensive drugs. The many different types available include diuretics, betablockers, vasodilators, and calcium antagonists. In the majority of cases, hypertension can be controlled by using one or a combination of these drugs. Initially, your blood pressure should be monitored, with readings taken every two to four weeks, so that the dosage can be adjusted as necessary. You should tell your doctor if you experience any side-effects while you are taking antihypertensive drugs.

STROKE

This is a potentially fatal result of hypertension. If the blood supply to the brain is interrupted, or blood leaks through the walls of blood vessels in the brain, damage to the brain will result. This can impair sensation, movement, or the function of the damaged area. Strokes are one of the major causes of death in the UK.

Sixty percent of strokes are caused by a cerebral thrombosis, when an artery in the brain becomes blocked by a clot (thrombus) that has built up in its wall. Thirty to 35 percent of strokes are due to a cerebral embolism – a blockage by a clot or air bubble that travels to an artery of the brain from another part of the body. When a thrombus or an embolus blocks an artery, the blood supply to the brain is interrupted, and the brain tissue does not receive sufficient oxygen. This results in the death of brain tissue. The other, and least common, cause of strokes is bleeding from ruptured blood vessels within or over the surface of the brain.

Risk factors Apart from age, risk factors include high blood pressure, atherosclerosis, heart disease, diabetes mellitus, smoking, a high level of fat in the blood, a high level of red blood cells, and taking the older type of contraceptive pill, which contained a high dose of oestrogen. Newer types of pill contain less oestrogen and the risk of stroke is now very low.

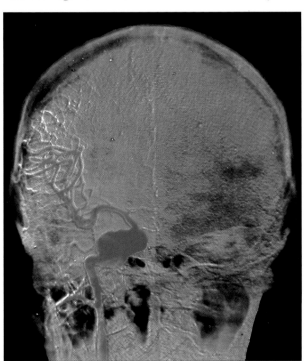

Aneurysm In The Brain
This is the balloon-like swelling of an artery, caused by blood pressing upon a weak point in the artery wall. A ruptured aneurysm results in bleeding over the surface of the brain (a stroke).

Possible complications in stroke victims include pneumonia due to lying in bed, and deep vein thrombosis – the formation of blood clots in the veins of the legs (thrombophlebitis), which are potentially fatal if they travel to the artery feeding the lungs, causing a pulmonary embolism.

Symptoms These include headaches, dizziness, visual disturbance, slurred speech, or loss of speech, and problems swallowing. If speech is affected, this may mean the dominant cerebral hemisphere of the brain is damaged.

Each side of the brain controls movement on the opposite side of the body, so damage in the right cerebral hemisphere can lead to weakness or paralysis on the left side of the body. One-sided weakness or paralysis of this kind is a very common effect of a serious stroke, and is known as hemiplegia.

In some cases, symptoms last less than 24 hours and the patient makes a full recovery. Such an episode is known as a transient ischaemic attack,

radioactive glucose into the bloodstream. Areas of dead tissue appear on the resulting scan as dark areas of the brain (see below). Other diagnostic techniques which may be used include chest X-rays, ECG, blood tests, and angiography.

Self-help After hospital treatment, stroke patients spend most of their recovery period at home relearning how to use the parts of their body that may have been paralyzed. There are many self-help aids available, such as easy-to-hold cutlery. Dressing in front of a mirror may speed up relearning.

Medical treatment If the patient is unconscious or semiconscious then the airway is kept clear, and feeding is carried out through an intravenous drip or gastric tube. The patient's position will also need to be changed regularly to avoid bed sores and pneumonia. There may be an accumulation of fluid within the brain, and this will be treated with diuretic drugs or corticosteroid drugs. If the stroke

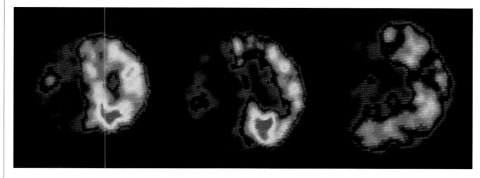

Decline In Brain Function Following A Massive Stroke
Deterioration and death of brain tissue occur rapidly after a serious stroke. The red and yellow areas in these three brain scans correspond to areas of high metabolic activity. The darker areas indicate brain tissue that has died.

and is probably caused by arterial spasm. It should, however, be regarded as a warning sign that insufficient blood is reaching part of the brain and that a stroke may be imminent.

About a third of major strokes are fatal. A third result in some disability, and a third have no long-term ill effects. Strokes are rare before the age of 60, but thereafter the risk increases rapidly.

Diagnosis To determine whether symptoms are the result of a stroke or of some other disorder, one of two types of brain scan may be carried out. A CT (computed tomography) scan produces a cross-sectional image of the brain constructed by computer from a number of X-rays. A PET (position emission tomography) scan is produced by injecting

has been caused by an embolism, then anticoagulant or, in some cases, thrombolytic (clot-dissolving) drugs may be given and the patient may have to go on taking these for a long time – in some cases for life. Aspirin is often prescribed as it thins the blood without risk of further haemorrhage, and reduces the risk of a stroke recurring. If the patient's movement or sensation have been lost, or speech is affected, physiotherapy or speech therapy will help.

Outlook About five percent of stroke sufferers will require long-term institutional care, but many patients recover more or less completely from a first stroke, and many people paralyzed by a stroke learn to walk again. Patients left with a disability may need occupational therapy.

OSTEOARTHRITIS

This is part of the normal ageing process of the joints, and most women over the age of 60 have some detectable form of arthritis. Under normal circumstances, the healthy joint is lined with smooth cartilage and lubricated by synovial fluid. In the osteoarthritic joint, the cartilage becomes rough and flaky, and small pieces break off inside the joint.

Osteoarthritis, which mainly affects the large joints of the lower back, hips, knees, ankles, and feet, leads to a thickening of the bone ends causing bony lumps to appear at the edges of the joints. Exactly the same process occurs at the surfaces of the vertebrae – often causing the sufferer to have a stiff neck that makes movement painful. Pressure from a bony outgrowth on a nerve may cause pain in the shoulder, elbow, and even the fingers. When bony outgrowths occur in the lower back, pressure on the sciatic nerve will cause pain in the buttock and the back of the legs, down to the sole of the foot. Postmenopausal women may find they suffer from Heberden's nodes – a thickening of bone affecting the joints at the ends of the fingers.

RISK FACTORS

Osteoarthritis develops as a result of excessive wear and tear on the joints due to obesity, slight deformity, or misalignment of bones in a joint. It is common in weight-bearing joints that have been subject to injury in youth, or joints that have been overused, such as knees affected by too much kneeling, or joints overused in certain sports.

SYMPTOMS

Osteoarthritis is aggravated by mechanical stress, and you may suffer pain, swelling, stiffness, and occasionally loss of function in the affected joint. This can interfere with activities such as walking and dressing, and may disrupt sleep. Weakness and shrinkage of the surrounding muscles also occurs if pain prevents the joints from being used regularly. Symptoms form the basis of a diagnosis and X-rays can confirm the presence of osteoarthritis.

SELF-HELP

Many sufferers are overweight, and losing weight often provides relief from symptoms. Physiotherapy, exercise, and heat treatment can also help.

MEDICAL TREATMENT

Although there is much relief available for osteoarthritis, there is no cure. Symptoms can be helped by painkillers and by non-steroidal anti-inflammatory drugs. An injection of a corticosteroid drug into the joint can sometimes ease the pain.

Surgery for severe osteoarthritis includes joint replacement surgery (see page 88), particularly of the hip, and arthrodesis, which immobilizes a painful joint completely, rendering it pain-free.

RHEUMATOID ARTHRITIS

This is a serious type of inflammation that typically affects the smaller joints in the fingers, wrists, and toes. It usually takes the form of recurrent moderate attacks, with affected joints becoming painful, stiff, and swollen. In severe cases the joints may become deformed. The frequency and severity of attacks and the number of affected joints can vary. Rheumatoid arthritis is distinct from osteoarthritis, which is not inflammatory. Rheumatoid arthritis is an auto-immune disorder – that is, one in which the immune system attacks the body's own tissues. A few patients have been found to be sensitive to gluten, which is a protein in wheat. Rheumatoid arthritis occurs worldwide, affecting one or two percent of the population. The disease can start at any age and is two to three times more common in women than in men.

SYMPTOMS

The disease starts gradually, with mild fever and general aches and pains before the joints are affected, though in some cases joint inflammation develops suddenly. The early symptoms are accompanied by tiredness and you may feel as if you have flu. The affected joints look red and swollen, and feel painful, stiff, and warm. The ligaments, tendons, and muscles surrounding the joint may also become inflamed and weak. The joints in the fingers are the most commonly affected, causing a weak grip. Reynaud's phenomenon, a condition in which the fingers turn white when exposed to cold, may also occur. Swelling of the wrist may lead to a condition called carpal tunnel syndrome (see page 89), caused by pressure on the median nerve, resulting in pain and tingling in the fingers. The tendon sheaths in the wrist may become inflamed and painful, a condition known as tenosynovitis.

When the feet are affected by rheumatoid arthritis, pain may be experienced in the toes, the arches of the feet, and the ankles. The shoulders, knees, and neck joints may also be affected by the disease. Almost all sufferers experience stiffness in the morning, and may even have difficulty getting out of bed and dressing.

Soft nodules sometimes develop under the skin, especially in areas subjected to pressure and friction, such as the elbow. Some sufferers develop bursitis, in which the fluid-filled sacs surrounding the joint become inflamed. Many sufferers feel fatigued, partly as a result of the anaemia that sometimes accompanies the disease.

Rheumatoid arthritis can also cause complications in various parts of the body unrelated to the joints. The lungs and the membrane around the heart may become inflamed. Ulcers may appear on the hands and the feet as a result of circulatory problems. A condition called Sjogren's syndrome may affect the eyes and the mouth, producing excessive dryness, and a burning sensation in the eyes. This is due to the destruction of the glands that produce lubricating secretions. The lymph nodes may become enlarged, producing swellings in the arms, feet, groin, and neck. Enlargement of the spleen can exacerbate existing anaemia.

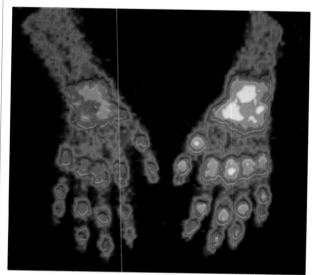

Rheumatoid Arthritis In The Wrists And Fingers
The hands can be very badly affected by rheumatoid arthritis, resulting in pain and a severely weakened grip. Arthritic joints are shown here as bright red and green areas.

DIAGNOSIS

The presence of morning stiffness and the appearance on X-rays of affected joints form the basis of a diagnosis. Blood tests will reveal signs of inflammation and specific antibodies known as rheumatoid factor. A person may have a negative test for rheumatoid factor but still appear to have rheumatoid arthritis; in such cases the condition is known as seronegative rheumatoid arthritis.

SELF-HELP

Muscle spasm and joint stiffness can be relieved by exercising in a warm hydrotherapy pool. Removable night splints worn on the hands can reduce pain and prevent deformities of the hand, and insoles and surgical shoes can help relieve pain in the feet.

Various household aids, such as special taps, knives, forks, door handles, and so on, are available to help make everyday tasks easier. There is no conclusive evidence that dietary changes are effective in relieving the symptoms of rheumatoid arthritis, but increased consumption of fish, or fish oil supplements, may be of some benefit. Acupuncture (see page 114) may be of help in relieving pain, but has no effect on the course of the disease.

MEDICAL TREATMENT

Drugs, physiotherapy, occupational therapy, or surgery can all be used to treat rheumatoid arthritis. Non-steroidal anti-inflammatory drugs (NSAIDs) are the main method of relieving pain and stiffness. Anti-rheumatic drugs, such as gold or penicillamine, may be used to arrest or slow the progress of the disease. Aspirin has anti-inflammatory properties, and in higher than usual doses, prescribed by your doctor, it can effectively relieve pain.

In severe cases, corticosteroid drugs or azathioprine can suppress the body's immune system. If anti-rheumatic drugs fail to control the disorder, or if they produce severe side-effects, corticosteroid drugs may also be injected into affected joints to provide local pain relief.

Surgery may sometimes be necessary to provide a substitute for a destroyed joint. The most common operations are hip and knee replacement (see page 88). Sufferers may have to take drugs for the rest of their lives, but effective control of symptoms often allows a return to a near normal level of activity. Modern methods of treatment have reduced the incidence of severe deformity and disability.

HIP REPLACEMENT

Osteoarthritis affecting the hip can sometimes be painful enough to immobilize you, and hip replacement may be necessary. This involves removing the head of the thigh bone (femur) and replacing it with an artificial joint. The procedure is also used for severe fractures at the top of the femur and for rheumatoid arthritis that affects the hip. Most patients report a return to normal mobility after surgery. Convalescence after the operation may take several weeks, and you will be counselled about movements that could damage the newly replaced joint.

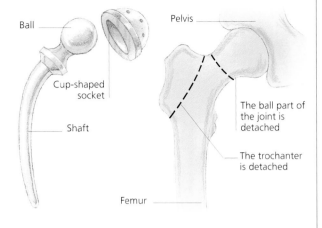

Ball

Cup-shaped socket

Shaft

Pelvis

The ball part of the joint is detached

The trochanter is detached

Femur

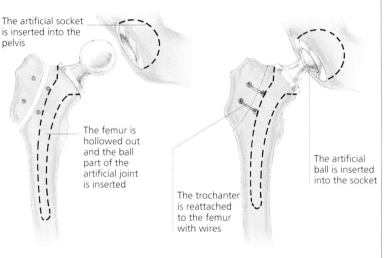

The artificial socket is inserted into the pelvis

The femur is hollowed out and the ball part of the artificial joint is inserted

The trochanter is reattached to the femur with wires

The artificial ball is inserted into the socket

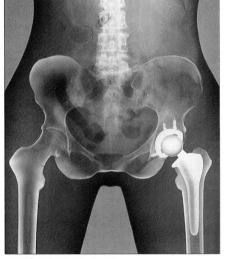

Artificial Joint In Position
This colour-enhanced X-ray shows how the two parts of the artificial joint are attached to the bone of the pelvis and the femur.

FRACTURES

Although bones can be broken at any time of life, some fractures become more common after the menopause, and are related to osteoporosis. Osteoporosis may cause bones to break with little or no provocation and certain bones – just above the wrist, for example – are more vulnerable to fracture than others.

The bones that make up the spinal column are the most frequently affected. After the age of 50, most women's bones become increasingly brittle and inefficient at keeping the intervertebral discs flat. The vertebrae are undermined by many tiny, undetectable fractures, and eventually they become compressed, causing a woman to lose height; about 15 percent of women lose up to 20 percent of their height between the ages of 50 and 70. The vertebrae become crushed and collapse inward causing a bent back, sometimes referred to as a "Dowager's hump", (see page 70) and severe pain.

The incidence of wrist and forearm fractures, known as Colles' fractures, increase as a woman ages. Such breaks usually occur when a woman puts out a hand to save herself from a fall and the weakened bone cannot provide support.

Hip fractures are costly to treat, disabling, and sometimes life-threatening. The hip joint is one of the major weight-bearing joints, and is constantly overstressed, especially in women who are over-weight. A hip fracture may be the result of falling over or a minor impact.

MEDICAL TREATMENT

X-rays are taken to confirm the diagnosis of fracture, and broken bones in the wrist and hip are realigned under general anaesthetic and kept immobilized until they heal. A Colles' fracture will usually heal within three weeks if it is immobilized in a plaster cast. Traction may be necessary to keep the thigh bone in position.

There is no treatment to restore fractured verte-brae to their former shape; instead, attention is paid to alleviating the painful effects of compression (see page 71).

PREVENTION

A fuller discussion of bone health is covered earlier in this chapter (see page 66). The main requirement for the prevention of fractures is to avoid falling. It is vital that a woman's surroundings are made as safe as possible. In the home, there should be adequate lighting; grab rails near the stairs, bath, shower, and other hard-to-negotiate areas; well-maintained floor surfaces (slippery rugs, worn and wet areas, and steep stairs should be avoided); and a lack of clutter. Outdoors, you should avoid icy or wet pavements. Try not to take medications that make you sleepy,

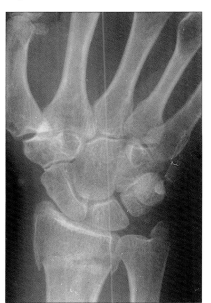

Colles' Fracture
This type of wrist injury is usually a result of breaking a fall with the hand. Although Colles' fractures can be painful, they are rarely serious and should heal within three weeks. The displaced fracture shown here is just below the wrist.

CAUSES OF FALLS

While severely diseased bone may break sponta-neously, falls are the most common and preventable cause. Not only is the older woman more at risk of falling, but compared to a younger woman, any falls she has will be more serious since she cannot break the impact so well, and her recovery will take longer.
Age-related factors: Due to impaired vision, poor balance, lack of mobility, and slow reflexes, older women are more likely to trip over rugs and items in the home, and on wet or slippery surfaces both indoors and outdoors.
Medical problems: Various diseases more common in middle to old age can affect mobility. These include arthritis, Parkinson's disease, strokes, cataracts, and blood pressure disorders.
Medications: Drugs for the above diseases may adversely affect balance, reaction times, and general awareness and alertness.

disorientated, or impair your coordination, and wear proper supportive shoes. It is also important to have regular eye tests.

CARPAL TUNNEL SYNDROME

Around the time of the menopause, women may experience numbness in the fingers and hands, and a sensation of pins and needles in the arms. This is due to a narrowing of the "tunnel" in the wrist that carries the nerves passing messages from the brain to the hand. Small joint changes coupled with water retention – due to fluctuating levels of hormones – put pressure on the median nerve, and may result in pain severe enough to require medication.

SELF-HELP

As an immediate, though temporary measure, raise your hands above your head to allow fluid to drain back down your arm and decompress the tunnel. You can also place your wrists under cold running water or apply an ice pack to reduce swelling.

MEDICAL TREATMENT

HRT helps alleviate carpal tunnel syndrome in some women, and this should be tried first of all. Diuretic drugs may be prescribed to relieve fluid retention, along with steroids to reduce inflammation. Surgery opens the constricted tunnel with a small incision.

UROGENITAL COMPLAINTS

UROGENITAL AGEING

Oestrogen receptors are found in abundance in the genital organs, the lower urinary tract, and the bladder, which makes it possible to treat the genital and the urinary organs as one system. When oestrogen is plentiful, the receptors keep this system healthy and resistant to infection. When hormone levels fall during the menopause, the receptors can no longer bind with oestrogen, and, as a result, are unable to keep organs strong and healthy. The urogenital system thins, atrophies (wastes away), and becomes susceptible to infection.

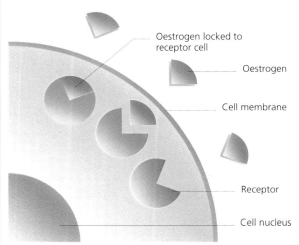

Oestrogen locked to receptor cell

Oestrogen

Cell membrane

Receptor

Cell nucleus

Oestrogen Receptors
This is the lock and key mechanism by which hormones exert their effects on the body. Oestrogen binds with special sites called receptors inside body cells, and this initiates a response in the cell.

SYMPTOMS
Signs of genital atrophy include a dry, itchy vagina and vulva, which causes pain during sex. These symptoms are often combined with the frequent, urgent desire to urinate, and incontinence. This combination of symptoms, known as urogenital syndrome, is the most common reason for women over the age of 55 to visit a gynaecologist.

DIAGNOSIS
A bladder pressure reading will show if the bladder muscle contracts spontaneously causing urine to dribble away, leading to the symptoms of urgency and sometimes incontinence. A smear test will determine whether the vaginal lining has atrophied, with a loss of the protective acid vaginal secretions.

MEDICAL TREATMENT
The first line of treatment should be oestrogen therapy. Research shows that oestrogen creams applied to the vagina diffuse through the urethra and the bladder and relieve symptoms in days. Oestrogen pessaries and rings are almost 100 percent effective. Oral and skin patch HRT also eliminate symptoms.

CYSTITIS

Oestrogen is so crucial to the health of the urinary tract that after the menopause the bladder is far more susceptible to bacterial infection. Cystitis is much more common in women than men anyway, because women have a shorter urethra (the tube leading from the bladder to the outside of the body). Nearly all infections that reach the bladder are due to bacteria entering the urethra from outside and then spreading upwards and inflaming the lining of the urethra and bladder.

You should treat cystitis promptly because if it is allowed to recur it can become chronic, making it very difficult to eradicate.

SYMPTOMS
Only a woman who has suffered from cystitis knows how agonizing the following symptoms can be:
- The urgent need to pass urine frequently. You may start to pass urine involuntarily, and then find there is very little urine to pass. This irritability of the bladder muscle is due to inflammation of the bladder lining. Even a few drops of urine can stimulate the bladder to contract.
- Severe pain when you pass urine. This pain may occur when the flow begins and the bladder muscle starts to contract down on the inflamed lining, it may be during urination, or it may be at the end, when the muscle squeezes the last few drops of urine out of the bladder.
- A dragging pain in the lower abdomen that may radiate up into the back. (Severe back pain could mean that you have a kidney infection and you should see your doctor immediately.)
- Blood in the urine – whether obvious streaks of red or simply a pale pink coloration – indicates severe inflammation of the bladder lining.

THE PATH OF BACTERIAL INFECTION

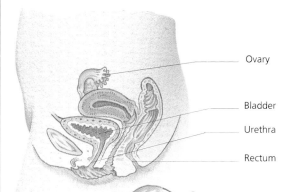

Ovary

Bladder

Urethra

Rectum

Bacteria from the rectum travel down to the vulva where they move up into the urethra and bladder and cause infection.

Bacteria spread from the rectum to the skin of the perineum

Bacteria move down to the vulva and up the urethra

CAUSES

The most common cause is infection from the bacterium E.coli. E.coli is normally present in the rectum, intestines, and on the anal skin, and does not usually ascend the urethra to cause infection. Some of the factors that cause infection are as follows:

- Unhygienic toilet habits allowing bacteria from the anal area to come into contact with the urethra.
- A sudden increase in the frequency of intercourse, resulting in excessive friction on the urethra.
- Insertion of a catheter into the bladder combined with bad hygiene.
- A chronic infection of the vagina or cervix.
- A prolapse of the front wall of the vagina, causing a hernia of the bladder down into the vagina.

- An allergic reaction to perfumed toiletries, such as a vaginal deodorant or a douche.
- Irritation of the urethral opening by soap or bath toiletries, or just from scrubbing yourself too hard.
- Hormonal deficiency after the menopause that causes thinning of the urogenital system.
- Vaginal irritation caused by a poorly fitting diaphragm, overuse of pessaries, careless use of spermicides, or leaving a tampon in for too long.
- Irritation of the urethra from tight clothing.

DIAGNOSIS

Your doctor will ask for a sample of your urine for analysis and for growing bacteria in a culture to see which particular bacterium is causing your symptoms. This will enable him or her to prescribe an antibiotic specifically to treat the bacterium.

SELF-HELP

You should drink lots of water or diluted fruit juice at the beginning of an attack. E.coli cannot multiply in alkaline urine, and you can make your urine alkaline by taking a teaspoonful of bicarbonate of soda in a glass of water. Drink this three times within five hours of the first twinge. Soluble aspirin and a hot water bottle can help to relieve pain.

Each time you pass urine, pay attention to hygiene and wash your hands carefully. You should also wipe your perineum from front to back once with damp cotton wool. Soap and water can dry out the perineum and vagina and make you more prone to infection. When you dry yourself, pat gently – don't irritate the urethra by rubbing briskly.

If your cystitis is provoked by intercourse, it is probably best to refrain from sex until you are more comfortable. Otherwise, reduce friction with a lubricating jelly and experiment to find the most comfortable sexual position. You should also wash carefully and pass urine after sex.

MEDICAL TREATMENT

Make an appointment to see your doctor as soon as possible, and take a specimen of urine in a clean receptacle with you. You will need a course of antibiotics and you should take the full course even though the symptoms may disappear within 36 hours. A minimum course for mild cystitis is five days, and in the case of a severe attack seven to ten days. With chronic infections, you may need to take antibiotics for three to six weeks.

Oestrogen cream applied to the vagina will do a great deal to help prevent cystitis; oestrogen diffuses through the vaginal wall to reach the urethra where oestrogen receptors make the urethral lining healthy and resistant to infection.

PRURITIS VULVAE

Itching is a sign of oestrogen deficiency, and chronic, uncontrollable itching of the vaginal area is usually worst in hot weather or at night. Diabetes, vaginal yeast infections, such as thrush, and urinary tract infections, can all cause pruritis vulvae. However, it can be psychogenic in origin. Repeated scratching can become more and more pleasurable, even to the point of orgasm. Eventually, the sufferer will develop profound soreness and thickening of the skin in the vaginal area.

SELF- HELP
You can prevent pruritis vulvae from getting worse by trying not to scratch the vaginal area. Consult your doctor if the condition persists for more than two days – if you don't, you may find yourself in an unbreakable itch-scratch-itch cycle. Pay particular attention to normal hygiene but, if possible, avoid the use of soap and detergents as they will strip the skin of oils and make it more sensitive. Use only warm or cool water, and try applying a silicone-based hand cream to the itchy area after each wash. Ice packs may also help to numb the itch too. Don't use local anaesthetic creams and sprays as these may cause allergic reactions.

MEDICAL TREATMENT
Pruritis vulvae usually responds well to oestrogen cream. Your doctor can also prescribe an emollient cream that keeps the skin soft and well lubricated. You should apply these creams as directed. If there is excessive inflammation your doctor may give you a cream containing hydrocortisone. If infection is suspected, he or she may give you a mild hydrocortisone cream containing an antibiotic. Oestrogen vaginal pessaries should also help.

If pruritis vulvae does not respond to treatment, your doctor can refer you to a dermatological specialist for further assessment.

INCONTINENCE
This occurs when the sphincter muscle at the base of your bladder becomes so weak (or the bladder muscle becomes overactive) that you have little or no control over the flow of urine. Although this condition is not life-threatening, it can be debilitating and embarrassing, and may make you housebound. Oestrogen helps to keep the sphincter muscle tight, and when oestrogen levels decline during the menopause, the muscle can become weak and flaccid, allowing leakage of urine.

The other probable causes of incontinence at or after the menopause are an irritable bladder, diabetes mellitus, or local infections such as cystitis. The three types of incontinence are as follows:
- Stress incontinence is the leakage of a small amount of urine caused by an increase in pressure inside the abdomen when you sneeze, cough, laugh, or lift a heavy object.
- Urge incontinence occurs if you wait until you need to urinate urgently. The bladder starts to contract involuntarily and empties itself. This type of incontinence is often triggered by a sudden change in position, such as standing up.
- Mixed pattern incontinence is a combination of both urge and stress incontinence, and may be the result of two faults in bladder function.

DIAGNOSIS
To determine the cause of your incontinence, your doctor will test a sample of your urine, and may examine your urethra with an instrument called a cystoscope, and recommend tests of your bladder function, called urodynamic studies.

SELF-HELP
Mild incontinence is often due to weakened pelvic floor muscles, and you can improve your bladder control by doing Kegel exercises. These involve repeatedly contracting and relaxing the muscles of the urogenital tract (see page 50). If you are suffering from urge incontinence, self-help measures include emptying your bladder every two hours, and avoiding diuretic drinks such as tea and coffee. There are a number of aids available for incontinence sufferers.

These include waterproof bed sheets, incontinence pads, female urinals, and waterproof pants. However, you should consult your doctor long before these become necessary. If you suffer from stress incontinence when you exercise, try emptying your bladder beforehand. Wearing a tampon during exercise can act as a splint to the urethra.

MEDICAL TREATMENT

Sometimes all you need to combat stress incontinence is oestrogen cream. Other forms of HRT will also help. Treatment may also include anticholinergic drugs (to treat an irritable bladder), an operation for stress incontinence, and bladder retraining.

PROLAPSE

Prolapse, or "pelvic relaxation", occurs when the pelvic musculature is unable to support the pelvic organs and allows them to drop out of position. The affected organs include the uterus, bladder, rectum, and urethra. The uterus is the most likely to prolapse. Because of advanced age, childbirth, and a decline in oestrogen levels, the uterine muscles become weak and sag. The pull of gravity is a contributing factor. Prolapse is especially noticeable when abdominal pressure is increased by coughing or straining during a bowel movement.

TYPES OF PROLAPSE

Uterine Prolapse This is due to a weakening of supporting pelvic ligaments and muscles. The uterus may descend from the pelvic cavity down into the vagina, causing irritation to the vagina, slight backache, and sometimes a sensation that your insides are going to fall out. The dropped cervix will also prevent deep penile penetration during intercourse.

First degree prolapse is when the uterus begins to descend into the vagina; second degree prolapse is when the cervix begins to protrude from the vagina, and third degree prolapse is when the cervix and uterus protrude outside the body. This is extremely uncomfortable and debilitating.

Prolapse is often the result of childbearing, especially if the pelvic floor muscle or the cervix was injured during delivery of a baby. Occasionally, the same conditions that have produced hernias in men, such as strenuous physical or athletic activity, may produce prolapses in women. Obesity and complaints such as constipation and chronic

UTERINE PROLAPSE
Prolapse occurs when the pelvic musculature becomes weak and can no longer support the pelvic organs.

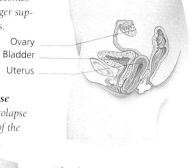

Ovary
Bladder
Uterus

First Degree Prolapse
Mild or first degree prolapse describes the descent of the uterus into the vagina.

Third Degree Prolapse
Second and third degree prolapse are more severe. In second degree prolapse the cervix is outside the body and in third degree prolapse the uterus also protrudes outside the vaginal opening.

Uterus

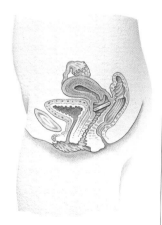

Ring pessary

Ring Pessary In Position
If the prolapse is relatively mild the uterus can be held in position with a ring or shelf pessary.

coughing all aggravate the condition because they increase the intra-abdominal pressure and cause the pelvic muscles to become weak and slack. Increased pressure can also lead to stress incontinence, in which you leak small amounts of urine when you cough, laugh, sneeze, or lift heavy objects.

Urethrocele The urethra bulges into the lower front wall of the vagina. Irritation of the urethral lining can lead to frequent urination.

Rectocele The front wall of the rectum bulges into the rear wall of the vagina. Extreme discomfort is experienced during defecation. In fact, it may only be bearable if a finger is inserted into the vagina to support the rear wall.

Cystocele The bladder bulges into the upper front wall of the vagina and is nearly always accompanied by bladder problems, such as recurrent cystitis. Sometimes the bladder sags below the level of the urethral outlet, which makes emptying the bladder extremely difficult. In such cases, it may be emptied by inserting a finger into the vagina and pushing up the sagging part.

SELF-HELP
Discomfort may be relieved to a certain extent by wearing a girdle as this counteracts the dragging feeling that you may have. Backache is a common symptom and it is very important to avoid standing for long periods, to maintain good posture, and to rest whenever you can with your feet up.

You can protect yourself from prolapse by performing pelvic floor exercises (see page 50), avoiding over-strenuous activity, losing weight, and giving up smoking, especially if you have a cough. Eat plenty of fibre, fruit, and vegetables to keep your bowels regular and the stools soft.

MEDICAL TREATMENT
In the early stages of prolapse, HRT may help rebuild tissue structures that are inclined towards atrophy because of low oestrogen levels. For older women, whose prolapse is not very severe, or where infirmity makes a general anaesthetic inadvisable, a ring pessary can be placed in the vagina where it supports the cervix and uterus. It should not be worn for very long periods because it may erode the thin atrophied tissues by friction.

Severe prolapse needs surgery. An operation is performed through the vagina and is tailored to the individual woman's problems. The anterior and posterior walls of the uterus can be repaired and the supports of the uterus shortened. If the uterus is severely prolapsed it can be removed, but discuss this thoroughly with your doctor.

MENORRHAGIA
This is the term used to describe excessive menstrual blood flow due to abnormalities in the uterus, such as fibroids, polyps, endometriosis or reproductive cancer, or a failure in the normal mechanism that stops bleeding. The main problem in diagnosing menorrhagia is differentiating between bleeding that is heavier than a woman is used to, and heavy bleeding that is abnormal. In a normal menstrual bleed 30–50 ml (one to two fluid ounces) of blood is lost, whereas in an abnormal bleed 80 ml (two to three fluid ounces) or more blood is lost.

Many women who consult their doctor about increased menstrual flow at the menopause may not technically be suffering from menorrhagia, and as long as they have no uterine abnormalities, heavy bleeding may disappear spontaneously. Some women will notice increased flow at the menopause because of the absence of progesterone, the hormone that is responsible for initiating a menstrual bleed. The uterine lining builds up and proliferates, unopposed by progesterone, until finally it breaks down naturally, resulting in a heavy and prolonged bleed. This type of bleeding can be diagnosed by a blood test that reveals the absence of progesterone. It can be successfully treated by taking progestogen.

DIAGNOSIS
Your doctor will need to exclude any uterine abnormalities and disorders in the way your blood-clotting mechanisms work. You will need to have a blood test, a general gynaecological examination, and an ultrasound scan. In women over 45, the uterine lining should be checked to exclude cancer. This can be done by D&C (see page 199), but a simpler procedure involves the use of a fine suction curette that removes small samples of endometrium without the need for an anaesthetic. If your bleeding has an unusual pattern as well as being heavy, your doctor may decide to look at your uterine cavity in a procedure called hysteroscopy.

SELF-HELP
Bioflavonoids, which are found in citrus fruits, may alleviate heavy bleeding. Other useful nutrients are vitamins A and C, and iron. Regular strenuous exercise and keeping your weight down may also be helpful. Avoiding alcohol may help relieve menorrhagia, since heavy drinking can inhibit the formation of blood platelets, which means blood

does not clot as well as it should and may flow more profusely during menstruation. The same is true of aspirin. Hot showers or baths during menstruation can also increase bleeding because heat dilates the uterine blood vessels and increases flow.

If you do suffer from menorrhagia, have your blood checked regularly for signs of anaemia. If your haemoglobin is low, eat more iron-rich foods and ask your doctor about iron supplements.

MEDICAL TREATMENT

Drugs are the first option in the treatment of menorrhagia. You may be prescribed an antifibrinolytic drug, such as tranexamic acid, that will increase the ability of your uterus to stop bleeding, or the combined contraceptive pill. Less effective, but sometimes helpful are the antiprostaglandin group of drugs, for example, diclofenac. If you have a condition such as fibroids, this will be treated. Menorrhagia can also be treated by destruction of the endometrium using lasers or diathermy (heating tissues by means of ultrasound or microwaves). In very severe cases hysterectomy may be necessary.

FIBROIDS

The exact cause of these slow-growing uterine tumours is unknown, but is thought to be related to oestrogen levels. Fibroids are benign and grow in or on the uterine wall. Women who are below the age of 20 rarely suffer from fibroids, but they affect a fifth of women between the ages of 35 and 45, and a quarter of women over the age of 80.

The relatively unopposed oestrogen of the perimenopausal years (progesterone production declines as women near the menopause) may be responsible for the increasing number of fibroid tumours. Decreased levels of oestrogen after the menopause usually causes fibroids to shrink. When fibroids do increase rapidly in postmenopausal women, there are grounds for concern because these tumours

have the greatest potential for becoming cancerous. Current dosages of HRT are not thought to be sufficiently high to affect postmenopausal fibroids one way or the other.

SYMPTOMS

Small fibroids may be symptomless. However, if a fibroid distorts the size or shape of the uterus, it may cause heavy or prolonged periods and anaemia. Large fibroids may press on the bladder, causing discomfort or frequent and urgent urination. Pressure on the bowel causes backache or constipation. Occasionally, a fibroid attached to the uterine wall becomes twisted on its stalk and can cause sudden pain in the lower abdomen.

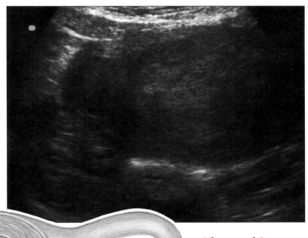

Ultrasound Scan

Fibroids are visible in X-rays of the pelvis. The rounded pale grey mass in the pelvic cavity shows a fibroid that has grown very large.

Uterus

Ovary

Small fibroid in uterine wall

Fibroid on the uterine lining

Large fibroid distorting uterine shape

Cervix

Vagina

Uterine Fibroids

Fibroids are benign lumps of tissue that form in and on the walls of the uterus. Large fibroids can cause heavy menstrual bleeding by increasing the surface area of the uterine lining.

DIAGNOSIS

Fibroids can cause the uterine wall to become lumpy and bumpy. If your doctor notices abdominal swelling he or she may recommend an ultrasound scan to confirm whether fibroids are present.

MEDICAL TREATMENT

Small symptomless fibroids, which are often discovered during a routine pelvic examination, usually require no treatment except monitoring. Surgery is required only for fibroids that cause symptoms such as pain or heavy bleeding, and a hysterectomy (see page 76) may be considered if there are a large number of fibroids or if you are experiencing significant pain or pressure.

Myomectomy, which involves shelling the fibroid out of its capsule, saves the uterus and is an alternative. If you are experiencing hot flushes and other menopausal symptoms, you should not necessarily be deterred from using HRT because you have fibroids. However, your doctor will want to carry out regular abdominal or internal examinations. Both the uterus and fibroids tend to shrink at the menopause, and the benefits of HRT in promoting good bones, a sense of well-being, and improved sexual function need to be weighed against the inconvenience of symptoms due to fibroids.

OVARIAN CYSTS

Although some cysts may be malignant, most are benign. As a cyst expands, the ovarian tissues thin out to surround it completely. Cysts have been known to grow up to 50 cm (20 in) in diameter. They are filled with a gelatinous fluid that very occasionally escapes into the pelvic cavity.

SYMPTOMS

Small ovarian cysts give rise to few or no symptoms, but, as they get bigger, you may notice an abdominal lump or swelling. When the cysts are very large, they may cause pressure leading to breathlessness, frequent urination, pressure on the veins of the legs causing varicose veins, swelling of the ankles, and digestive problems such as vomiting or constipation. Ovarian tumours cause irregular vaginal bleeding only if they are producing oestrogen.

Sudden severe pain occurs if an ovarian cyst growing on a stalk becomes twisted. Sudden abdominal pain must be investigated by a doctor.

DIAGNOSIS

An ovarian cyst may be discovered during a routine pelvic examination. To exclude other causes of abdominal swelling, you may need to have an ultrasound examination or a laparoscopy (examination of the abdominal cavity through a viewing tube).

MEDICAL TREATMENT

Surgical removal is always required, whatever the type of ovarian cyst, as only microscopic examination of the cyst distinguishes a malignant tumour from a benign one. The likelihood of the cyst being cancerous increases as you get older.

SKIN COMPLAINTS

LEUKOPLAKIA

Raised white patches on the inside of the mouth and on the tongue or around the vaginal opening are due to the thickening of tissue. Leukoplakia is most prevalent in elderly women.

Leukoplakia in the mouth, most commonly on the tongue, is usually due to smoking or to the rubbing of a rough tooth or denture. It is not known what causes leukoplakia to develop in the vulva or on the vaginal opening. The patches develop slowly, cause no discomfort, and are usually harmless. But occasionally they may undergo malignant change, and for this reason, leukoplakia should always be reported to your doctor.

MEDICAL TREATMENT

Once the underlying cause of leukoplakia in the mouth has been treated, it should clear up. If the condition persists, the patches can be removed under a local anaesthetic. The same treatment is used for leukoplakia of the vulva. The removed tissue is examined under a microscope, and if there are any signs of malignant change, the patches are treated radically with surgery or laser therapy.

AGE SPOTS

These brownish-yellow, sometimes slightly raised spots (seborrhoeic keratoses) may start to appear on the skin after the menopause. They can occur anywhere and sometimes get caught on clothing. Sun spots (solar keratoses) start to appear on the backs of the hands and face or any part of the body exposed to the sun. Red, pin-point spots – De Morgan's spots – appear on the trunk. Only solar keratoses need treatment, since they may become cancerous. They can be removed under local anaesthetic or frozen with liquid nitrogen. Any blemish that grows or bleeds should be seen by a doctor.

CHLOASMA

Blotches of pale-brown pigmentation on the face are called chloasma. They sometimes develop in pregnancy, and occasionally the patches become fused together, forming "the mask of pregnancy". They can also appear after use of the contraceptive pill and at the menopause. The pigmentation is aggravated by sunlight and may be a reaction to HRT – switching brands of hormones may help.

BROKEN VEINS AND SPIDER NAEVI

As the skin thins and loses colour during the menopause, dilated veins become more visible. Hot flushes, when blood capillaries dilate to fill with blood, may leave behind permanent broken veins. A spider naevus is a tiny, raised, red dot on the skin from which widened blood capillaries radiate outwards (spider naevi). If spider naevi outnumber seven on the face they are thought to indicate underlying liver disease.

If broken veins are particularly unsightly, they can be treated with procedures such as electrocautery or desiccation, (see page 171) or they can be camouflaged using make-up. Although spider naevi do not require any medical treatment, you should point them out to your doctor.

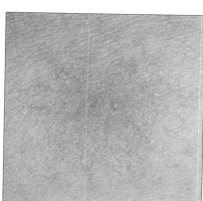

Spider Naevi
Dilated broken veins become more visible after the menopause. Although they may make the skin appear flushed, they are not harmful.

HORMONAL COMPLAINTS

HYPOTHYROIDISM

The underproduction of thyroid hormones is caused by the body developing antibodies to its own thyroid gland, preventing the production of thyroid hormones. Hashimoto's thyroiditis is an example of this. More rarely, hypothyroidism may result from an operation to remove part of the thyroid gland, or from taking radioactive iodine as a treatment for hyperthyroidism (overactivity of the thyroid).

Hypothyroidism affects one in 100 of the adult population and, although it can occur at any age, is most common in elderly women.

SYMPTOMS

A deficiency of thyroid hormones can cause generalized tiredness and lethargy, muscle weakness, cramps, a slow heart rate, dry and flaky skin, hair loss, a deep and husky voice, and weight gain. A syndrome known as myxoedema may develop, in which the skin and other body tissues thicken. In some cases a goitre – an enlargement of the thyroid gland – develops (although not all goitres are due to hypothyroidism). The severity of symptoms is dependent on the degree of thyroid deficiency. Mild deficiency may cause no symptoms, severe deficiency may produce the whole range of symptoms.

MEDICAL TREATMENT

Once diagnosed by tests that measure the level of thyroid hormones in the blood, treatment consists of replacement therapy with the thyroid hormone thyroxine. In most cases, hormone medication must be continued for life. If this treatment does not cure a goitre, surgery may be required.

DIABETES MELLITUS

This is a deficiency of the hormone insulin. Sufferers who produce no insulin by themselves and are dependent on insulin injections have type I diabetes. The type of diabetes that usually affects women over 40 is type II diabetes, in which insulin is still produced, but in insufficient quantities. This type of diabetes has a slow onset and may only be discovered during a routine medical examination.

Insulin, produced by the pancreas, controls the effective use of glucose in the body. Insufficient insulin makes the glucose level in your blood rise

SYMPTOMS OF DIABETES

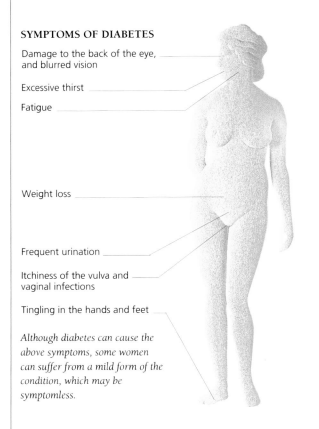

Damage to the back of the eye, and blurred vision

Excessive thirst

Fatigue

Weight loss

Frequent urination

Itchiness of the vulva and vaginal infections

Tingling in the hands and feet

Although diabetes can cause the above symptoms, some women can suffer from a mild form of the condition, which may be symptomless.

dramatically, and you start to excrete glucose in your urine instead of using it as energy, or storing it. The fact that you cannot utilize your most accessible form of energy has a detrimental effect on the body, and you may experience fatigue, weight loss, excessive thirst, the need to pass large amounts of urine, blurred vision, and itchiness or redness of the vulva.

RISK FACTORS
Obesity is associated with diabetes. If you are overweight and have a high intake of carbohydrates, the amount of glucose in your blood will be high, and your pancreas may not be able to cope. Losing weight and changing your diet may be helpful. Other risk factors are heredity – a third of diabetics have a family history of the condition – and old age.

DIAGNOSIS
Your doctor will test your urine for glucose and a substance called ketones (a byproduct of fat breakdown). He or she may also take a sample of your blood after you have not eaten for a few hours. If both your urine and blood are found to contain significantly high levels of glucose and ketones, diabetes is likely.

SELF-HELP
It is important to monitor the amount of glucose you are ingesting. Too much glucose in the blood (hyperglycaemia) will exacerbate your diabetic symptoms, and too little (hypoglycaemia) will cause dizziness, weakness, confusion, and eventually unconsciousness. You can monitor your glucose levels with a kit, which your doctor will give you, by dipping an impregnated strip into a sample of your urine and then comparing the colour change against a chart.

Your doctor will advise you about dietary control of diabetes, but, as a rule, you should avoid all sugar. Eat small amounts of carbohydrates at regular intervals so that you do not have drastic fluctuations in glucose levels, and eat plenty of fibre. In mild cases of diabetes, which are due to obesity, simply cutting out sugar and reducing your weight if you are obese will improve your condition dramatically because your pancreas will be producing enough insulin to cope with your reduced body size.

MEDICAL TREATMENT
Serious cases of type II diabetes may require hypoglycaemic drugs to lower blood glucose. Insulin injections are prescribed only for sufferers of diabetes mellitus type I.

The complications that can arise from severe diabetes mellitus include damage to the retina at the back of the eye (retinopathy), damage to nerve fibres (neuropathy), damage to the kidneys (nephropathy), atherosclerosis (see page 79), hypertension, and gangrene.

Both diabetes and HRT alter the way that you metabolise carbohydrates, and for this reason HRT may be relatively contraindicated for diabetics (see page 135). However, if your diabetes is stable, if you test your urine regularly, and if you liaise closely with your doctor, it may be safe, particularly in the very low dose skin patch form.

5

MANAGING
YOUR
MENOPAUSE

*Although many women seek medical help during their
menopausal years, there are many strategies that you can
adopt by yourself to manage your own treatment,
including a range of alternative therapies, from yoga to
aromatherapy. Also, if you understand the effects of
different types of HRT on your body, you can negotiate
with your doctor on your own terms.*

OVERCOMING STEREOTYPES

Referring to the menopause as "the change of life" is misleading and can be counterproductive. The menopause isn't the only change that will occur during your life and it is unlikely to be the most significant change. Life is a series of gradual changes – we don't suddenly reach a turning point and start growing old when we reach midlife. Ageing is a continuous process that begins the moment we are born. I believe that a healthy attitude to the menopause is to see it as a time in which to rediscover yourself, to assess your life and its purpose, and to establish new aims and goals.

Many of us have spent much of our lives trying to please other people. We put a great deal of effort into taking care of our children, our husbands, our parents, and friends. We try to be what they would like us to be, and very often we lose sight of who we are and what we want. By trying to become everything to everyone, we can end up being nothing to ourselves. By the time we reach middle age most of us carry around the received "wisdom" of society, left-overs from old customs and traditions, fears that are often obsolete, and beliefs that may be borrowed. Without clearing out all these redundant feelings, we can lose touch with our inner selves.

It is important to resist negative stereotypes associated with the menopause. These are often culturally created, and do not reflect the reality of our individual experiences. In countries where age is venerated and older women are respected for their experience and wisdom, fewer physical and psychological symptoms of the menopause are reported (see pages 25–28). Many Asian, Arabic, and African women positively welcome the end of fertility and childbearing, and, perhaps as a result, they seem to encounter fewer difficulties than Western women. In countries that lack a tradition of myths and misconceptions about the menopause, ageing seems to be regarded as a more natural process; women aren't adversely affected by negative images and may feel less confused by what is happening to them.

If you believe that in order to be beautiful and successful you must be young, then you may not enjoy your middle age to the full. If you are convinced that the quality of life deteriorates from the age of 50 onward, this can become a self-fulfilling prophecy; because you believe it is going to happen, you may inadvertently make it happen by not taking care of yourself and adopting resigned, negative attitudes.

TAKING CONTROL OF YOUR BODY

The first step toward taking charge of your life and managing your menopause is to take charge of your body. You need to take an active role with your medical and health carers, be aware of all your options and exercise them, in order to eliminate as many health problems as you can. The strategy you choose to deal with any menopausal symptoms you may have is up to you. You may decide to try self-help measures or complementary medicine. Alternatively, you may feel that your symptoms warrant medical help.

To achieve these goals, you need to have a sense of self-worth and optimism about the future, and you must be prepared to make an effort. As soon as you start to take control of your menopausal symptoms, your health and sense of well-being will benefit enormously.

YOUR MEDICAL ADVISOR

Ideally, the doctor you consult at the menopause will be a doctor who has treated you over several years, and who is well acquainted with your medical history. The best doctor–patient relationships are those in which you receive full attention and satisfactory answers. You should be able to visit your doctor with a complete list of questions to which you require answers.

Unfortunately, although this kind of easy relationship should be the norm, some women encounter entrenched conservative opinion that dismisses the menopause as a woman's legacy, requiring neither help nor treatment. If your doctor espouses these attitudes, my advice is to change to a more sympathetic doctor as soon as possible. Don't continue with a doctor with whom you have little rapport. Some of the symptoms you may experience will require you to be open and confident enough to discuss them in intimate detail. If you feel at all inhibited, that doctor is not for you. Remember, doctors are there to help you and provide a service. Shop around until you can find a doctor who really suits you. He or she must be able to tailor your treatment to your individual needs in the light of your medical and gynaecological history. Your doctor should be aware of the side-effects you can encounter while taking hormone replacement therapy (HRT; see chapter six), be responsive to your comments about a particular HRT regime, and be able to implement changes over a period of several months until you are absolutely happy with your treatment. A GP who is not well versed in menopausal medicine may not be able to provide quite such an individual service, in which case you should seek specialist advice from menopause or well-woman clinics, or from a gynaecologist.

MANAGING HORMONAL MEDICATION

Not all women who should get HRT do get it, and many women who are prescribed HRT do not take it for a sufficiently long period to prevent their bone mass declining and to protect them against cardiovascular disease. Such women are usually anxious about side-effects, have read panic stories in the press, or have misconceptions about their treatments. In my opinion, more women should consider trying HRT and more doctors should be prepared to prescribe medication over a four-month trial period. Research carried out on the oral contraceptive pill shows that four months is the minimum trial period for hormone-based medication because it takes your body that long to settle down and achieve a comfortable balance. Within four months it is possible for your doctor to adapt the treatment so that you can find the regime that suits your body most. It is worth embarking on the search for the right dose and type of HRT because it can have a profound effect on your physical and emotional well-being.

Only a sixth of the women who start taking HRT continue to take it for a year. The main reason given for this low compliance rate is side-effects. However, it is worth remembering that certain side-effects, such as headaches, indigestion, and tender breasts can occur whether you're taking hormones or not. In several well-controlled studies, women who were told they were taking HRT, but were actually taking a placebo, had as many symptoms as women taking HRT. The important factor seems to be how well informed you are about the side-effects; women who are warned of potential minor problems seem to cope with them better than women who are not so well informed.

A MONTHLY BLEED?

The first decision for you and your doctor to make when you are contemplating taking HRT is whether or not to have a withdrawal bleed. The consensus of medical opinion is that if you have an intact uterus, you should have a menstrual bleed at regular intervals. Two new approaches – combined continuous therapy (see page 132) and a progestogenic drug called tibolone – have allowed some women to avoid bleeding altogether, and various menopause experts have been researching three-monthly, rather than monthly withdrawal bleeding. This research has found that women only need to menstruate every three months in order to maintain a healthy uterine lining. At one time (and I was involved in this research 25 years ago), it was thought that the HRT cycle should be similar to the natural menstrual cycle in that a bleed should take place every month. This was achieved by giving women progestogen for 11–13 days in the second half of the cycle. The current thinking is that this may be unnecessary for quite a number of women – your doctor may be able to carry out a test on you to be absolutely certain that it is safe for you to bleed as infrequently as once every three months (see page 198).

Doctors involved in research at the Medical Care Programme in Oakland, California, hypothesized that the addition of progestogen every three months instead of every month would be safe. To evaluate the acceptability of this regime 200 women, who had previously taken progestogen on a monthly basis, were asked to complete a daily diary and, at the conclusion of the study, to complete a preference questionnaire about which HRT regime they felt suited them best. On the three-monthly regime, the average duration of

A New Way Of Taking HRT
Unlike the usual method of taking HRT, which works in monthly cycles, this regime involves taking oestrogen continuously and then taking progestogen for 12 days at the end of every third month. The advantage of this is that women experience a withdrawal bleed once every three months instead of once every month. The long-term safety of this regime is still being evaluated.

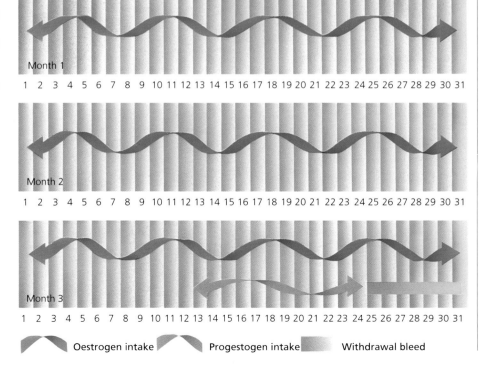

Month 1
1 2 3 4 5 6 7 8 9 10 11 12 13 14 15 16 17 18 19 20 21 22 23 24 25 26 27 28 29 30 31

Month 2
1 2 3 4 5 6 7 8 9 10 11 12 13 14 15 16 17 18 19 20 21 22 23 24 25 26 27 28 29 30 31

Month 3
1 2 3 4 5 6 7 8 9 10 11 12 13 14 15 16 17 18 19 20 21 22 23 24 25 26 27 28 29 30 31

Oestrogen intake   Progestogen intake   Withdrawal bleed menstruation was two days longer than it had been formerly. The safety of the treatment was checked by performing a physical examination and carrying out biopsies on the uterine lining at the beginning of treatment and after one year.

The results of the preference questionnaire showed that women preferred the three-monthly progestogen regime to the monthly one, despite the fact that their periods were longer and heavier. In addition, a reduction in blood pressure occurred over the year of the study. Biopsies of the uterine lining did not reveal any abnormalities, suggesting that three-monthly progestogen is as safe as monthly progestogen. Although this way of taking HRT is still being evaluated for its long-term safety, you could discuss it with your doctor.

There is also another way of taking HRT, which allows you to take progestogen "on demand". Research shows that it is possible to monitor growth (induced by oestrogen) of the endometrium, or uterine lining, with a technique called vaginosonography, in which an ultrasound picture shows the thickness of the uterine lining. This technique can also monitor endometrial shedding after the addition of progestogen. Vaginosonography enables us to find out which type and dose of oestrogen causes the lowest endometrial growth for you, and which type and dose of progestogen causes the best endometrial shedding, with minimal withdrawal bleeding. A study carried out in the Netherlands found that the sensitivity of the menopausal endometrium to oestrogens and progestogens is unique to each woman. Another remarkable discovery was that the endometrium could shed itself without withdrawal bleeding after the addition of progestogen – certain progestogens cause shedding of the endometrium without withdrawal bleeding more often than others. Vaginosonography is still at the experimental stage, and not widely available.

CONTROLLING SIDE-EFFECTS OF HRT
If you experience side-effects while you are taking HRT, there are several ways that you and your doctor can bring them under control. With time and patience you can adapt your regime by changing the type of hormones, the dose, the route of administration, or the medication regime.

Changing The Types Of Hormones   Certain side-effects may indicate that the hormones you are taking do not suit you. Tender and enlarged breasts, general bloating, fluid retention, headaches, and weight gain are oestrogen-related symptoms. Mood changes, sadness, depression, irritability, short-temperedness, and possibly weight gain may result from taking some progestogens.

Oestrogens can be divided into synthetic types (such as mestranol and ethinyl oestradiol) and natural types (such as conjugated equine oestrogens and oestradiol varieties). Synthetic oestrogens in higher dosages than those normally used in HRT may increase the risk of thromboembolism. Although it is usual to prescribe natural oestrogens in HRT, you should find out which of these two types you are taking and suggest to your doctor that you switch from a synthetic hormone to a natural one, or, if you are already taking a natural oestrogen, that you try a different brand.

The main progestogens used in HRT are dydrogesterone, medroxyprogesterone acetate, norethisterone, and norgestrel. These vary quite markedly in their effects, and if you have side-effects, lowering the dose or switching to another type of progestogen may help. A drug called tibolone (see page 102) has few progestogenic side-effects.

Changing The Dose Of Hormones Side-effects can also occur if you are taking more hormones than your body needs. As a woman's body gets older, it becomes more and more sensitive to female hormones, and a much lower dose is needed for HRT than is needed for contraception. The aim of HRT is to be effective at the lowest possible dose. For instance, if you are taking conjugated equine oestrogen, it is possible to halve the dose from 1.25 micrograms of oestrogen per day to 0.625 micrograms. Similarly, progestogen could be reduced from 500 micrograms of norethisterone acetate per day to 300 micrograms. These changes in your dose of hormones should be handled by your doctor in sequence rather than in parallel.

Changing The Route Of Administration Most doctors start women off on HRT in the oral form. However, this does not suit all women. For example, high doses of oestrogen can cause nausea (if you are affected in this way, try taking your tablet at night so that you sleep through any nausea).

As with any drug taken by mouth (rather than being absorbed through the skin or implanted in the fat layer), a larger dose than necessary is given because of the first-pass effect of the liver in which much of the drug is removed from the bloodstream after absorption. The tablet form of HRT contains more hormone than necessary to alleviate symptoms and this may explain why you experience side-effects.

If you cut your dosage of oral medication and you still have problems, try switching to a patch form of HRT (see page 129), which contains much less hormone than oral HRT, or ask your doctor about an implant, which is formulated to release oestrogen slowly and consistently over a period of four to six months.

If you find that your menopausal symptoms affect your urogenital tract more than any other part of your body, and you have symptoms such as a dry vagina, pain during sex, and frequent, urgent urination, then vaginal pessaries or cream may be sufficient to relieve your symptoms. Because these are applied locally, they prevent your whole body from being exposed to hormones. However, creams and pessaries will not have the protective qualities of oral HRT on your heart and bones.

Some women who experience progestogenic side-effects, such as mood changes, respond well to progesterone taken in a suppository form. This may be advantageous in that it

First-pass Effect Of The Liver
Oral HRT contains a larger dose of hormone than other types of HRT because, as it passes through the liver before entering the bloodstream, much of the hormone is lost. This is called the first-pass effect.

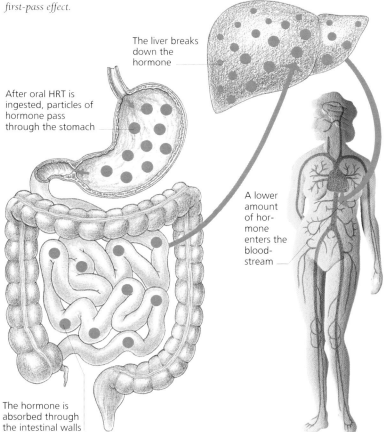

The liver breaks down the hormone

After oral HRT is ingested, particles of hormone pass through the stomach

A lower amount of hormone enters the bloodstream

The hormone is absorbed through the intestinal walls

contains true progesterone instead of its synthetic counterpart. Some women find that they can tolerate the natural hormone better than synthetic progestogen. However, bigger doses of natural progesterone are needed to control the HRT cycle than if synthetic progestogens are used (this is why progesterone is not widely prescribed). A combination of an oestrogen skin patch and a progesterone suppository may be the best route of administration for you.

Changing Your Regime The essence of success in HRT is matching the treatment to each individual woman. You and your doctor should work together to find the hormone combination that suits you best. In one recent survey of 100 women, it was found that only 17 percent had stayed on their first treatment over many years, and all the others had made one or two adjustments. If something does not seem right, discuss with your doctor whether the dose or route of administration is suitable. If you have premenstrual symptoms or troublesome bleeding, modification of the progestogen may help.

It is unwise to make rapid and frequent changes or to change more than one aspect of HRT at a time, since it often takes several weeks for a treatment to settle down. Most women will take continuous oestrogen and 10–14 days of progestogen each month. However, there are several variations in the way that HRT can be taken, one of which is sure to suit you.

If you are taking oestrogen tablets you can begin to leave a space between medications. With the supervision of your doctor, you could try taking your tablet two days out of three, three days out of four, or every other day, and see how you feel. Skin patches can be left on for four days at a time instead of three to four, or they can be left off for a day. This may be particularly helpful in relieving mastalgia and weight gain.

If you have progestogenic side-effects and you are taking HRT in which progestogen and oestrogen are combined, ask your doctor to prescribe different products in which the hormones are separate. For example, you could take oestrogen in a skin patch form and progestogen in tablet form. This way you and your doctor can juggle the dose of the progestogen so that you have a withdrawal bleed without troublesome side-effects.

MAXIMIZING YOUR INTERNAL OESTROGEN

If you have been taking HRT for some time, you may feel that you would like to see how you cope without it. Alternatively, you may opt not to take HRT in the first place. In either case, there are two ways in which you can boost your own internal oestrogen production to compensate for the low hormone levels in your bloodstream.

The first is exercise (see pages 160–163), which can be almost as good as HRT in the postmenopausal years when your body needs relatively little oestrogen to thrive. Your second source of internal oestrogen comes from your fat cells, which is why it is dangerous for peri- and postmenopausal women to diet excessively and become underweight. Thin women generally have an earlier menopause than overweight women, because fat cells all over your body manufacture oestrogen, and in their absence hormone levels can fall very low. If you don't wish to take HRT but are having symptoms of oestrogen deficiency, make sure you keep your weight up slightly. Whatever you do, don't lose so much weight that you have very little body fat – you will be depriving yourself of an important source of natural oestrogen.

ALTERNATIVES TO HRT

Not every menopausal woman will be prescribed HRT or choose to take it, and some women find that conventional medicine does not alleviate the changes or discomforts of the menopause. Luckily, there are plenty of other techniques and therapies to try. Some of them, such as yoga, will help to relieve emotional symptoms, by helping you to relax; others, such as homeopathy, will target specific menopausal symptoms, such as hot flushes. There are many therapies that may bring a tangible benefit in terms of fitness, mood, and spirit. All should be regarded as weapons for dealing successfully with the menopause.

Without doubt, exercise is the menopausal woman's best friend in that it allows you to control your body and emotions by using your internal resources. Each time that you take exercise, your adrenal glands are stimulated to convert the male hormone androstenedione into oestrogen. A minimum of four 30-minute exercise sessions a week will be enough to keep you topped up with oestrogen. As you become older, your cardiorespiratory fitness, your strength, and your flexibility begin to decline, but for people who remain active, they decrease at a lower rate (an average of five percent per decade after the age of 20, as opposed to nine percent per decade).

Long-term exercise also means that you will have stronger bones and a lower risk of osteoporosis than your non-exercising counterparts. Although every woman is different, most of us lose 25–35 percent of our bone mass by the time we reach the age of 65. Bone loss begins around the age of 35, proceeds slowly up to the menopause, and then accelerates during the five to seven years after the menopause, when oestrogen levels are low.

OVER-TRAINING

Although many of us don't take enough exercise, a small percentage of women become psychologically addicted to exercise, experiencing the need to train every day, and feeling guilty if they miss a single session. One reason for this may be that women are conditioned to want to look attractive and are influenced by the powerful cultural associations between thinness and beauty. A few women who have deep-rooted insecurities about their bodies may respond by channelling their anxieties into compulsive exercising.

If you are addicted to exercise, you may be afraid that if you stop, even for a while, you will become unfit and overweight. This is quite untrue. Even competitive athletes have breaks in which they train lightly or not at all. Going to extremes in exercise can affect every facet of your life. When you over-train, you can experience mood swings and problems with sleep and appetite. You're also more susceptible to colds and injuries, as intense physical exercise can lower the integrity of the immune system.

If you think you may be over-training, it may help to know in physiological terms how fit you are. If you see scientific data on your fitness and compare it with your own idea of how fit you are, you'll probably be surprised and more able to come to terms with the fact that you don't have to exercise so hard. If you feel your need to exercise is compulsive, or that it is accompanied by anxiety and depression, you should seek medical help. An exercise addiction will be taken as seriously as any other compulsive form of behaviour.

Women who do weight-bearing exercises, such as low-impact aerobics, walking, running, or weight training in their 20s and 30s can increase their bone density before loss sets in. Beginning exercise later in life can restore small amounts – around four percent – of bone. Unfortunately, you cannot "store" the benefits of exercise; it must be ongoing to confer its many benefits.

EXERCISE AS A MENTAL TONIC

Regular exercise may also have a significant effect on our mental agility by increasing the amount of oxygen supplied to the brain. In a comparison of sedentary older women and older women who took regular exercise, after four months the latter group processed information faster in tests. This effect of exercise is particularly marked in older people.

Apart from increasing the oxygen supply to the brain, exercise may also slow down the loss of dopamine in the brain. Dopamine is a neurotransmitter that helps to prevent the shaking and stiffness that can come with old age. A severe shortage of dopamine results in the exaggerated tremors of Parkinson's disease. Dopamine decreases in the brain by about one percent a year from our mid-20s, and if we lived to be a 100 years old, we would all appear to have Parkinson's disease. Since exercise can slow down dopamine loss, it is particularly beneficial as we grow older. Exercise can also prevent our reaction times from slowing down.

THE BENEFITS OF REGULAR EXERCISE
- A reduced risk of heart disease.
- A lower chance of developing diabetes.
- Maintenance of muscle strength.
- Higher levels of the healthy type of cholesterol in the blood.
- Better bone health and less chance of developing osteoporosis.
- A more efficient immune system.
- Reduced body fat.
- Better appetite control.
- Increased mental agility.
- Fewer headaches.
- Improved sleep quality.
- Flexible joints.

The type of exercise that you take will obviously depend largely on resources, how much time is available, and personal preference. In order to gain the most positive effect from exercise it is very important to find a form that you enjoy. Nowadays there are a wide range of opportunities available, not only in sport centres and fitness classes but, for women who need or prefer to exercise in their own home, there are lots of videos, audio cassettes, and publications on the market.

You may prefer a game sport such as tennis, badminton or squash, all of which offer the added attraction of meeting and socializing with people. Likewise, joining any aerobics, pop-mobility or "exercise" class can provide a social aspect that may encourage you to exercise regularly. Less rigorous and more traditional forms of exercise such as walking and swimming offer a viable alternative and will keep the body fit and supple.

Recently, there has been a move away from aerobic training towards strength training and weight bearing exercise. Research suggests that any exercise involving weights can delay loss of bone and muscle tissue, which is a natural consequence of ageing. Weight-bearing exercise also helps to normalize the flow of sugar from the blood into muscle tissue, where it can be properly metabolized. This may lower the risk of diabetes and heart disease.

NATURAL MEDICINE
As well as exercise, there are many practices, currently labelled "complementary" or "alternative" that can help women cope with menopausal discomforts. Although it can be helpful to visit a qualified practitioner in the first instance, many complementary therapies can be practised by women on themselves.

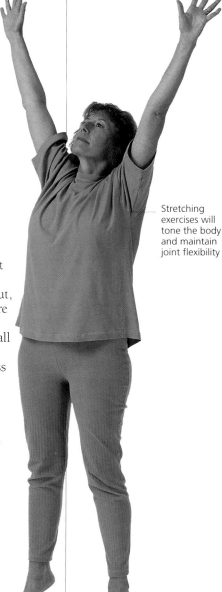

Staying Healthy
Exercise not only increases your physical fitness and resistance to disease, it also has an uplifting effect on your mood.

Stretching exercises will tone the body and maintain joint flexibility

COMPLEMENTARY THERAPY

Any medicine that heals or relieves discomfort without having any harmful side-effects is, in my opinion, good medicine. Although HRT is the major treatment advocated by the medical establishment, complementary medical practices offer many natural alternatives.

Orthodox medicine is based on allopathy, a doctrine that originated in Asia Minor in the first century BC. It followed a principle so simple that it soon became accepted as common sense: when the working of the body goes wrong, the symptoms should be counteracted. An example of this practice would be treating constipation with a laxative.

In contrast, the main branches of complementary medicine argue that our bodies have a life force that becomes disturbed when diseased but reasserts itself if the body stops being abused and is nourished correctly.

Just like the best orthodox medicine, the best unorthodox medicine is holistic – it treats the whole person, rather than an isolated symptom. The true naturopath is sceptical of symptomatic remedies because they fail to treat the root cause of the illness.

One reason that complementary medicine is not readily accepted by the medical profession is that its techniques are not usually subjected to scientific scrutiny and objective analysis. This is gradually changing and some excellent clinical studies have been conducted in osteopathy and chiropractic, which have proven to be more helpful in treating low back pain than routine hospital procedures. Aromatherapy is now accepted for the treatment of indigestion, migraine, and some bowel problems.

NATUROPATHY

Many types of complementary medicine are based on naturopathy. Its principles are as follows.

- The patient is treated, not the disease.
- The whole body is treated, not just a part of it.
- The underlying factors causing the disease must be removed.
- Disease is a disturbance of a life force, demonstrated by tension, rigidity, or congestion somewhere in the body, for example, the muscles.
- The patient's own life force is the true healer.
- The body must have a "healing crisis" in which the life force cleanses the body by eliminating accumulated "toxins". The use of drugs in orthodox medicine, while superficially curing the disease, drives it deep within the body, leaving behind a chronic condition for the future.

Naturopaths consider nutrition to be the anchor of health, and treatment usually involves fasting (one of the oldest therapeutic methods known to us) and other dietary constraints. You should drink pure water, and the food you eat should be organically grown, unprocessed, and, as far as possible, uncooked. Animal protein should not make up more than 25 percent of the diet. Food supplements from natural sources rather than vitamin supplements are recommended. Wheatgerm oil, kelp, and royal jelly can be particularly beneficial during the menopause.

Naturopaths also believe that health depends on adopting a healthy and well-balanced attitude of mind by practising relaxation exercises, yoga, meditation, and psychotherapy. Some naturopaths will also include hydrotherapy in their treatment programmes.

AROMATHERAPY

This is a fairly recent addition to complementary medicine, although its roots go back through the centuries. Human beings have a highly developed sense of smell and we can react to an odour within a split second. Babies bond with their mothers through scent and lovers are attracted by each other's pheromones, or chemical secretions. Smells can be mood-enhancing and they may relieve pain and illness. Massage using essential oils is relaxing and enjoyable, and beneficial in reducing many stress-related conditions.

The oil essences that are used in aromatherapy are pure distillations from plants, and are very concentrated. In a dilute form, they can be inhaled and absorbed through the lining of the air passages. The essential oils can be used singly or blended, and have different properties; some are anti-viral, some affect blood pressure, and some are general healers.

Essential oils are actually absorbed through the skin during massage or bathing, and through the lungs when inhaled. Oral doses are not generally used, except in the case of garlic, which may be taken in capsule form. The emphasis in aromatherapy is on the treatment of minor ailments and the promotion of health and well-being, both physical and mental. For this reason, the use of essential oils has achieved a wide popularity. The methods of inhaling essential oils are as follows.

- On a compress (although you should be careful not to apply neat essential oils to the skin because they are highly concentrated).
- Heating diluted essential oils on an oil burner.
- Inhaling as a vapour. Add three drops of essential oil to a bowl of steaming water and then cover your head with a towel and breathe in deeply. This method is good for skin problems.
- Inhaled on a handkerchief or pillow.
- Added to warm water in a bath. This method is good for nourishing the skin and relieving tension. It is one of the easiest ways of using essential oils – you should spend at least 15 minutes in the bath to derive the full benefit.
- Applied to the skin as massage oil. The essential oil is diluted with a base oil such as sweet almond oil or soya oil. About 20 drops of essential oil should be added to 100 ml (3.3 fl oz) of base oil.

Essential Oils

Burning essential oils in a burner (below) is a good way to fragrance a room. Essential oils can be preserved by keeping them in dark bottles (bottom), away from natural light.

The flame heats a mixture of oil and water in the dish above

Preserve essential oils in dark glass bottles

AROMATHERAPY REMEDIES FOR MENOPAUSAL SYMPTOMS

ESSENTIAL OIL	SYMPTOM
Cypress, geranium, rose	Heavy periods
Avocado, wheatgerm	Dry skin
Juniper, lavender, rosemary	Muscle and joint pain
Lavender, peppermint	Headaches
Basil	Fatigue
Neroli, lavender	Insomnia
Lemon grass, ylang-ylang	Premenstrual symptoms
Clary sage, rose	Depressed mood

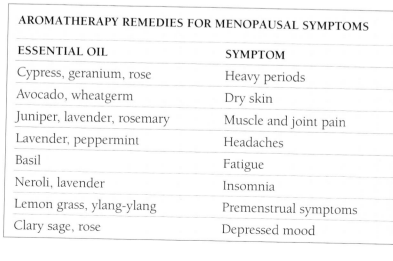

HOMEOPATHY

This is a form of natural healing based on the principle that a substance that produces the same symptoms as an illness will, in a very dilute form, help to cure that illness. Homeopathic remedies are derived from mineral, animal, or vegetable matter. Lachesis, which is the venom of the bushmaster snake, is very poisonous, but because it is used in such a dilute form, it is not toxic. The potency of remedies affects the efficacy of treatment – the more dilute the remedy, the higher the potency. Homeopathic remedies have a number after them that indicates how dilute they are. For instance, pulsatilla 30 is more dilute and therefore more potent than pulsatilla 6.

The homeopathic view of menopausal problems is that they are a manifestation of existing imbalances that can only be treated with regard to the mental and physical make-up of the individual. Women are encouraged to prepare for the menopause by looking at their overall health and developing a positive attitude of self before its onset.

The emphasis upon the individual and their physical and emotional history, rather than the illness they are suffering from, is fundamental to homeopathy. When consulting a homeopathic practitioner, not only are your symptoms assessed, but also your personality and constitution, likes and dislikes – all of this information is noted and used to form the basis of a decision as to which treatment should be given. For example, sepia is suited to someone who is irritable, moody, or dejected.

If you would like to treat your symptoms homeopathically, it is a good idea to consult a homeopathic practitioner. If you decide to treat yourself, bear in mind the following.

- You should stop taking a remedy as soon as your symptoms start to improve.
- If your symptoms are not relieved after six doses, increase the potency or seek medical advice.
- Homeopathic remedies should be preserved by storing them in a cool, dark place away from smells.
- Some substances, such as coffee, peppermint, menthol, and camphor, counteract the effects of homeopathic remedies and should be avoided.
- Some homeopathic pills are coated in milk sugar and you should avoid them if you are allergic to milk.
- If your symptoms are very acute, you can take a remedy hourly. For longer term problems, remedies can be taken in the morning and at night.

HOMEOPATHIC REMEDIES FOR MENOPAUSAL SYMPTOMS

REMEDY	SYMPTOM
Lachesis	Hot flushes
Pulsatilla	Insomnia, PMS, joint pain
Sepia	Dry vagina, prolapse, flushes, thinning hair
Sulphur	Dry itchy vulva and skin
Bryonia	PMS, mastalgia
Belladonna	Hot flushes and night sweats

HERBALISM

Some of the oldest methods of healing the sick are based on herbalism. Herbal law was handed down through families who had their own recipe books of tonics and teas. Treatments matured through centuries of hit-or-miss practice until particular herbs were linked to particular ailments.

Over the centuries, developments in orthodox medicine began to cast doubt on the efficacy of natural remedies, but since the 1950s herbalism has enjoyed renewed popularity, and can sometimes be compared favourably with modern drugs, which may create allergies or spread resistant strains of bacteria.

Like homeopathy, the aims behind herbal treatment are to remove the cause of the symptoms rather than merely the symptoms themselves, and to improve the patient's general standard of health. A disadvantage of herbalism is that agreement over which remedies should be used for particular disorders is still surprisingly limited. However, herbalism does offer an attractive alternative to other forms of treatment in that it may allow the patient to experiment with a variety of herbs without the complication of serious side-effects. It is also recognized that herbal remedies can work as a complement to orthodox medicine.

Modern herbalism aims to correct what is wrong with the body by strengthening its natural functions so that it may heal itself. Herbs can be very effective in relieving menopausal symptoms, but although there is valuable anecdotal information about their benefits, few remedies have been subjected to tightly controlled clinical trials.

GUIDELINES FOR TAKING HERBS

- Always use herbs in moderation.
- Discontinue use if you start to experience side-effects.
- Give each herb a week or two to assess its efficacy.
- Start by taking a herb in tea form. Increase the amount from half a cup a day to several cups a day, over a period of a week.
- Don't take herbs for longer than a few months without a break.
- If you are taking medication, you should check with your doctor before you take a herbal remedy.
- Don't defer seeking medical advice because you are taking a herbal remedy.

There are many herbs that can help to relieve both the physical and emotional symptoms of the menopause, but three in particular are sage, vitex agnus-castus, and black cohosh. Sage may help to alleviate hot flushes, and you can take it in tea form, made from fresh sage grown in the garden or dried sage bought from a supermarket or herbalist. Simply boil the leaves with one cup of water and strain. Sage tea has quite a strong taste, and whereas some women find it calming to the stomach, others find it unpalatable – if you don't like the taste, you can buy sage in tablet form from a herbalist.

The herb vitex agnus-castus (also known as vitex or chaste berry) has long been associated with menopausal disorders, and it may help to normalize hormone levels, acting as a natural type of HRT. Some herbalists recommend the following combination of herbs to treat hot flushes: blackcurrant leaves, hawthorn tops, sage, and vitex agnus-castus. This may be drunk in an infusion three times daily for six weeks. Black cohosh has oestrogenic properties and can help if you are feeling weak and tense. It also has anti-spasmodic and sedative properties and will help to alleviate premenstrual tension, pains, and bloating. Black cohosh works well in combination with vitex agnus-castus.

HERBAL THERAPY

Herbs have many diverse effects. Some have antiseptic, or anti-inflammatory properties, others act as natural sedatives, stimulants, diuretics, or general tonics. The therapeutic ways that fresh and dried herbs can be used are also various: you can drink them in tea form, as a decoction (the herb is boiled and then simmered for ten minutes), or as a tincture. You can also apply herbs to the skin as a compress or a salve.

BETH ROOT (right)
This is helpful for heavy periods, irregular periods, and breakthrough bleeding.

ALFALFA (right)
A plant rich in minerals, particularly calcium. Alfalfa also has oestrogenic properties.

SAGE (right)
This herb reduces sweating and can be drunk in tea form for hot flushes.

ST JOHN'S WORT
(right) Used to treat a range of symptoms from depression and lethargy to insomnia, poor memory, and hypertension.

FALSE UNICORN ROOT (below)
A herb used to treat prolapse, weak ligaments, and dragging pains.

SCULLCAP (left)
A sedative herb used to alleviate nervousness and irritability. It can be combined with the herb balm to treat anxiety that leads to insomnia.

VERVAIN (left)
This is good for emotional symptoms, such as anxiety. It should be drunk as a tea or taken as a tincture.

ELDERFLOWER (right) Helps to calm inflammation and soothe the skin, when used as elderflower water.

BLACK COHOSH (left)
Contains oestrogenic substances and will help menstrual irregularities, PMT, and cyclical skin complaints.

WILD YAM (right)
Helpful for ovarian and uterine pains and increasing the production of female hormones.

VITEX AGNUS-CASTUS (left)
This is a good general herb for the menopause and will help to alleviate hot flushes and night sweats.

CHINESE HERBS

Eastern medicine views illness as a result of an imbalance or disturbance in the body's two energy forces, yin and yang. Whereas Western medicine treats one illness with one drug, Chinese medicine tailors its remedies and dosages to the individual woman and her symptoms. Viewed this way, every woman's menopause is different and her symptoms may result from a number of different energy disturbances. The herbs below are *examples* of remedies – you should consult a Chinese doctor for an individual diagnosis.

Night sweats
Nuo dao gen
Wu wei zi

Hot flushes
Qing huo
Mu dan pi

Thinning hair
Bao shao yao
Sang shen zi

Sore, dry vagina
Tu fu ling
She chaung zi

Dry, itchy skin
Di fu zi
Chi shao yao

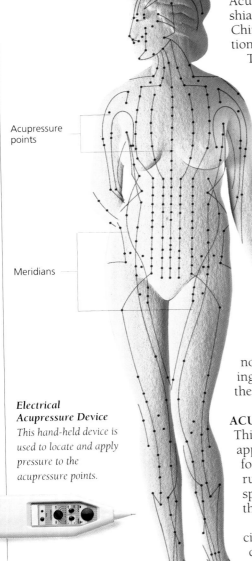

The Meridians
Acupuncture and acupressure are based on the theory that our life force flows along channels called meridians. When the flow of energy is disturbed, we become ill.

Acupressure points

Meridians

Electrical Acupressure Device
This hand-held device is used to locate and apply pressure to the acupressure points.

ACUPUNCTURE

This word comes from the Latin and means "to pierce with a needle". Acupuncture reputedly originated when it was noticed that Chinese soldiers wounded in battle by arrows, not only recovered from the arrow wound, but gained relief from other ailments as well. From this observation, the technique of inserting needles into the body for therapeutic purposes evolved. The use of acupuncture in China has been common for 5,000 years, but has only been acknowledged in the West in this century. Acupuncture is just one of the oriental therapies (others include shiatsu, acupressure, and Chinese herbalism), and if you consult a Chinese doctor, he or she may recommend acupuncture in conjunction with another therapy.

The theory behind acupuncture is that a life or energy force flows through the body along channels called meridians, which are quite distinct from the lines followed by nerves. This life force must flow unimpeded if bodily health is to be maintained. When we become ill, the energy flowing along a particular meridian may be affected at a site considerably distant from the sick part of the body. The acupuncturist aims to restore the flow of energy in the affected meridian by the use of copper, silver, or gold needles superficially inserted into the flesh at specific points along the meridian. These needles are so fine that they can hardly be felt as they enter the skin. Depending on the position of the selected point, the needles may be inserted vertically, at an angle, or sometimes almost horizontally. The needle is then rotated, moved up and down, or used to conduct heat or a mild electric current. This is thought to set up some kind of current along the meridian line. It passes to the central nervous system and has an effect on the organ or area that is malfunctioning by re-establishing the flow of energy through the meridian.

Acupuncture is one of the few Eastern practices that is widely accepted in the West, although its applications are not nearly so widespread here. In China, major operations, including heart transplant surgery, may be performed using acupuncture as the only form of pain relief.

ACUPRESSURE

This is similar to acupuncture, but pressure, rather than needles, is applied to the energy meridians. A form of neuromuscular massage forcefully performed with the thumb is intended to restore interrupted energy flow along the meridians. Pressure is applied to specific points, with the aim of stimulating the nerves that supply the affected organ.

Acupressure is claimed to improve overall health, and to help specific organs by releasing blocked energy. Unlike acupuncture, you can practice acupressure on yourself, although you may find it hard to locate the right acupressure points at first. Acupressure can be used to alleviate pain, to improve your general well-being, or to target specific symptoms, such as joint stiffness.

HYDROTHERAPY

As its name suggests, this involves the use of water, either to drink or to bathe in. Hydrotherapy was popular in Roman times, and some of the spas used by the Romans are still in use today. As well as "taking the waters", the patient is required to immerse the body, or part of it, in water. Hydrotherapy aims to increase the blood flow to the skin and eliminate toxins (this should be viewed with scepticism as toxins cannot be eliminated through the skin – we have a liver to do that). It is also designed to draw blood and nourishment to internal organs and then flush it out again.

Most forms of hydrotherapy use hot and cold water alternately. The hot water dilates the blood vessels, increasing blood flow to the skin. This part of the treatment may last five, ten, or 15 minutes, according to the severity of the condition and the patient's frailty (it should be avoided if you have any kind of heart condition as hydrotherapy can put an enormous strain on the heart).

The second stage of therapy involves douching, sluicing, or showering in cold water, which causes the blood vessels to constrict, reducing blood flow, and driving blood back to the heart and the purifying organs, such as the liver.

Sauna Originally, this was a succession of hot baths interspersed by cold showers. The Finns, who developed modern saunas, substituted intense dry heat from a stove for the hot bath, and this is followed by a cold shower, and then a second, shorter period in the sauna, followed by a scrub-down with a towel. The initial period in the sauna is designed to make you sweat profusely, and the overall treatment is said to improve circulation, tone up muscles, cleanse the skin, and produce a feeling of well-being. As mentioned above, it should be avoided by anyone who has heart disease.

Scotch Douche Hot and cold water are sprayed alternately up and down the spine. This is supposed to stimulate the spinal nerves by sluicing blood in and out of the spinal area. At the end of a therapy session, there is a tingling sensation in the spine. This treatment is thought to relieve pain such as migraine.

Sitz Bath This type of bath has two sections, one contains hot water and one contains cold. You sit with your buttocks and hips in the hot water for five to ten minutes while your feet are immersed in the cold water. This constricts the blood vessels in the feet and forces blood to the area where the skin is warm. You then transfer to a cold sitz bath and immerse the feet in hot water. This forces blood away from the pelvis and down into the legs. The effect of both stages is to flush blood into the pelvic area to nourish it and then out again to carry off waste material.

Steam Cabinets This is another form of panthermal treatment that works very much like the traditional Turkish bath, except that the head is outside the steam area. Since the heat is wet rather than dry, it produces sweat faster and is said to clear the skin of waste materials more efficiently. Because the sweat does not have the chance to evaporate from the skin, the body feels hotter than it would in a sauna and some people may find the process fairly debilitating.

After about 15 minutes in the steam cabinet, the bather takes a cold shower to restore the skin temperature to normal. Treatment should be followed by rest. Never take any heat treatment without checking with your doctor first.

BALNEOTHERAPY (Bath Therapy)

Baths have always been centres of physical and mental rejuvenation, and different constituents in water are supposed to help particular ailments. For example, the sulphurous water of the Dead Sea may benefit skin complaints such as psoriasis.

Therapeutic substances used in baths are Epsom salts; mud, which draws out impurities from the skin; mustard, which warms the skin and helps arthritis; oatmeal and peat, which help to hold heat in the skin; and pine, which invigorates the skin and tranquillizes the bather.

Foot baths are recommended for sore, tired feet, or to ward off a chill (particularly if they contain mustard or eucalyptus).

In Germany, scrubbing baths, in which you are scrubbed all over with a stiff brush, and then rubbed down with a towel, are popular. This is followed by bed rest.

Another popular bath is the jet bath, or whirlpool, in which the body is bombarded with jets of water from all directions. This is very relaxing and recommended for people with arthritis, or muscular and rheumatic complaints. No form of balneotherapy should be taken by someone who has eczema or dermatitis.

MASSAGE

Many claims are made about the virtues of massage, some are false, some plausible, and some indisputable. For example, massage does not help to break down fat, but it may relieve emotional tension, and it definitely speeds up local circulation and improves nourishment of tissues. During a massage, parts of the body are treated in a specific order. The direction of massage is always towards the heart, assisting the return of venous blood (containing waste) to the heart and cleansing oxygenation in the lungs. The patient lies down and the masseur massages each foot and leg in turn. Next comes the abdomen, followed by the arms, wrists, hands and fingers, and then the back of the body.

Swedish massage involves vigorous massage strokes, such as beating with the sides of the hands from the base of the spine to the neck and back again. Although massage is generally a very safe therapy, you should avoid vigorous massage if you have any sort of skin disease, or if your skin has been injured.

Neuromuscular massage consists of pressing with the fingertips, and was adapted from an Indian technique in the 1930s by Stanley Leif, an osteopath who wanted to find a way of relaxing patients' muscles before osteopathic manipulation. Specific motor points in the muscles are deeply massaged in an

TYPES OF MASSAGE STROKE

Pressing

Localized pressure can be given using the thumbs – either in static form, pressing in one position, or circular, moving the thumbs in small circles.

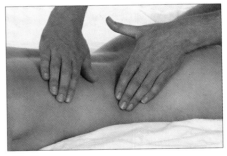

Circling

This is a simple stroke, in which you use the fingers and palms to massage the skin in firm, circular movements.

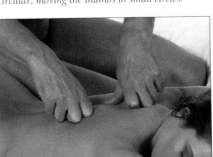

Knuckling

Here, the knuckles are used to exert pressure below the shoulder blades. This is good for getting rid of tension in painfully knotted muscles.

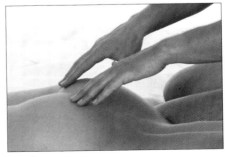

Feathering

This playful and gentle massage stroke involves skimming the fingertips and fingernails across the surface of the skin.

attempt to damp down the output to the sensory nerves to the area, and break the vicious circle of pain and muscle spasm from which we can sometimes suffer. Once muscular tension has been relieved using this technique, the muscle will be less likely to spring back into its previous tense position.

YOGA

This is probably the best known of all meditation and movement therapies. Yoga's holistic approach, encompassing stretching movements, mental relaxation, and deep breathing can help you to deal very effectively with menopausal symptoms.

Yoga is a vast philosophy, and the form that has been embraced by the West is Hatha yoga, which has been practised in India for 6,000 years. The basic aim of the exercise is to encourage a healthy mind to exist in a healthy body and bring both into harmony. Yoga consists of a series of postures, called *asanas*, which promote a relaxed and supple body and a peaceful state of mind. Anyone can take up yoga, whatever their age – you simply do as much as you find comfortable. Many people find that it helps them to overcome specific problems, such as smoking or excessive drinking. Some studies have demonstrated that yoga can help to reduce high blood pressure and alleviate menstrual problems.

Yoga must be learned slowly, avoiding all strain. No special equipment is needed, except perhaps a mat, a quiet room, and comfortable, loose clothing. Some people find it easiest to have some tuition to start with so that they can master the breathing techniques (*pranayama*).

Unlike most forms of exercise, asanas seem to be a very static way of conditioning the body. If you achieve the correct posture, however, each limb and muscle is extending and stretching. After a series of asanas, you should allow yourself a period of complete relaxation in order to discipline and focus the mind, and create a calm mood.

Although medical opinion is divided over some of the more extravagant claims for yoga, it is generally felt that yoga promotes good posture and mental tranquillity, which may alleviate backache, mild depression, and problems sleeping. Yoga can be practised by all – the young and old, the stiff and the supple – but if you suffer from severe back disorders, dizziness, heart trouble, or any other serious medical conditions, it is wise to consult your doctor before taking up yoga.

GUIDELINES FOR PRACTISING YOGA
- Breathe deeply and rhythmically through your nose.
- Some yoga positions can feel uncomfortable at first – try not to force yourself into a difficult position.
- Work slowly at becoming supple.
- Hold a posture for as it long as is comfortable. Aim for about 30 seconds initially in standing and sitting postures.
- Wear loose clothing and keep your feet bare to stop yourself slipping.
- Don't practice yoga for at least four hours after a large meal.

Vicious Circle of Pain
Massage can relax the muscles and break the vicious circle of muscle tension and pain.

YOGA POSITIONS

Movement therapies, such as yoga, aim to stretch the body and increase its suppleness. The slow, restful nature of these positions is designed to make you feel relaxed and tranquil. Deep breathing will focus the mind and passive stretching movements will counteract the effects of gravity and improve your sense of posture and balance.

Rest your head on a cushion and let your shoulders fall forward

Your arms should rest on the floor. Your palms should be face up

Use your hands to give support to your lower back

Touch the floor behind your head with your toes

THE BABY POSE
This natural resting pose (above) will help you to relax and unwind. Lie with your forehead or cheek against the floor and let your shoulders and arms relax, with your palms facing upwards.

THE PLOUGH
Begin by lying on your back and raising your legs over your chest, supporting your waist with your hands. Then push yourself up and over so that your feet touch the ground behind your head (above). Hold this position for as long as is comfortable and then bring your legs down very slowly in a smooth uncurling motion (right).

The slower you uncurl from this position the better toned your stomach muscles will be

Lean back, keeping your head level with your partner's

Rest your body weight on your partner

This position will stretch and tone your calf and thigh muscles

Use an exercise mat or cushions

THE SANDWICH

This passive stretching movement (above) will stretch your spine and help to relax you. Lean back over a friend, let your neck muscles relax, and then stretch your arms out behind you.

PASSIVE BACKWARD BEND

Choose a curved object, such as a bolster (below), a pouffe, or even some pillows, and position the small of your back against the curve. Then stretch out your legs and arms to lengthen your body. Breathe deeply.

Lengthen your spine by stretching as much as you can

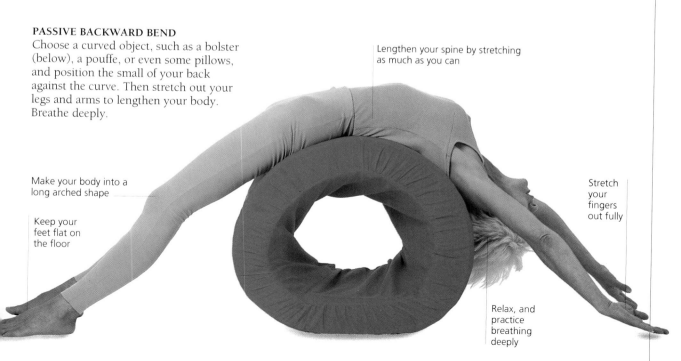

Make your body into a long arched shape

Keep your feet flat on the floor

Stretch your fingers out fully

Relax, and practice breathing deeply

119

OSTEOPATHY

Manipulation was one of the earliest forms of medical practice – its benefits are listed in the *Kung Fu*, written 5,000 years ago. Modern osteopathy is based on the theory that our bodies have the ability to regulate and heal themselves, provided that they are structurally sound and blood and nerve impulses are able to move freely.

Harmful structural changes to the body may result from poor posture, physical trauma, a sudden awkward movement, or sleeping on a bed that is too soft. Osteopathic stimulation tries to rectify these damaging changes by manipulating the spinal vertebrae, which allows the nervous system to resume healthy functioning. Osteopaths also believe that relief of muscle spasm cures illnesses stemming from muscular stress and strain.

The two basic techniques of osteopathy are the massage of muscles in spasm and the manipulative correction of misaligned bones in the spinal column. This involves gentle leverage of one part of the body against another, for example, the chin against the neck to adjust the position of the vertebrae at the base of the skull. A new cranial technique aims to make minute adjustments to the bones of the skull by manipulating the spine, sacrum (the fused vertebrae in the lower part of the back), and pelvis. This is claimed to treat not only muscle, bone, and joint illnesses, but also disorders of the liver, heart, and kidneys. Osteopathy can claim many well documented cures and is rapidly gaining acceptance by the medical profession. Before you have osteopathic treatment, you should request X-rays to exclude the possibility that you have osteoporosis (see page 66).

CHIROPRACTIC

This term is derived from two Greek words, *cheir*, meaning "hand", and *praktikos*, meaning "practitioner". Chiropractic was founded by Daniel Palmer in the 1890s in rather bizarre circumstances. Palmer overheard his janitor explaining how he had suddenly lost his hearing some 17 years earlier when he had bent over and felt something "go" in his back. On examining the janitor's back, Palmer found a vertebra that was slightly out of place; he proceeded to adjust the position of the vertebrae by manipulation and managed to restore the janitor's hearing.

Chiropractic focuses on the anatomy of the spinal cord and the nerves that branch out from it. Nerves run through each vertebra to the skin, bone, muscles, blood vessels, and organs; and the theory is that manipulating a particular vertebra will influence the health of a particular organ. For example, because the liver is supplied by nerves from the middle thoracic (chest) vertebrae, manipulating these vertebrae will affect liver function. Even minor deviations of the anatomy of the spinal cord caused by bad posture or inflammation can impair the working of a nerve and the body part it supplies.

Practitioners manipulate the vertebrae using short, sharp thrusts designed to "spring" a bone back into place. This procedure demands great precision in placing the adjusting hand, and timing and directing the thrust. The movements are quite different from those used in osteopathy.

Symptoms that respond best to chiropractic techniques are neck, muscle, shoulder, and joint pain. As with osteopathy, chiropractic should be used with extreme caution in any menopausal women who might be suffering from osteoporosis or who show signs of very low bone mass.

MAINTAINING BIRTH CONTROL

For many women, one of the best things about the postmenopause is no longer needing to worry about contraception and pregnancy. However, even from the age of 35 onwards, ovulation can be erratic, and contraception must not be neglected – not even when periods become irregular.

Because your fertility is declining in the years leading up to the menopause, a contraceptive that may have been only 90–95 percent effective when you were 20 might prove to be almost 100 percent effective when you are 40. This means that perimenopausal women can take very low dose oral contraceptives or rely on the oestrogen-free mini-pill, which does not inhibit ovulation, but still has an efficacy rate in excess of 90 percent.

Mechanical methods might also suit you. A simple barrier method like the diaphragm that worried you in your younger years because of its potentially high failure rate may be suitable now. It is essential that whatever method you and your partner choose, you discuss it with your doctor or gynaecologist.

INTRAUTERINE DEVICE (IUD)

IUDs are specifically recommended for women over 35 who have completed their families. Although the IUD has been criticized because it can cause irregular bleeding and cramping pain on insertion, most women have no problems, and it is a very effective method of contraception. Modern designs, such as progestasert and the copper T, should be the first options you discuss with your doctor. IUDs have the advantages of being effective, inexpensive, unobtrusive, and needing to be changed only every four or five years, or longer. In the over-35 age group, the risks associated with IUDs, such as perforation of the uterus, and pelvic inflammatory disease, are extremely rare. Research on IUD use in women who are over the age of 35 shows that failure rates are extremely low, and that removal of the device is easy and painless.

BARRIER METHODS

Contraceptives that physically prevent sperm from coming into contact with an ovum (egg), such as the diaphragm and condom used with a spermicide, are good alternatives for many couples. They have a higher failure rate than the IUD, but the fact that you are less fertile may compensate. (If you want to absolutely minimize the risk of getting pregnant, you should choose a contraceptive that is 99–100 percent effective.)

The condom used with a spermicide containing nonoxynol–9 is popular, because it prevents the transmission of sexually-transmitted diseases, including the AIDS virus. Condoms are widely available and are a satisfactory contraceptive choice for women over 35 (as long as spermicide is also used). The efficacy of female condoms is predicted to be similar to that of male condoms.

COMBINED BIRTH CONTROL PILL

The latest generation of oral contraceptives contain far less oestrogen and progestogen than those marketed 30 years ago. They are easier to take and they are virtually free of side-effects. The pills of the 1960s contained what we would describe now as high dose, high potency hormones. Current pills contain low doses of much gentler hormones and, if taken properly, they are 100 percent effective. If you want to make absolutely sure that you don't get pregnant, this is the most reliable form of contraception.

BIRTH CONTROL

*Although the menopause signals the end of fertility, women should
continue to use birth control for at least one or two years after their
last menstrual period – a date that can only be identified retrospectively. A common
method of contraception chosen by women who have completed their families is the
intra-uterine device or IUD, but other methods, such as the pill or condoms, are
convenient and highly effective.*

The condom is the
most widely available
and popular method
of barrier
contraception

SPERMICIDAL JELLY

This is designed for use with a cap or a diaphragm.
The jelly is squeezed into the diaphragm, which
is then inserted into the vagina so that it
covers the entrance to the cervix.
Spermicidal creams and
jellies are not effective contraceptives on their own.

Contraceptive jelly con-
taining vaginal spermicide

MALE CONDOM

This is the most widely used contraceptive in the
world and it works by preventing sperm from
entering the woman's body. It is rolled on to the
erect penis before penetration and should be
removed immediately after intercourse.

THE PILL

Combination pills contain oestrogen and
progestogen; triphasic pills contain
three different doses of oestrogen and progestogen;
mini-pills contain
progestogen only.

The diaphragm prevents
sperm from entering the
uterus

Triphasic pill

Mini-pill

DIAPHRAGM

This is a soft rubber device with a
flexible metal rim, designed to fit
over the cervix. It is used with
spermicidal jelly.

Combination pill

INTRA-UTERINE DEVICE (IUD)
This small plastic device is inserted into the uterus so that the thread hangs down into the top part of the vagina. After insertion, an IUD can remain in place for several years.

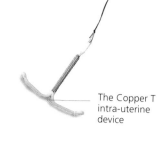

The Copper T intra-uterine device

VAGINAL SPONGE
This is impregnated with spermicide and should be put in water until it becomes foamy. It is then inserted deeply into the vagina, where it will remain effective for up to 24 hours.

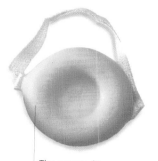

The sponge fits snugly over the cervix

FEMALE CONDOM
This is the newest type of barrier contraceptive. It is inserted into the vagina before sexual intercourse and removed immediately afterwards. The open end of the female condom sits outside the body on the vulva.

The female condom is lubricated with spermicide for extra protection

TYPES OF CONTRACEPTION

TYPE	ADVANTAGES	DISADVANTAGES
Diaphragm and Spermicide	*The spermicide can act as a lubricant.* *Can be inserted before lovemaking, and does not interfere with sex.*	*Difficult to use if you have a slight prolapse.* *May make urinary infections more likely, since the front rim of the diaphragm can press on the urethra.*
Condoms (Male and female)	*Widely available without the need for a prescription.* *Protects against sexually transmitted diseases, such as the HIV virus.*	*Effectiveness is lower than that of the pill or the IUD.* *Condoms may sometimes interfere with a man's erection as he gets older.*
Vaginal Sponge	*Easily available and can be self-fitted before intercourse.*	*Has the highest failure rate of all barrier contraceptives.*
IUD	*Very effective as a contraceptive.* *After insertion you can forget about it.*	*Requires insertion by a doctor.* *Some IUDs have to be removed due to symptoms such as pain, irregular bleeding, or infection.*
Combined Pill	*High success rate.* *Offers protection against the risk of endometrial and ovarian cancer.*	*Carries more risk than barrier methods, e.g. thrombosis.* *Disguises the menopause by regularizing menstrual periods.*
Mini-pill	*Suitable if you are advised not to take oestrogen.*	*Has a slightly higher failure rate than the combined pill.*

Some studies on the older types of pills suggested that women over 35 who used this type of contraception were at a higher risk of heart attacks, high blood pressure, and strokes than women who did not take the pill. Further studies have contradicted this: only pill takers who are obese, or smoke cigarettes, or whose blood pressure is already high are at a greater risk.

Either the combined or triphasic low dose pills are good oral contraceptives. A good hormone combination would be no more than 35 micrograms of ethinyl oestradiol or 50 micrograms of mestranol, and a low dose of progestogen, say 300 or 500 micrograms of norethisterone acetate. There is no strict evidence to suggest that one combination pill is better than another, so long as you take the lowest dose possible that will give protection.

The conclusions of the Harvard Nurses Health Study in 1989 were extremely reassuring for menopausal women. This study found that women over the age of 40 who have taken oral contraceptives – even for a long period of time – do not have an increased risk of breast cancer.

As women age, there are certain contraindications to taking an oestrogen-containing oral contraceptive. These are a history of heart disease, liver cancer, breast cancer, diabetes, high blood pressure, and obesity. Women who smoke should know that taking oestrogen substantially increases their risk of suffering from cardiovascular disease.

PROGESTOGEN-ONLY ORAL CONTRACEPTIVES
If you have a contraindication to taking oestrogen in oral contraceptives, you could consider taking the progestogen-only contraceptive, or mini-pill. This does not contain oestrogen and is increasingly being prescribed for women over the age of 40. It does, however, have a marginally higher failure rate than the combined pill and it may occasionally cause irregular bleeding due to the lack of oestrogen. In women over the age of 35, the failure rate is about one percent (one woman in 100 would get pregnant during 12 months of use), and irregular bleeding is experienced less and less as you get older.

SWITCHING TO HORMONE REPLACEMENT THERAPY (HRT)
HRT is not a contraceptive and some form of birth control must be used for at least one year from the time of the last period (or two years if you are aged under 50). If you are taking the pill, you will not know whether you are menopausal or not, but it will probably safe to switch to HRT at the age of 51.

6

MEDICAL
MANAGEMENT
OF THE
MENOPAUSE

Since oestrogen replacement therapy was first prescribed in
the 1950s, medication has been progressively refined, and
there are now very many ways to take HRT, so that
menopausal symptoms are alleviated and side-effects are
kept to a minimum. There are also non-hormonal drugs
available to combat emotional symptoms and hot flushes.

TYPES OF MEDICATION

The mainstay of orthodox medical treatment is hormone replacement therapy (HRT), which treats the menopause as a hormone deficiency condition that can be alleviated by replacing the oestrogen and progesterone that a woman's ageing ovaries no longer secrete in sufficient quantities. Because of the diverse range of HRT products, and the number of ways in which they can be administered, most women can find an HRT regime that matches their needs and produces few side-effects. However, for women who don't wish to take HRT or have a contraindication to its use, alternative medications are available.

The basis of all HRT regimes is oestrogen; progestogens are added solely to induce a uterine bleed with shedding of the endometrium, or uterine lining. Although the main way of treating menopausal symptoms is to prescribe oestrogen and progestogen in the form of HRT, other hormonal treatments are available, such as medroxyprogesterone acetate or norgestrel (usually used as a contraceptive). These are both progestogens and may alleviate hot flushes.

HORMONAL MEDICATION

HRT is a substitute for the female sex hormones oestrogen and progesterone; it is prescribed when the body's levels of female hormones are low, most usually at or after the menopause. The main oestrogens used in HRT are chemically similar to oestradiol, which is produced by the ovaries. Some HRT products contain conjugated equine oestrogen, which is harvested from the urine of pregnant mares. Progestogen is the synthetic form of progesterone. Because natural progesterone is rapidly metabolized by the body, it does not produce a sustained effect when taken in tablet form. Oestrogen is given to maintain the female sex organs and breasts; it also helps to keep the lining of the vagina and other body tissues moist and elastic. Progestogen causes the uterine lining to shed, which prevents over-thickening and cancer of the uterus.

The normal menstrual cycle depends on the sequential production of oestrogen and progesterone, so it makes sense to include these ingredients in menopausal replacement therapy. Another vital hormone is testosterone, which is also manufactured by the ovaries; if you have your ovaries removed, there will be 50 percent less testosterone in your bloodstream. High levels of oestrogen in HRT can also deplete the amount of available testosterone. Much of the female sex drive is attributed to this male hormone, and if you are taking HRT and suffering from a lack of libido, try discussing the possibility of low-dose testosterone supplements with your doctor.

When long-term hormonal medication was prescribed to women in the 1960s and 1970s, it consisted of oestrogen on its own (ERT). Later on, in the mid-1970s, there were reports that women who were taking ERT had higher rates of uterine cancer than non-users – from 5–14 times higher in some studies. Since this time, oestrogen has been prescribed together with progestogen, which ameliorates the effects of oestrogen by causing a withdrawal bleed and preventing the build-up of the uterine lining. Used in this way, HRT, rather than ERT, eliminates the risk of uterine cancer and can even protect against it. However, not all doctors have been willing to prescribe HRT after the initial scare. This is particularly true of doctors in America, who have been slow to combine oestrogen with progestogen.

By understanding the benefits of HRT you have the knowledge to make an intelligent choice. Only you have the final responsibility for your own health care. It is important to gather as much information as you can and maintain the motivation to keep yourself in the best possible health. On average, women taking HRT live three to four years longer than their contemporaries. So on balance, not taking HRT seems riskier than taking it.

THE BENEFITS OF HRT

In this age of preventive medicine, HRT should be hailed as one of the most effective treatments for counteracting long-term disease. Our whole orientation in medicine should be towards prevention rather than cure, and any regime that can cut down on expensive treatments, hospital admissions, and serious disease should be embraced enthusiastically by the medical profession.

Prevention Of Heart Attacks And Strokes Acute coronary artery disease is a major cause of death in women aged over 50, and kills one woman in every four. Taking oestrogen in HRT has been shown to reduce the risk of acute coronary artery disease by up to 50 percent.

Maintenance Of Healthy Organs, Bones, And Muscles HRT has also proved successful in maintaining the health of all the reproductive organs, including the uterus and cervix. In addition to keeping the tissues of the vagina supple and moist, it can prevent atrophy and thinning of the urinary tract, with associated infections and incontinence. Oestrogen contributes to the health, strength, and functioning of the bones, muscles, and joints and can help to prevent backache – a problem that is common in menopausal women due to osteoporosis of the spine. The general toning effect of HRT on the musculo-skeletal system means a return of strength, stamina, and energy.

Improvement In Shape There are three ways in which menopausal women can change shape. First, by loss of muscle and ligament strength, second, by the tendency towards male fat distribution on the waist and abdomen, and third, by the changes caused by osteoporosis. HRT can prevent these changes, which may be partly why some people perceive hormonal medication as youth-promoting. Don't make the mistake of thinking that oestrogen is a dietary or weight-control product – it is not a substitute for good nutrition and exercise.

Increased Well-being Beta-endorphins are chemicals from the central nervous system that are associated with a general sense of well-being and euphoria. Reduced beta-endorphins are associated with depression, and it is thought that HRT will increase beta-endorphin levels. Taking hormones during and after the menopause can directly raise your mood, your feelings of self-worth, and alleviate anxiety. Your sense of emotional well-being is likely to improve – the so-called "mental tonic" effect of HRT. You may be able to work better and feel revitalized. Although HRT may alleviate depressed moods, it should not be considered an antidepressant drug.

Relief Of Menopausal Symptoms Women who have hot flushes and night sweats find relief when they take oestrogen, regardless of the form of administration. In over 90 percent of women, symptoms disappear completely, and 98 percent

ABOUT OESTROGEN

Both natural and synthetic forms of oestrogen are available, as are other chemicals that have an oestrogenic effect, but are not, strictly speaking, oestrogens. Natural oestrogens, derived from human or animal metabolism, are absorbed and excreted by the body more easily than synthetic ones.

Synthetic oestrogens are much more potent than naturally occurring ones and may have some unwanted effects on the body, such as increasing the risk of thrombosis. However, most oestrogens used in HRT are natural and have minimal effects on the metabolism. Also, with the wide range of products and potencies available, there is great scope for adjusting the treatment and for finding a product that is suitable for each individual woman.

ABOUT PROGESTERONE

This naturally occurring hormone has two synthetic forms, progestin and progestogen. Originally, HRT consisted only of oestrogen, and was known as ERT. Progestogen was added when it was found to lower the rate of endometrial cancer, and HRT then became the norm for women with a uterus.

Taking progestogen has the disadvantage of a monthly withdrawal bleed. Moreover, a small number of women (about 10–15 percent) experience side-effects, similar to premenstrual syndrome.

Fortunately, these side-effects subside in about four months for half the women taking HRT. Progestogen intake can be reduced by taking it only once every three months (see pages 102–103).

find that HRT alleviates their symptoms. Very heavy periods (menorrhagia) can be experienced by women in their late 40s and early 50s. This can be helped by HRT, although severely abnormal bleeding may need the addition of a low-dose contraceptive. The symptoms of vaginal dryness, soreness, and painful intercourse may also be soothed by taking oestrogen. Headaches can become more frequent at the menopause and oestrogen can bring relief.

Intellectual problems such as an inability to concentrate and difficulty making decisions tend to disappear within a month or so of taking HRT. In one study, women found relief from panic attacks when they took HRT and received psychotherapy.

The response of the libido to HRT is different for every woman. You may notice an increase in sexual enjoyment, but not necessarily an increase in sex drive. There are low-dose testosterone products, such as testosterone undecanoate, which, if taken daily, can bring about a subtle return to sexual vitality without side-effects such as facial hair or lowering of the voice.

Studies from sleep laboratories show that oestrogen changes the proportion of sleep time spent in the rapid eye movement (REM) stage that is characteristic of dreaming. Women may dream more when they take oestrogen and dream less when they are oestrogen deficient. As REM sleep increases, your general state of peacefulness improves and you feel more rested after sleep.

Your skin will respond to oestrogen by showing increased tone and suppleness. Your hair will be stronger and less prone to dryness and brittleness. Similarly, nails that were brittle and prone to splitting become stronger. Gum recession around the time of menopause can also be alleviated by HRT.

HRT PRODUCTS

As mentioned previously, the usual way for women with an intact uterus to take HRT is in a combined form with both oestrogen and progestogen. Doctors often prescribe these two hormones in tablet form, so that you take oestrogen every day, and progestogen for around 12 days in each month or cycle. The latter induces a withdrawal bleed. However, your doctor may also prescribe a patch, an implant, or an oestrogen cream. These different forms of HRT are known as routes of administration (see the advantages and disadvantages of each opposite), and they are all very effective at relieving menopausal symptoms, with the exception of oestrogen cream, which only treats local urogenital symptoms, such as dryness, soreness or itchiness. It will not help symptoms such as hot flushes, and it will not prevent a decline in bone density, as other routes of administration can.

The skin patch releases oestrogen transdermally (across the skin), which means that, unlike oral HRT, hormones do not have to pass through the liver – this is advantageous for some women. You may be prescribed progestogen tablets with your patch, or you may be prescribed a combined patch, already containing progestogen. Patches need to be changed every three or four days.

Implants also avoid the passage of oestrogen through the liver, and once they are inserted into the fatty tissue underneath the skin of the abdomen or thigh they last for up to six months.

New HRT products that may be on the market in the future include vaginal rings containing oestrogen, a gel containing a synthetic form of oestradiol to be rubbed into the skin, and an intra-uterine device (IUD) that delivers progestogen or progesterone directly into the uterus.

TYPES OF HORMONE REPLACEMENT THERAPY

TYPE	ADVANTAGES	DISADVANTAGES
Oral HRT (Tablets)	*Highly effective in combating physical and emotional symptoms.* *Tablets containing oestrogen, progestogen, and testosterone are available.* *The appropriate dose will offer a high level of protection against osteoporosis.* *You can stop taking it immediately if it doesn't suit you.* *You are responsible for your own medication.*	*You may experience side-effects such as breast tenderness and nausea* *You may experience breakthrough bleeding if you forget to take a tablet.* *May be unsuitable if you have a history of high blood pressure, blood clotting, or liver trouble.*
Local Vaginal Treatment (Creams and pessaries)	*Helps to alleviate slight incontinence.* *Creams containing oestrogen and progesterone are available.* *Easy to apply.* *Eliminates vaginal dryness and irritation.*	*Does not protect against osteoporosis.* *Not effective in combating hot flushes and night sweats.*
Transdermal HRT (The patch or gel)	*Equally effective as oral HRT in treating most menopausal symptoms, and preserves bone in 85–95 percent of women.* *Easily changed and simple to stop using.* *You can wear a combined oestrogen and progestogen patch so that you don't need to take additional progestogen orally.* *Since a low dose of hormone is absorbed, the patch has few side-effects.*	*A very few women develop red, itchy skin at the site of the patch. This may get worse in a hot climate.*
Subcutaneous HRT (Implant)	*Excellent relief from physical symptoms.* *Some women find that problems such as depression and irritability disappear more readily than with other forms of HRT.* *You can forget you are on HRT because the implants are changed so infrequently.* *Testosterone can also be given as an implant.* *Protection against osteoporosis is high.*	*Wrong doses cannot be easily modified.* *Some women experience symptoms at ever decreasing intervals – too frequent implants lead to a hormone overdose.* *If you decide to stop using HRT, implants are difficult to remove.* *Administration is controlled by your doctor, and you need a minor surgical procedure for insertion of the implant.*

TYPES OF HRT

The form in which you are offered HRT depends on your doctor. A GP is likely to offer you tablets, which are the most widely available, but HRT also comes in the form of implants, pessaries, transdermal patches, and vaginal creams. Not only do the forms of HRT differ, but there are differences in the effects of individual brands. This large choice of product makes it easier to find a form of HRT whose method of application and effects will suit your personal needs.

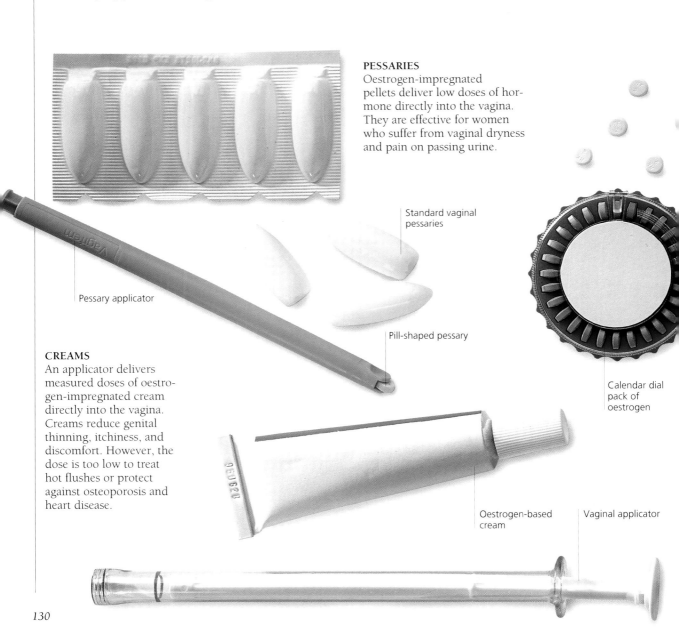

PESSARIES
Oestrogen-impregnated pellets deliver low doses of hormone directly into the vagina. They are effective for women who suffer from vaginal dryness and pain on passing urine.

Pessary applicator

Standard vaginal pessaries

Pill-shaped pessary

Calendar dial pack of oestrogen

CREAMS
An applicator delivers measured doses of oestrogen-impregnated cream directly into the vagina. Creams reduce genital thinning, itchiness, and discomfort. However, the dose is too low to treat hot flushes or protect against osteoporosis and heart disease.

Oestrogen-based cream

Vaginal applicator

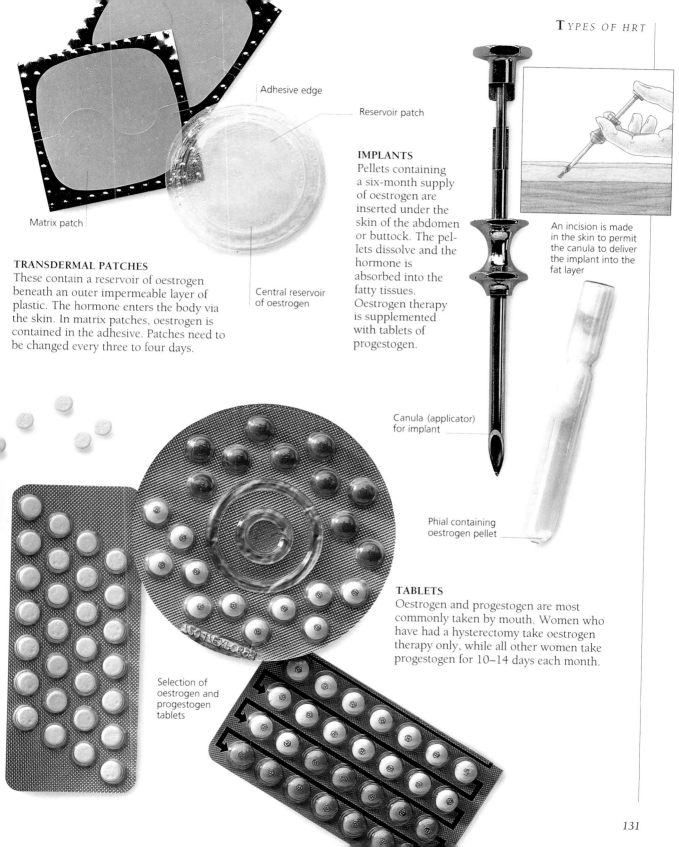

Adhesive edge

Reservoir patch

Matrix patch

TRANSDERMAL PATCHES

These contain a reservoir of oestrogen beneath an outer impermeable layer of plastic. The hormone enters the body via the skin. In matrix patches, oestrogen is contained in the adhesive. Patches need to be changed every three to four days.

Central reservoir of oestrogen

IMPLANTS

Pellets containing a six-month supply of oestrogen are inserted under the skin of the abdomen or buttock. The pellets dissolve and the hormone is absorbed into the fatty tissues. Oestrogen therapy is supplemented with tablets of progestogen.

An incision is made in the skin to permit the canula to deliver the implant into the fat layer

Canula (applicator) for implant

Phial containing oestrogen pellet

TABLETS

Oestrogen and progestogen are most commonly taken by mouth. Women who have had a hysterectomy take oestrogen therapy only, while all other women take progestogen for 10–14 days each month.

Selection of oestrogen and progestogen tablets

131

WAYS OF TAKING HRT

Just as there are several different forms of HRT, there are also several ways the medication can be administered. The main difference is in the bleeding pattern that results. The three main HRT regimes are described below.

Continuous Therapy Continuous oestrogen therapy with added progestogen medication has now become the most common way to take HRT. You can take a daily tablet of oestrogen or wear a skin patch twice a week. Progestogen is taken either in pill form or in a combination skin patch for 12–14 days. Over 90 percent of women will have a monthly bleed on this regime if the uterus is intact. Take notice of your bleeding pattern, which should occur after you stop taking progestogen. If bleeding begins before you stop taking progestogen, the dose of progestogen may be too low for you and should be adjusted.

Cyclical Therapy Oestrogen and progestogen taken cyclically is a less common method of taking HRT. Oestrogen is taken from the first to the 21st day of the cycle, and progestogen for the last 12 or 13 days of the cycle. Both medications are stopped on the 21st day and a withdrawal bleed will occur between the 22nd and 28th days; the patch or pill-free days. Over 90 percent of women who have not had a hysterectomy will experience a withdrawal bleed in the interval between ending one treatment and beginning the next. However, bleeding usually lessens over time and may disappear altogether.

The latest way to take cyclical therapy is to take progestogen once every three months. This means that you go two months without a bleed, then bleed in the third month, so that you have four periods a year (see pages 102–103).

Combined Continuous Therapy (No-bleed HRT) This method of taking HRT involves taking continuous daily doses of oestrogen combined with a very low dose of progestogen. The aim of this continuous therapy is to avoid periods, and even if you do have withdrawal bleeding at first, it will probably stop within a few months. No-bleed HRT is popular among women on long-term treatment. Between 60 and 90 percent of women find this regime successful.

COMMON HRT REGIMES

Although new ways of taking HRT are being investigated, these three regimes are currently the most usual ways to take oestrogen and progestogen.

KEY

Bleeding

Oestrogen

Progestogen

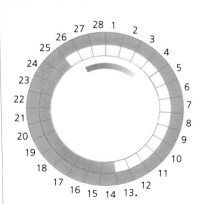

Continuous Therapy
Oestrogen is taken every day and progestogen is taken from day 14 to day 25, to induce a withdrawal bleed.

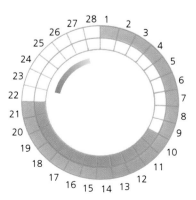

Cyclical Therapy
Oestrogen is taken for 21 days and progestogen is added for 12 days. This is followed by seven tablet-free days.

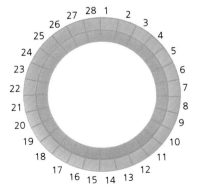

Combined Continuous Therapy
Taking both oestrogen and progestogen continuously means that you probably won't experience a withdrawal bleed.

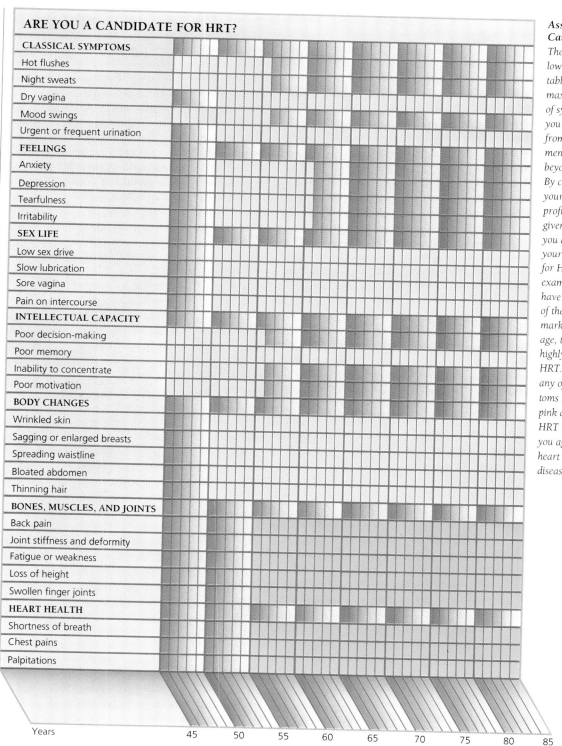

ARE YOU A CANDIDATE FOR HRT?

CLASSICAL SYMPTOMS
Hot flushes
Night sweats
Dry vagina
Mood swings
Urgent or frequent urination

FEELINGS
Anxiety
Depression
Tearfulness
Irritability

SEX LIFE
Low sex drive
Slow lubrication
Sore vagina
Pain on intercourse

INTELLECTUAL CAPACITY
Poor decision-making
Poor memory
Inability to concentrate
Poor motivation

BODY CHANGES
Wrinkled skin
Sagging or enlarged breasts
Spreading waistline
Bloated abdomen
Thinning hair

BONES, MUSCLES, AND JOINTS
Back pain
Joint stiffness and deformity
Fatigue or weakness
Loss of height
Swollen finger joints

HEART HEALTH
Shortness of breath
Chest pains
Palpitations

Years   45   50   55   60   65   70   75   80   85

Assessing Your Candidacy

The pink and yellow panels in this table tell you the maximum number of symptoms that you may suffer from during the menopause and beyond.

By comparing your symptom profile with that given for your age, you can assess your candidacy for HRT. For example, if you have two or more of the symptoms marked for your age, then you are highly eligible for HRT. If you have any of the symptoms shown in the pink area, then HRT may protect you against future heart and bone disease.

FINDING THE RIGHT DOSE

Many people believe that if something is doing you good, more will be even better for you. This is not a maxim to which doctors subscribe. As a general principle, doctors prefer you to take the lowest possible dose for the maximum effect and for the fewest side-effects. As a rule of thumb, medication should be taken for the shortest possible time – HRT is a rare exception to this rule.

It may take a little time to find your optimum dose, and you and your doctor may have to experiment a little because there is no way of anticipating how each individual woman will respond to the many different oestrogens that are available. When you begin to take HRT, it is wise to have a minimum of a four-month trial because it takes that long for your body to settle down. If necessary, your doctor can assess whether your hormone dose is correct by measuring the amount of oestrogen in your bloodstream. Even in low doses, hormones are powerful substances and it is unwise to change your dose without consulting your doctor first.

MONITORING HRT

As you approach the menopause you should be seeing your doctor for annual blood pressure checks, regular cervical smear tests, and mammography. Your doctor should also check your weight and carry out a pelvic and breast examination before you take HRT. Once you're taking hormones, you should have these examinations annually, and your weight and blood pressure should be checked every six months. Bone density scans to check on the health of your bones may also be appropriate.

SIDE-EFFECTS AND RISKS

Only about nine percent of menopausal women in the UK are taking HRT – the majority of those who try it give up after a few months. According to a survey conducted by the Amarant Trust in 1992, women were much more likely to give up HRT if their doctors had given them insufficient information. Those who were given a sympathetic hearing and who had the opportunity to discuss the benefits and side-effects had a more realistic view of HRT.

The main reasons why women give up HRT are the side-effects of progestogen, the inconvenience of monthly bleeds, and a fear of breast cancer. As far as the latter is concerned, the consensus of medical opinion is that there is no added risk as long as HRT with progestogen supplements are taken. Indeed, the progestogen may help to prevent breast cancer.

About 10–15 percent of women find progestogenic side-effects so troublesome that they decide to stop taking HRT. To varying degrees, women complain of symptoms such as weight gain, fluid retention, abdominal cramps, backache, acne, greasy skin, irritability, aggressiveness, moodiness, tearfulness, and loss of libido. The diversity of natural and synthetic hormone products on the market should enable your doctor to prescribe an alternative progestogen, or a smaller dose if symptoms are troublesome.

Women who take oestrogen only (if they have had a hysterectomy) don't usually experience discomfort. However, if the dose is too high, there may be oestrogenic side-effects such as breast tenderness, weight gain, or headaches. Always check with your doctor – he or she will probably suggest reducing the oestrogen dosage – tablets can be broken in half or you may be prescribed a lower dose product.

Hypertension As hypertension is known to increase the risk of heart attack and strokes, it is a condition that should be taken very seriously in postmenopausal women. Oestrogen will not alter your blood pressure unless you are specifically sensitive to it; a very rare phenomenon. This means that you can take HRT even if you do have raised blood pressure, but you should make sure that your blood pressure is checked shortly after starting HRT. If the reading is high, switch from tablets to the patch as oral administration occasionally causes the liver to produce chemicals that raise blood pressure.

Breast Pain HRT may cause the type of breast tenderness that is characteristic of the week prior to menstruation. In the first half of the month, the oestrogen in HRT stimulates growth of milk glands and ducts. In the second half of the cycle the progestogen may cause fluid retention within the breast. At this point, the breast may feel as though it is full of orange pips – these are swollen milk glands. Breast swelling and tenderness may lessen if you reduce your intake of salt, coffee, and chocolate. Small doses of vitamin B6 can also reduce breast pain, and modifying the progestogen dose may help. Breast pain that occurs throughout the HRT cycle is usually due to a dose of oestrogen that is too high.

Fibroids Benign lumps in the uterine lining may become more widespread if you take HRT. However, if your menopausal symptoms are severe, fibroids should not deter you from taking HRT. Women of any age should have fibroids monitored or removed.

Diabetes If you are diabetic, it is essential that you discuss your health with your doctor before embarking upon a course of HRT. This is because carbohydrate metabolism is altered by HRT. If you are prescribed HRT, you should check your blood sugar and urine frequently.

Gallstones Between the ages of 50 and 75, three women in 100,000 are estimated to die from complications of gallbladder disease. This increases to six women in 100,000 among women taking HRT. This is because oestrogen therapy increases the concentration of the bile in the gallbladder. Obesity is also associated with an increase in gallstone disease and so it is important to reduce the amount of cholesterol in your diet and to take HRT in a form that does not pass through the liver. The skin patch will be better than a tablet at reducing the possibility of gallstones.

Migraine The response of migraine to HRT is unpredictable. Some women find that migraines disappear completely while others experience worse attacks. The usual complaint is that migraines occur during the progestogen phase or just after the progestogen is completed. These migraines can often be alleviated by changing the type or dose of progestogen. Migraines that occur at other times of the cycle may be due to an oestrogen dose that is too low.

Irregular Bleeding Occasionally, HRT can lead to irregular bleeding, and your doctor will need to take a sample of the uterine lining by dilatation and curettage (D & C; see page 199) to check that there are no abnormalities. You may consider a D & C an inconvenience, but it is best to have an early examination to clear up any possible medical complaints.

Cancer The possibility of a link between HRT and uterine and breast cancer is a major concern. Fortunately, we now know that the use of progestogen eradicates the risk of uterine cancer and may give future protection. However, the debate surrounding breast cancer is complicated, as experts do not agree. A persuasive body of evidence indicates that in almost all cases of breast disease, HRT plays no causative role. If you are not at any increased risk of breast cancer (you are not obese, you don't smoke, and breast cancer does not run in your family), then the evidence seems to weigh in favour of HRT (see page 8).

CONDITIONS REQUIRING SPECIAL CARE
The term "contraindication" refers to a medical condition that may be exacerbated by a particular drug. In the case of HRT, there are some conditions that are thought to be "absolute contraindications", such as breast cancer or uterine cancer. However, some doctors now believe that there is no such thing as an absolute contraindication, and that only "relative" contraindications exist, provided that the dose and route of administration is individually tailored. Other doctors subscribe to the theory that the medical conditions listed below make it risky to take HRT. These are conditions that have made doctors anxious about prescribing HRT in the past, but they need not be a cause of anxiety now. The items in this list are still frequently quoted as contraindications, but when they are scrutinized, the dangers diminish (and in some instances disappear). This is partly because of increased medical understanding, but mainly because theoretical disadvantages of HRT can be overcome by careful adjustments to therapy and tailoring HRT to suit each patient.
- Any type of abnormal vaginal bleeding.
- Breast cancer.
- Ovarian cancer.
- Uterine cancer.
- Recent stroke.
- Pancreatic disease.
- Recent heart attack.
- Recent liver disease.
- Recent venous thrombosis (clots in the veins), or pulmonary embolus (see page 79).

In older lists of this kind, angina and a family history of heart attacks, strokes, and venous thrombosis may have been included. Now, these conditions are regarded as indications for HRT, since HRT will protect you against them.

PUTTING CONTRAINDICATIONS INTO PERSPECTIVE
The first warnings about contraindications were based on the oral contraceptive pill (which contains a much higher dose of hormones than HRT), and they are therefore not directly referable to HRT. Lists of contraindications for HRT are usually supplied by drug companies who have special reasons (such as avoidance of litigation) for including a wide range of conditions that do not necessarily reflect medical thinking or practice.

You need to evaluate the pros and cons of HRT. Although it treats your menopausal symptoms, if you have had a condition such as breast cancer your doctor may be reluctant to prescribe HRT. These decisions should be negotiable. If you cannot cope with hot flushes and night sweats, go to a gynaecologist or a menopause clinic who may try to find a suitable form of HRT for you.

HRT AND YOUR MEDICAL HISTORY

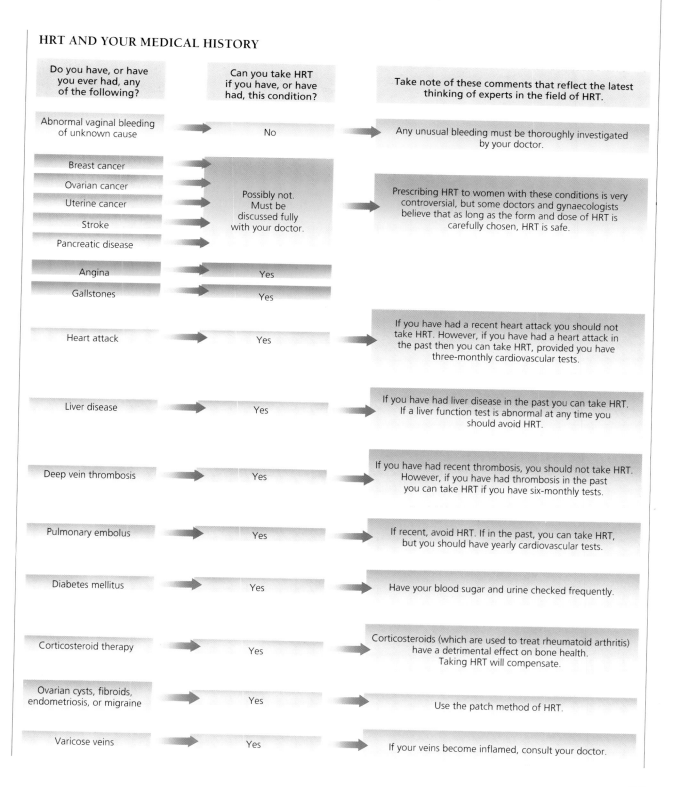

Do you have, or have you ever had, any of the following?	Can you take HRT if you have, or have had, this condition?	Take note of these comments that reflect the latest thinking of experts in the field of HRT.
Abnormal vaginal bleeding of unknown cause	No	Any unusual bleeding must be thoroughly investigated by your doctor.
Breast cancer	Possibly not. Must be discussed fully with your doctor.	Prescribing HRT to women with these conditions is very controversial, but some doctors and gynaecologists believe that as long as the form and dose of HRT is carefully chosen, HRT is safe.
Ovarian cancer		
Uterine cancer		
Stroke		
Pancreatic disease		
Angina	Yes	
Gallstones	Yes	
Heart attack	Yes	If you have had a recent heart attack you should not take HRT. However, if you have had a heart attack in the past then you can take HRT, provided you have three-monthly cardiovascular tests.
Liver disease	Yes	If you have had liver disease in the past you can take HRT. If a liver function test is abnormal at any time you should avoid HRT.
Deep vein thrombosis	Yes	If you have had recent thrombosis, you should not take HRT. However, if you have had thrombosis in the past you can take HRT if you have six-monthly tests.
Pulmonary embolus	Yes	If recent, avoid HRT. If in the past, you can take HRT, but you should have yearly cardiovascular tests.
Diabetes mellitus	Yes	Have your blood sugar and urine checked frequently.
Corticosteroid therapy	Yes	Corticosteroids (which are used to treat rheumatoid arthritis) have a detrimental effect on bone health. Taking HRT will compensate.
Ovarian cysts, fibroids, endometriosis, or migraine	Yes	Use the patch method of HRT.
Varicose veins	Yes	If your veins become inflamed, consult your doctor.

STOPPING HRT

If you stop taking HRT after a short length of time, symptoms such as hot flushes may recur in a more severe form than before. An oestrogen-deficient body means that your bones will become fragile, your blood cholesterol higher, and your vaginal walls thinner and dryer. Each of us is born with a blueprint that determines how long menopausal symptoms will last and HRT may help you pass more comfortably through these years. You may opt for a medium-term course of HRT, or choose long-term treatment in order to ensure healthy bones, heart, and blood vessels. Although it is a personal decision, you should consult your doctor before you stop taking HRT.

LONG-TERM USE

If you are not told what to expect from HRT, and you experience uncomfortable side-effects, you may discontinue therapy and lose out on the long-term benefits. HRT must be given for at least five years if it is to prevent bone loss and heart problems. Every woman is different and several attempts may be necessary before the most suitable treatment is found. Ask your doctor to explain the side-effects of HRT so that you have a realistic idea of what to expect. It is absolutely crucial to be involved in the choice of your HRT. If you choose the precise regimen you are on, it will be more likely that you will have confidence in the treatment. Beware of having unrealistic expectations. Media hype about the beauty benefits and prospects of staying young forever is not to be trusted. Don't make the mistake of thinking that the problems with HRT are trivial. Be sure to clarify all possible setbacks with your doctor.

CONTRACEPTION AND HRT

Some form of birth control is required for two years after your last menstrual period for women who are under 50. Women who start HRT prior to the menopause will need to use contraception up to the age of 52. Remember, HRT alone will not act as a contraceptive.

NON-HORMONAL TREATMENT

The consensus of medical opinion is that non-hormonal drugs have a secondary role in the management of menopausal symptoms. However, if you are experiencing symptoms and you fall into one of the following groups, you may want to try alternative medical treatments:

- You do not want to take HRT because you feel that it interferes too radically with your metabolism and you would like to try to alleviate your symptoms in other ways.
- Your doctor says that you have a contraindication to HRT, such as undiagnosed vaginal bleeding.
- You find that HRT causes side-effects that are very difficult to tolerate, such as nausea, profound fluid retention, or severe weight gain.
- HRT has not significantly helped your menopausal symptoms (this may be because the type and dose of your HRT was not appropriate).

If one of these descriptions applies to you, there is a range of non-hormonal treatments that you can try. These include antidepressants, tranquillizers, sedatives, and drugs such as clonidine and propranolol. Dietary and complementary remedies are also useful.

SEDATIVES

These are drugs that damp down the centre of the brain and as a result they may make you feel drowsy. Sedatives are less effective than HRT at reducing menopausal symptoms but they may help to reduce the number of hot flushes that you experience. They rarely help in relieving emotional symptoms such as anxiety and irritability.

TRANQUILLIZERS

Doctors who believe that menopausal symptoms are "neurotic" are inclined to prescribe tranquillizers and antidepressants rather than replacing lost hormones with HRT. Tranquillizers in fact are not very effective in treating menopausal symptoms unless HRT is given as well. Given on a short-term basis in conjunction with HRT, they can relieve agitated states, such as excessive anxiety, irritability, and insomnia.

Several tranquillizers have been associated with over prescription by doctors and long-term abuse by patients, resulting in dependency. Tranquillizers may be useful for a few weeks to help get over a particularly stressful situation or a life event, such as a bereavement, separation, or divorce, but you should try to avoid taking them for long periods of time. Once you are taking tranquillizers, you should not stop taking them suddenly. Instead, attempt to wean yourself off them gradually by reducing your dose by half a tablet every five days, until you are completely free of medication. If you feel that you are becoming dependent on tranquillizers – or any other drug that you have been prescribed – seek medical advice.

ANTIDEPRESSANTS

Mild depression that occurs in the years around the menopause is usually due to hormone deficiency, and I believe that HRT should be the first line of treatment. If a woman does not respond to hormones, then antidepressants can be added to her HRT regime. Only about a fifth of cases of depression respond to treatment by antidepressants alone.

The most commonly prescribed antidepressants are amitriptyline, imipramine, and drugs such as monoamine-oxidase inhibitors (MAO) and selective serotonin inhibitors. Nearly all antidepressants have side-effects and you should ask your doctor about this before you start treatment. You should also be aware of any interactions with other medications or foods. For example, if you are taking a monoamine-oxidase inhibitor, you should not eat cheese or yeast-based products, such as yeast extract.

Drugs such as antidepressants and tranquillizers are much more effective at treating menopausal symptoms when they form part of a total programme that includes counselling or psychotherapy.

CLONIDINE

This is occasionally helpful for hot flushes. It was first used as a treatment for migraine and later for high blood pressure. It was noticed that it seemed to reduce the number of hot flushes in women and it is now prescribed for this purpose, although not all women respond to it. Studies have also shown that clonidine may reduce cravings in people who are trying to give up smoking, alcohol, or drugs. If it's impossible for you to take HRT for hot flushes, clonidine is worth trying.

PROPRANOLOL

This is a betablocker used for the treatment of hypertension and migraine headaches. Some studies have shown that it is helpful in the treatment of hot flushes and you should discuss the option of taking it with your doctor.

ETIDRONATE

This is a drug that treats spinal osteoporosis. It works by inhibiting osteoclasts (bone-resorbing cells) and allowing osteoblasts (bone-rebuilding cells) to work more effectively (see page 40).

VITAMIN B6

There is some research to show that vitamin B6 taken in doses of 100 mg a day can alleviate the fluid retention and depression that is sometimes caused by oestrogen and progestogen, both in oral contraceptives and HRT. Vitamin B6 should not be taken in high doses for long periods as it is toxic and can cause nerve damage. Always seek advice from your doctor before taking it.

VITAMIN D

An adequate supply of vitamin D is vital for menopausal women as it can preserve bone health and prevent the symptoms associated with osteoporosis (see page 66), such as stiff joints, and back and neck pain. Vitamin D facilitates the uptake of calcium from the intestine, and also helps us to absorb phosphorus. Having said this, it is very rare for menopausal women to suffer from vitamin D deficiency as it is readily available from food, and we can manufacture it ourselves from sunlight. Too much vitamin D can be harmful, and can even lead to bone thinning in postmenopausal women.

VITAMIN E

To date there is no conclusive scientific evidence to show that vitamin E effectively treats hot flushes or other menopausal symptoms. However, many women claim that it has helped them. Very high doses – mega doses – are advocated in order to relieve hot flushes, but this is not verified medically.

CALCIUM

This mineral is essential for long-term bone health, and the prevention of heart disease and high blood pressure. Calcium tablets are derived from different sources and there are many products on the market so you should consult your doctor about the best one for you. In order for calcium to be absorbed by the body, oestrogen and small amounts of vitamin D must be present. This is why calcium supplements work well in conjunction with HRT.

7

MAXIMIZING YOUR RESOURCES

The menopause is sometimes incorrectly stereotyped as the start of a gradual decline into old age, when your body loses its feminine qualities and becomes sexually redundant. Women know from experience that this is far from the truth. With care, your body remains one to be proud of, your mental resilience continues to be great, and you still have a valuable role to play in society.

POSITIVE ATTITUDES

While health and vigour during the menopausal years depend a great deal on eating a good diet and exercising, these are not the only resources you have to draw upon. Rest, relaxation, and a variety of leisure activities will help you to keep active and mentally alert. You also need self-affirming thoughts to maintain your self confidence and prevent self-criticism. Never allow yourself to think that you are unattractive, lack-lustre, or out-of-touch. The strong interaction between your mind and your body means that you can make your menopause more difficult with negative thoughts. In other words, if you believe you're sick, you can start to behave like a sick person.

If you repeat some of these statements like a mantra each day, you will gradually become convinced of their truth. Positive thoughts and attitudes will maintain your self-esteem.

- My body is strong and healthy and can become healthier each day.
- My female organs are in good shape.
- My body chemistry is effective and balanced.
- I eat healthy nourishing food.
- I'm learning to handle stress.
- I'm calm and relaxed.
- I work efficiently and competently.
- I have the freedom and confidence to enjoy life.
- I can be happy and optimistic at this time of my life.
- My life belongs to me and it brings me pleasure.
- I devote time to myself each day.
- My friends and family are more enjoyable than they have ever been.
- I'm going through the menopause more easily and more comfortably with each passing day.

GOOD FOODS AND NUTRIENTS

As you get older, the digestive tract becomes less efficient and digestion takes longer; your body no longer finds it so easy to cope with foods that contain a lot of calories but little nourishment. Although you need fewer calories, you still need the same amount of vitamins and minerals. The healthiest diet during the menopause is one consisting of unprocessed fresh foods, such as wholegrains, vegetables, fruits, seeds, nuts, seafood, lean meats, fish, some oil, and the occasional egg. Healthy foods are becoming widely available in the high street so it has never been easier to be experimental. Concentrate on building up a diet of unprocessed, high-grade carbohydrates to which protein can be added as a "condiment".

As your body's metabolism and chemical reactions slow down, an adequate intake of vitamins and minerals is essential; eating the right diet can have a powerful and beneficial effect on menopausal symptoms, making you independent of doctors and drugs.

Some protein is essential for health, but too much, especially in the form of fatty meats, can lead to deficient calcium absorption. If you've been a heavy meat-eater in the past, this could increase your risk of developing osteoporosis (see page 66). Start to cut down on the amount of meat in your diet, and try to eat more rice, beans, vegetables, and pasta.

A certain amount of fat is needed for functions that cannot be performed by any other nutrient; essential fatty acids are necessary for the metabolism of calcium, and they cannot be manufactured by the body. The best forms of fat are those found in whole natural foods, such as vegetable oils and fish oils. Fats to avoid are saturated fat, fats that are solid at room temperature, and certain vegetable oils, such as coconut or palm oil found in processed foods.

Fermented milk products, such as yogurt, are effective at encouraging calcium absorption. Even people who cannot tolerate whole-milk products can tolerate fermented milk products because they are partially predigested.

VITAMIN A

This is necessary for the health and growth of the skin, eyes, and mucous membranes. Vitamin A deficiency can cause night blindness, increased suscep-tibility to infections, and rough, scaly skin. Low vitamin A may contribute to heavy menstrual bleeding (and possibly cervical cancer), and skin conditions related to the ageing process, such as leukoplakia (see page 96).

VITAMIN B COMPLEX

Several B vitamins are helpful during the menopause. If you're taking hormone replacement therapy (HRT; see chapter six) you may want to take a vitamin B6 supplement because HRT can lead to a deficiency, which may make you prone to depression. Folic acid (another B vitamin) may help to prevent precancerous changes in the cervix (see page 195).

All the B vitamins work in harmony. Their effects include helping us to han-dle sugar, keeping the liver healthy, and stabilizing brain function. Low levels can lead to emotional distress, fatigue, and irritability.

VITAMIN C

This is the healing vitamin; it helps to mend wounds and burns, and it maintains collagen (see page 53), so, to a degree, it could be called an anti-wrinkle vitamin. Since the need for collagen regeneration increases with age, vitamin C is needed in greater amounts as we get older. Vitamin C also helps the adrenal glands and the body's immune system to fight infections and allergies.

VITAMIN D

Along with calcium and oestrogen, vitamin D is essential to maintain bone mass and prevent osteoporosis (see page 66). Vitamin D promotes the absorp-tion of calcium and phosphorus from the intestine and, although vitamin D deficiency is rare, all menopausal women should include adequate quantities of vitamin D in their diets to maintain strong, straight bones in later life.

VITAMIN E

Dubbed "the menopausal vitamin" because it may have chemical activities sim-ilar to oestrogen, vitamin E has been used with some success in America as an oestrogen substitute. It is possible that vitamin E may relieve hot flushes and psychological symptoms of the menopause, but this has not been medically verified. It may also go some way to relieving vaginal dryness when applied as an oil directly to your vagina, as well as when it is taken in the diet. Vitamin E also acts as an antioxidant, which means that it helps to keep your cells healthy and disease-free.

VITAMINS THAT WILL BENEFIT MENOPAUSAL COMPLAINTS

VITAMIN	SOURCE	COMPLAINT
Vitamin A (Retinol and carotene)	carrots, spinach, turnips, apricots, fresh liver, cantaloupe melons, sweet potatoes	excessive menstrual bleeding, cervical abnormalities, fibrocystic disease and cancer of the breast, leukoplakia and other skin conditions
Folic Acid (Vitamin B complex)	green leafy vegetables, nuts, peas, beans, liver and kidney	cervical abnormalities and cancer, osteoporosis, diabetes mellitus
Vitamin B3 (Niacin)	meat and poultry, fish, pulses, wholemeal wheat, bran	hyperlipidaemia (high concentration of blood fat), hypoglycaemia (low blood glucose)
Vitamin B6 (Pyriodoxine)	meat and poultry, fish, bananas, wholegrain cereals, dairy products	deficiency as a result of taking HRT, cervical abnormalities and cancer, diabetes mellitus
Vitamin B12 (Cyanocobalamin)	fish, poultry, eggs and milk, B12 enriched soya produce, (no vegetable contains B12)	anxiety, depression, mood swings, fatigue
Vitamin C (Ascorbic acid)	citrus fruits, strawberries, broccoli, green peppers	excessive menstrual bleeding, cervical abnormalities and cancer, chloasma
Vitamin D (Calciferol)	sunlight, oily fish, fortified cereals and bread, fortified margarine	poor calcium absorption, leading to an increase in the risk of osteoporosis
Vitamin E (Tocopherol)	vegetable oils, green leafy vegetables, cereals, dried beans, wholegrains, bread	hot flushes, anxiety, vaginal problems (e.g. dryness), hypothyroidism, chloasma and other skin conditions, atherosclerosis, osteoarthritis, fibrocystic disease of the breast

CALCIUM

The National Osteoporosis Society of Great Britain recommends that women over 40 who are not on HRT should take the equivalent of 1,500 mg of calcium a day, women over 40 on HRT should take 1,000 mg, and women over 60 should take 1,200 mg. Calcium is essential for long-term bone health, it will protect your heart, it helps to control high blood pressure, and it lowers blood fats. It is possible to get enough calcium by eating a varied diet of peas, beans, green leafy vegetables, fish, seeds and nuts, yogurt, dried skimmed milk, wholemeal bread, and cheese.

Calcium Absorption   There is a misconception that in order to increase your daily calcium intake you can simply take calcium tablets. Unfortunately, calcium tablets taken on their own are hardly absorbed, and the calcium that is absorbed cannot be utilized by the bones and is excreted in the urine. To maximize the effect of calcium supplements, it is essential that both oestrogen and small amounts of vitamin D are present.

Menopausal women who control their weight with a low-fat diet may be lacking in calcium, which puts them at risk of osteoporosis (see page 66). In fact, three-quarters of all women over the age of 35 have a diet that supplies only half their daily calcium needs, and postmenopausal women who are not on HRT receive about a third of the required amount of calcium.

While calcium absorption varies from individual to individual, at best only 20–40 percent of the calcium you eat is absorbed, and even that decreases with age. Your genetic make-up determines whether or not you absorb calcium efficiently, but disease or illness can decrease the amount that you retain. Oestrogen enhances calcium absorption, which helps to explain the rapid loss of bone that occurs when oestrogen levels decline after the menopause. Other factors that impede calcium absorption, and increase excretion, are inactivity, medicines, drugs, smoking, caffeine, and stress. Lack of other nutrients will deter absorption – especially the vitamins C, D, K, and the minerals magnesium and phosphorus. As you can see, drinking a glass of milk at night or taking a calcium tablet isn't enough to prevent or reverse bone loss. A total programme is vital for women who are seriously at risk.

Calcium Supplements   If you think you need a calcium supplement, you should seek medical advice. There are many calcium products on the market, and deciding which one to use is a decision you should reach with your doctor. Different tablets are derived from different sources, and some are combined with other nutrients for better absorption or because the nutrients work as a unit within the body.

A calcium and magnesium combination is excellent because the two function together and are required by the body in a specific ratio. Calcium carbonate and calcium gluconate are among the more easily absorbed supplements (although calcium carbonate can cause constipation). Calcium citrate is a good choice for postmenopausal women since it is better tolerated by individuals with low stomach acid – a condition more common with age.

Calcium And Phosphorus   Taken correctly, phosphorus will enhance the amount of calcium absorbed by the bones; the ideal ratio of calcium to phosphorus being two to one. However, with the abundance of phosphorus in foods, the

GUIDELINES FOR A CHANGED DIET

● *Keep your meals simple and easy. Cut down preparation time.*
● *Eat the biggest meal of the day early; have a hearty breakfast, a light lunch, and an even lighter dinner.*
● *Eat a variety of foods so that you get a range of nutrients; don't eat the same foods every day out of habit.*
● *Make the transition to raw, high fibre food slowly; don't worry if it takes a few months to change your dietary habits.*
● *Identify any "high stress" foods and start substituting these with low stress ones (see page 152).*

MINERALS THAT WILL BENEFIT MENOPAUSAL COMPLAINTS

MINERALS	SOURCE	COMPLAINT
Calcium	milk and milk products, dark-green leafy vegetables, citrus fruits, dried peas and beans	osteoporosis, hyperlipidaemia (high concentration of blood fat), hypertension
Magnesium	green leafy vegetables, nuts, soya beans, wholegrain cereals	osteoporosis, fatigue, diabetes mellitus, coronary artery disease, anxiety, depression
Potassium	orange juice, bananas, dried fruits, peanut butter, meat	fatigue, heart disease, hypertension, anxiety, depression
Zinc	meat, liver, eggs, poultry, seafood	osteoporosis
Iron	nuts, liver, red meats, egg yolk, green leafy vegetables, dried fruits	excessive menstrual bleeding
Iodine	seafood, fish, seaweed	hypothyroidism, fibrocystic disease of the breast
Chromium	meat, cheese, wholegrains, breads	hypoglycaemia (low blood glucose)
Selenium	seafood, meat, wholegrain cereals	fibrocystic disease of the breast and breast cancer
Manganese	nuts, fruit and vegetables, wholegrain cereals	atherosclerosis (see page 79)
Bioflavonoids	all citrus fruits, especially the pulp and pith	hot flushes, excessive menstrual bleeding, vaginal problems, anxiety, irritability, and other emotional problems

ratio is one to four. This retards calcium retention and accelerates bone demineralization by stimulating the parathyroid glands, which secrete a bone-dissolving hormone.

To re-establish the correct mineral ratio, you should reduce your intake of high-phosphorus foods drastically. This means eliminating processed foods (such as tinned meats, processed cheeses, instant soups and desserts, and soft drinks), which offer little nutrition anyway. Check the labels of packaged foods and avoid foods containing sodium phosphate, potassium phosphate, phosphoric acid, pyrophosphate, or polyphosphate.

OTHER BENEFICIAL MINERALS

Magnesium is instrumental in converting vitamin D to its usable form and keeping calcium soluble in the bloodstream. It may also help you if you have low energy and a lack of vitality. A magnesium deficiency disturbs the calcification of bone, impairs bone growth, and reduces calcium levels; diets deficient in magnesium may lead to skeletal abnormalities, including osteoporosis. Potassium is essential for normal muscle contraction and heart function; zinc is needed for hormone and brain function, and for building new cells. Fortunately, many foods contain magnesium, potassium, and zinc together.

Calcium, vitamin D, and phosphorus all increase magnesium requirements, thus emphasizing the importance of nutrient inter-relationships. Evidence suggests that the balance between calcium and magnesium is especially important. If the calcium level is raised, magnesium intake needs to be raised as well. The optimum calcium/magnesium ratio is two to one. Thus if you are taking 1,000 mg of calcium, you'll need 500 mg of magnesium to maintain a balance.

FIBRE

Roughage is very important in the diet. It keeps your gut healthy and promotes regular bowel movements. This helps to prevent the distention, gas, and bloating that many women experience during the menopause. It also helps bowel complaints such as diverticulitis (an inflammatory condition of the gut) and irritable bowel syndrome. Fibre gives you a feeling of fullness and satisfaction that will help you to control your appetite, combat cravings, and avoid binges. There is good evidence to show that a woman who eats a high-fibre diet is less likely to suffer from a variety of cancers, including colonic and breast cancer. It may also protect against heart disease. Here are some suggestions for increasing the amount of fibre in your diet.

- Switch to a high-fibre bread.
- Have a high-fibre bran cereal for breakfast.
- Eat high-fibre soups – bean, lentil, or sweetcorn for example.
- Use beans and peas in your green salads, such as chick peas, green beans, kidney beans, or butter beans.
- Use dark salad greens, such as spinach, rocket, and endive, instead of pale iceberg lettuce.
- Eat bean dips with raw vegetables or wholewheat pitta bread.
- Use unprocessed wheat bran in recipes for pies, cakes, and biscuits.
- Use wholewheat flour in your standard recipes.
- Snack on wholegrain crackers and dried fruits.
- Use nuts and sesame seeds in recipes.
- Eat wholemeal muffins instead of cakes and biscuits.

THE IMPORTANCE OF WATER

About 55–65 percent of the human body is made up of water and it is very important that we keep ourselves hydrated. If we are dehydrated, it may become impossible for us to regulate our body temperature and we will be much more vulnerable to other health problems. Fortunately, our natural thirst mechanism ensures that we drink enough water to enable our basic body functions to take place. Excessive perspiration, which is caused by physical exertion, being in a hot climate, fever, or hot flushes, may mean that we lose more fluid than we take in – as long as we aware of this, we can compensate by drinking extra water.

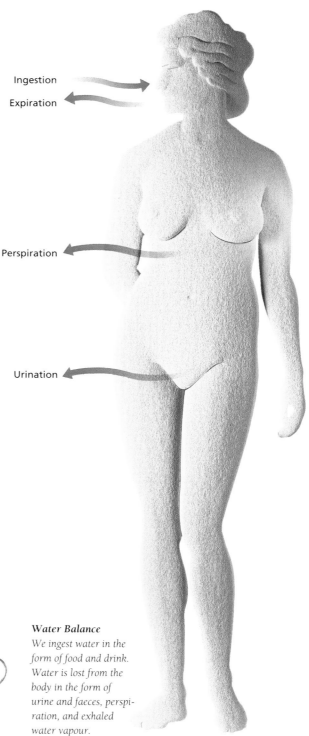

Ingestion

Expiration

Perspiration

Urination

Urine Colour

The appearance of our urine is a useful way of telling whether we are drinking sufficient fluids. If your urine looks very dark and concentrated, you are probably dehydrated and need to drink more water. Healthy urine is a pale yellow colour.

Dark concentrated urine

Healthy pale urine

Water In Foods

Much of the water we ingest comes from the food we eat. Fruits and vegetables contain a very high percentage of water. Some, such as watermelon and cucumber, are almost entirely water. Others, such as carrots, bananas, and courgettes, are 70–90 percent water.

Foods with high water content

Healthy Drinks

Some drinks are better at maintaining the water balance in our bodies than others. Drinks such as fresh orange juice and mineral water provide us with nutrients, as well as keeping us hydrated.

Orange juice   Mineral water

Unhealthy Drinks

Some drinks, such as coffee, are not so efficient at maintaining our water balance since they act as diuretics, making us excrete more urine. Canned drinks often contain caffeine and sugar, which are both nutrient depleters.

Cola drink   Coffee

Water Balance

We ingest water in the form of food and drink. Water is lost from the body in the form of urine and faeces, perspiration, and exhaled water vapour.

WATER

Few of us think of water as nutritious, but it is a much neglected nutrient that is very important to women during the menopause. Water performs a wide range of functions in the body: it acts as a solvent for nutrients, oxygen, homones, antibodies, and waste products; it helps to eliminate waste from the body as urine; it keeps the skin and mucous membranes plump and moist; and it lubricates the joints.

Water leaves the body in the form of urine and faeces; it is also expired as water vapour, and perspired as sweat. It serves as the body's natural radiator, keeping the skin cool – when perspiration evaporates from the surface of the skin, it turns into water vapour, using the body's internal heat to do so.

On average, you need about two to three litres (about four to six pints) of water each day, simply to replace the amount you lose through urine, faeces, perspiration, and exhalation. Half of the water we need comes from food, in the form of fruit and vegetables. Bananas are 76 percent water, carrots 88 percent and courgettes 75 percent; meat and poultry are a half to two-thirds water; even bread is one-third water.

The other half of our water must come from drinking – approximately six to eight glasses a day. Any fluid is better than no fluid, but pure water is best, followed by fruit juices, and low-fat milk. Beverages containing caffeine or alcohol are not good choices because they can increase the amount of water we lose. Drinks containing lots of sugar are fattening, bad for the teeth, and will nullify the positive effect of the fluid.

Fluid intake should be increased if you are active for long periods, the weather is very hot, or you're at high altitudes. If you are suffering from hot flushes and night sweats, you will be losing water through perspiration and you will need to drink more than usual.

As a general rule, if the colour of your urine appears dark yellow or orange, it means that it is very concentrated and you're not drinking enough water to excrete waste products from the kidneys. Urine should always be a pale lemon colour – the paler the better (see opposite).

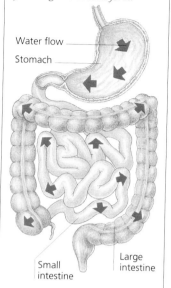

Absorption Of Water
After passing through the stomach, water is absorbed in the large and small intestine, and undigested food is egested in solid form.

Water flow

Stomach

Small intestine

Large intestine

BAD FOODS

There are two food groups that are detrimental to menopausal women: "non-foods", such as sugar, which are high in calories but low in nutrients; and highly processed foods, which are nutritionally inferior and don't contain the mysterious micronutrients, enzymes, and trace elements that are found in natural foods. That is why nutritionists prefer foods to pills and supplements.

There are also foods and processes that can be described as "nutrient depleters" because they diminish the effect of many healthy foods. For instance, vitamin A is depleted by coffee and processed foods; vitamin E is lost from polyunsaturated fats by freezing; vitamin B is depleted by sugar, processed foods, dieting, coffee, and tea; calcium by sugar, fat, and spinach; and potassium by fasting, sugar, and coffee. Try to keep your intake of nutrient depleters low. For example, always use wholegrain flour, which is high in vitamin D and other essential nutrients, in place of white flour. Use fresh vegetables rather than tinned or frozen ones, and keep to a low-fat diet. Two substances, alcohol and caffeine, and one practice, cigarette smoking, have such deleterious effects that they are treated separately (see page 164).

SALT

High blood pressure, bloating, and fluid retention are all adversely affected by salt. Unfortunately, salt is present in many of our favourite prepared foods, such as hamburgers, olives, salad dressings, hot dogs, pizzas, and French fries, and is often difficult to avoid. Always look for brands that have no added salt.

Fruits, vegetables, meat, and grains naturally contain all the salt we will ever need. You can enhance natural salt in foods by using flavourings such as garlic, herbs, spices, and lemon juice. If you can't avoid adding salt, substitute potassium-based salt for table salt (sodium chloride) – it's healthy and doesn't exacerbate high blood pressure or heart disease. Season vegetables with powdered seaweeds, such as kelp or nori, that can also be added to rice and salad. They're rich in essential iodine and many trace elements.

OTHER VITAMIN AND MINERAL DEPLETERS

DEPLETER	VITAMIN OR MINERAL
Alcohol	*Vitamins A, B, and C; magnesium and zinc*
Cigarettes	*Vitamins A, C, and E; calcium and selenium*
Caffeine	*Vitamins C and B, especially thiamine (B1); calcium, potassium, and zinc*
Nitrites (found in processed and smoked meats)	*Vitamins A, C, and E*
Oestrogen	*Vitamins E and B, especially pyriodoxine (B6); magnesium and zinc*
Aspirin	*Vitamins C and B, especially pyriodoxine (B6) and folic acid*
Antibiotics	*Vitamins B, C, and K; potassium*
Antacids	*Vitamin B, especially thiamine (B1); phosphorus*
Antihistamines	*Vitamin C*
Barbiturates (sedative drugs)	*Vitamins A, C, D, and folic acid*
Cortisone (anti-rheumatic drug)	*Vitamins A, C, D, and B, especially pyriodoxine (B6); potassium, zinc*
Indocin (anti-rheumatic drug)	*Vitamins C and B, especially thiamine (B1)*
Laxatives and diuretics	*Vitamins A, D, E, and K; potassium*

SUGAR

Many people in the Western world eat too much sugar. Convenience food, relishes, salad dressings, tomato sauce, cakes, biscuits, sweets, and fizzy drinks all have high levels of sugar, and many people turn to them for solace and instant gratification. Refined carbohydrate foods such as white flour, white bread, white sugar or white rice also have a high proportion of raw foodstuffs removed and are, therefore, low in fibre content.

Eating too much refined carbohydrate can contribute to obesity and is also associated with a high intake of fat. Excess sugar in the diet will accelerate the development of diabetes mellitus (see page 97) and will also disturb the blood sugar balance, which leads to mood swings, irritability, and anxiety. Sugar also reduces the supply of vitamins and minerals. When cooking, you can cut the amount of sugar in a recipe by one-third without spoiling the taste.

You can reduce cravings for chocolate and other sweet foods with healthier sweet alternatives, such as fruit and fruit juice. A high-fibre diet will fill you up so that you are less likely to want a snack. If you have a sweet tooth, substitute a more concentrated healthy sweetener, such as honey, which has a sweeter taste weight for weight. You can also substitute fruit for sugar in pastries, cakes, and biscuits. Artificial sweeteners sweeten without adding calories, and carob can replace chocolate and cocoa. Carob is a member of the same family as peas and beans and is very high in calcium. It tastes similar to chocolate but is better for you and can control a sugar craving. Unfortunately, like chocolate, carob is high in fat and should only be eaten occasionally.

FAT

Most of us consume nearly half our calories in fat, and most of this comes in the form of saturated fat, from dairy products such as cheese, butter, and cream, and from meat products such as beef and pork. Saturated fat is found in many processed foods too. It is particularly dangerous for menopausal women because it is linked to heart disease, strokes, high blood pressure, cancers, and obesity. However, polyunsaturated fats, such as those found in certain vegetable and fish oils, can help remove cholesterol from the tissues and transport it to the liver for excretion. Because of this, polyunsaturated fat can help protect the heart against heart disease.

The easiest ways to reduce your fat intake are to cut the fat off meat, avoid fried food and sauces that are made with butter, cream, or cheese, and cut out solid fats such as lard. Eat lean meat and grill or broil rather than frying.

To obtain the essential fats and oils, eat raw seeds and nuts sparingly. Cook with vegetable oils such as corn, canola, sunflower, soya-bean, safflower, or olive oils. When frying or baking, rub oil lightly around the pan, and sauté or stir-fry instead of deep frying. Eat low-fat dairy products, such as skimmed milk, which in powdered form is also high in calcium. Substitute natural yogurt for cream in desserts and main dishes. Be very sparing when cooking with cheese; cut down the amount you use by a half to two-thirds so that it becomes a flavour or garnish, rather than a main ingredient. You can shred or grate cheese whenever possible to help a little go a lot further. Goat's or sheep's cheese is better for you than cheese made from cow's milk, since the fat it contains is more easily utilized by the body. Alternatively, replace cheese with tofu, which is high in calcium content. You can also replace milk in recipes with soya milk, nut milk, or grain milk.

HIGH-STRESS FOODS

These are substances, such as sugar, caffeine, and alcohol, that contribute to various menopausal problems. High-stress foods contain few nutrients and, in some cases, they may be addictive. The chart below outlines substitutes that can be used. If possible, avoid black pepper, monosodium glutamate, and very hot spices (which worsen hot flushes), or cut down the amount by half.

SUBSTITUTES FOR HIGH-STRESS FOODS

HIGH-STRESS FOOD	SUBSTITUTE
135 g (4 oz) white flour	135g (4 oz) wholewheat flour, less two tablespoons
1 square chocolate	1 square of carob or 1 tablespoon powdered carob
1 tablespoon coffee	1 tablespoon decaffeinated coffee
$\frac{1}{2}$ teaspoon salt	$\frac{1}{2}$ teaspoon of one of the following: potassium salt substitute, yeast extract, basil, tarragon, oregano
125 ml (4 fl oz) wine	125 ml (4 fl oz) light wine
250 ml (8 fl oz) beer	250 ml (8 fl oz) light beer
250 ml (8 fl oz) milk	250 ml (8 fl oz) soya milk, nut milk, or grain milk
150g (5 oz) sugar	One of the following: $\frac{1}{4}$ cup molasses, $\frac{1}{2}$ cup honey, $\frac{1}{2}$ cup maple syrup, $\frac{1}{2}$ cup barley malt, 2 cups apple juice

HEALTHY COOKING

There are three important principles for cooking a healthy menopause diet:
- Use nutritious, good quality food.
- Prepare food quickly and easily.
- Use cooking methods that preserve nutrients.

CHOOSING AND PREPARING FRUIT AND VEGETABLES

When buying fruit and vegetables, the key factor is freshness. Vegetables that are in season and grown locally have more flavour than vegetables that are shipped from abroad. Reject any produce that is limp, wrinkled, or faded – not only does it look unpleasant, but most of its essential nutrients will have disappeared. Frozen vegetables are preferable to canned ones.

Blending is a quick and easy way to prepare many nutritious foods, particularly soups, and vegetable and fruit purées. You can make sauces and delicious milkshakes using non-dairy or low-fat milk.

Any food that requires chopping, grating, and shredding can be prepared with a food processor in a fraction of the time it would take by hand. If you're going to eat lots of salads, a food processor is invaluable.

Try to serve fruit and vegetables whole, or cut them into the largest pieces possible. The less surface area of a fruit or a vegetable that is exposed to air, the better, since some of the essential nutrients will be degraded by oxidation. Vegetables, such as carrots, broccoli, celery, spinach, tomatoes, mushrooms, and cucumbers, are delicious when served raw with dips or dressings. Green, leafy vegetables are pleasant to eat, and the darker green the leaves, the more nutritious they are. Also use parsley, watercress, lambs lettuce, and any dark-green lettuce. Beans of all kinds are good salad ingredients and sources of protein.

When preparing leaf vegetables, tear the leaves by hand to preserve their vitamin C. Never add salad dressing until immediately before serving. Keep any left-over salads and ingredients in well-sealed plastic bags. Store produce in the salad drawer of your fridge and, if possible, buy small quantities often in order to preserve freshness.

CHOOSING AND PREPARING MEAT, FISH, AND POULTRY

Red meat should be eaten once a week at most. A steak once a month is all that we need nutritionally in the context of a well-balanced diet. Don't forget that too much red meat exacerbates oestrogen deficiency.

If you can, buy lean free-range meat and poultry, and make sure that the animals have not been given hormones, antibiotics, or growth-promoters. Also avoid meat that is marbled with fat, or cuts such as chuck steak, where the fat is abundant. Trim away the extra fat from meat and remove all the skin from poultry before cooking.

You should try to eat fish at least twice a week; it is very low in fat and high in iodine, which keeps the thyroid gland active. It is low in calories, and a good deal easier to digest than meat. Fatty fishes are extremely nutritious because fish oils have cardioprotective properties.

COOKING TECHNIQUES

Grill fish rather than frying it, and avoid using deep-fried batters as they soak up a lot of fat in the cooking process. You can replace hot oil with hot water, broth, or a sauce. Meat, poultry, and fish can all be cooked well by steaming, stewing, and simmering. If you are roasting meat, try to cook it on a spit so that the fat runs off. Gravy is usually made with white flour and a lot of fat, so try to serve your meat, poultry, and fish with only their own juices.

Cooking with very little water means that foods are virtually steamed, sealing in the goodness. Steaming is excellent because it requires no fat for cooking. It's quick, and vegetables retain their texture, vitamins, and minerals. A wok is useful for stir-frying food in the minimum of fat or oil; vegetables can be cooked very quickly and eaten while still crisp, which means that fragile vitamins like vitamin C remain intact.

We now know it is better not to use aluminium or copper pans for cooking, since the metal can contaminate your food. Acidic foods can react chemically with aluminium, forming compounds that may be toxic. In addition to this, Alzheimer's disease has been connected with excessive aluminium intake. Iron cookware is useful because iron from pans can enter the food, which is good for menopausal women who may have low iron levels.

WHY TOO MUCH MEAT MAY BE HARMFUL

- *Red meats (beef, pork, and lamb) are very high in fat. High-fat diets are known to increase the risk of obesity, hypertension, atherosclerosis, and cancer.*
- *Red meats aggravate premenstrual syndrome (PMS) and can cause menstrual cramps.*
- *Red meats are high in phosphates, which increase the loss of calcium from the bones, creating a greater risk of osteoporosis.*
- *Large amounts of protein put a strain on the kidneys because they form organic compounds containing nitrogen waste.*
- *Too much protein may deplete vitamins B6 and B3 (pyriodoxine and niacin), calcium, and magnesium.*
- *Processed and smoked meats, such as bacon, ham, salami, and luncheon meats, contain a lot of salt, nitrates, and nitrites, which can lead to the formation of cancer-causing nitroscamines in the body.*

CONTROLLING YOUR WEIGHT

Being thin at any time of life means that a woman is unhealthy. Thinness can lead to infertility, and studies have shown that many women athletes who are underweight don't menstruate. Some fat is essential for true health and this is never more true than at the time of the menopause. We now know that women are healthier after the menopause if they're 13–18 kg (6–8 lb) heavier than their premenopausal weight, so don't worry about maintaining your former slimness – it could be bad for your health. Here is the most up-to-date weight table. You will see that there is only one frame size and women can weigh the same as men of similar height.

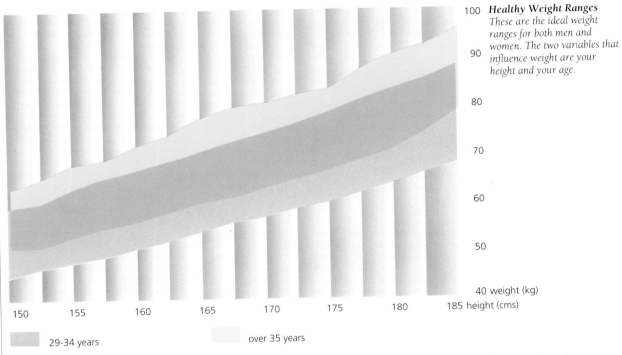

100
Healthy Weight Ranges
These are the ideal weight ranges for both men and women. The two variables that influence weight are your height and your age.

90

80

70

60

50

40 weight (kg)

150   155   160   165   170   175   180   185 height (cms)

29-34 years   over 35 years

Weight increase is gradual in both men and women as they age, but for women it may become especially noticeable during the menopausal and post-menopausal years. There are at least two factors involved here. First, lack of oestrogen leads to a change in body shape and fat distribution (see page 43), so that the waist thickens and fat is deposited on the front of the abdomen (fat cells all over the body also increase in size). Second, the metabolic rate slows down as we mature and, by the age of about 55, we need fewer calories. Unless we have a regular and frequent exercise regime incorporated into our lives, continuing to eat at our usual rate will lead to weight gain. To combat this we need to stick to a sensible calorie intake, which in practical terms means that we have to eat less and take more exercise.

Although we need fewer calories, our body's nutritional needs remain the same. Calorie counting may be too time consuming for anyone to maintain in the long term, so it's much better to eat a diet that is well balanced and contains no "empty" high-calorie foods, such as sugar and fat. It's within your power to change not only what you eat, but how you eat. As we get older, we often find we can't manage three main meals a day. Try eating five or even six small meals at regular intervals so that the nutritional load is spread. This eating habit is very effective in terms of weight control because each time you eat, you use energy for digestion and, if you eat very small quantities, the amount of energy expended in digestion can help compensate for the energy absorbed from the food. Small frequent meals prevent troughs of low blood sugar, which are accompanied by cravings for food. By eating little and often you will gain confidence in your ability to control your appetite.

Many studies have been carried out to show the differences between people who eat small, frequent meals and those who eat fewer and larger meals. The latter invariably have more body fat than the former. Some slimmers find that a diet designed on a nibbling pattern helps to prevent hunger pangs, and there is evidence that this may speed up weight loss. Your digestive system will prefer a nibbling pattern, particularly if you suffer from indigestion or peptic ulcers. Reducing the fat content in your diet will greatly help you to maintain your weight, and it will also protect you from a range of diseases.

Try not to attempt crash diets or long-term diets that are little more than starvation. The initial weight loss may be impressive – as high as three to five kilograms (6–11 lb) in the first week – but less than half of this will be fat; most of it will be water, and it could even include some of your precious body protein. A diet that restricts total calorie intake to below a thousand calories is only just adequate. Very strict diets, those around 500 calories, cannot provide all the required nutrients for an adult woman.

The attraction of a micro-diet is that it offers severely obese people a chance to lose up to half a kilogram (a half to one pound) a day, or one to two kilograms (three to six pounds) per week. However, there is much research to show that towards the end of a long period of this kind of dieting, the rate of weight loss not only decelerates, but the weight starts to go back on. In other words, the body adapts itself to starvation.

The fewer and fewer calories we give the body, the less and less it needs, until it can finally get by on less than 300 calories a day. A return to a normal eating pattern will cause an inevitable increase in weight as body stores of glycogen are replaced. This is extremely depressing if you have made a great effort to shed excess weight. It is common for a person coming off a starvation diet to go on eating binges and find themselves on a treadmill of intermittent starving and bingeing that is extremely damaging to their health and self-image.

SUGGESTED MEALS

Rather than having a set menu for breakfast, lunch, and dinner, think in terms of what food you would *like* to eat and how much time and energy you have to prepare it. For example, choose a time-consuming meat meal at the weekend when you have plenty of time, and a nutritious soup meal when you are busy or feeling tired.

Healthy options for breakfast include fruit, such as prunes, apricots or melon; cereals, wholemeal muffins, wholemeal bread, low-fat yogurt, low-fat cheese (goat's or sheep's cheese, if possible), and nuts (in moderation).

For lunch and dinner, choose soup, salad with a low-calorie dressing, nutritious wholemeal bread sandwiches, raw or lightly cooked vegetables, poultry, fish, and milk or custard-based puddings that are high in calcium.

RELAXATION

If you are relaxed, you will be better able to deal with problems and conflicts at home and work, and you will find personal relationships easier to manage. Irritability and aggressiveness will dissipate and you will find you have energy to spare. Relaxation can often help you to deal with menopausal symptoms such as hot flushes. Bear in mind, too, that if you are relaxed, energized, and positive, these feelings will extend to people around you.

DEEP MUSCLE RELAXATION

This technique was devised at Stanford Heart Disease Prevention Centre and has been taken up by most relaxation experts around the world. It may take a little time to learn, but it will help you cope with stress, lower your blood pressure, decrease your chance of getting headaches, and make you sleep better.

1 Find a peaceful place, lie on your back or sit in a comfortable chair, and close your eyes.
2 Begin by tensing your right hand (or left, if you are left-handed), and then letting it go loose. Now imagine that your hand feels heavy and warm. Repeat with your right forearm, upper arm, and shoulder, and then move on to the right foot, the lower leg, and the upper leg. Now do exactly the same thing with the left side of your body. By the time you have finished, your hands, arms, and legs should feel heavy, relaxed, and warm. Give yourself a few seconds for these feelings to develop and to get used to the sensation.
3 Now relax the muscles around your hips and waist. Let the relaxation flow up the abdomen into the chest. A good trick is to try to imagine the surface under you pushing up into your back, so that you get a sensation of heaviness. You will find your breathing starts to slow down.
4 Now let the relaxation go up into your shoulders, jaw, and facial muscles. Pay special attention to the muscles around your eyes and forehead – tense them and then let the frown melt away. Finish by imagining that your forehead feels cool and smooth.

If you can, you should practice this twice a day for 15–20 minutes each time. However, even as little as three minutes will be sufficient time to give you a sense of well-being. The best time to practice is just before mealtimes or an hour afterwards. Once you've mastered deep muscle relaxation, you're ready to go on to deep mental relaxation.

DEEP MENTAL RELAXATION

This is designed to clear your mind of stressful thoughts, anxieties, and tension. It is a form of meditation in which you attempt to separate your body from your thoughts in order to create a personal space that is free from worry and negative thoughts. You can retreat or escape to this whenever you want to. Find a place where you know you will not be disturbed and lie down or make yourself comfortable in a chair. Close your eyes and start by breathing deeply several times.

1 Allow thoughts to freely associate in your head.
2 Stop any recurring thoughts by simply saying "no" to them under your breath, and repeating "no" until they go away.
3 With your eyes closed, imagine a tranquil scene such as a clear blue sky and a calm blue sea. Whatever you imagine, try to see the colour blue, as this is a very therapeutic colour.

4 Concentrate absolutely on your breathing – make sure that it is slow and natural. Follow each breath as you inhale and exhale.

5 By now, you should be feeling calm and rested. You may find it helpful to repeat a soothing word or mantra, such as "love", "peace", or "calm". Think of a calming sound like "ah", and say it silently to yourself in your mind when you're breathing out.

6 Remind yourself to keep the muscles of your face, eyes, and forehead relaxed, and imagine that your forehead is cool and smooth.

When you've mastered both deep muscle and deep mental relaxation, they can be done together. They're fairly easy to combine once you've mastered them, and you should practice them twice a day until you've become competent. Other techniques you can employ to help your body overcome tension and anxiety are instant relaxation and mental imagery.

INSTANT RELAXATION

Once you have trained your body to achieve deep muscle and mental relaxation, you should be able to achieve partial relaxation within about 30 seconds. If you are feeling stressed, these steps will help to calm you.

1 Sit or lie comfortably. You can also teach yourself to stand comfortably, even when you're waiting in a queue or just before you know that you are going into a stressful experience.

2 Take a deep breath to the count of five, and then breathe out slowly.

3 Tell all your muscles to relax.

4 Repeat this two or three times until you're feeling relaxed.

5 Imagine yourself in a pleasant situation, such as walking along a beach or swimming in a pool. If a situation suddenly panics you, regain control by breathing deeply and slowly.

MENTAL IMAGERY

Use your imagination to get in touch with your body so that you have greater control over it. For example, focus on your left hand and make it feel warm. Now concentrate on your right thigh and make it feel warm and heavy. Now try to imagine that one leg is heavier than the other. Once you've mastered this, you can apply it in any situation by imagining that your body has the inner resources to overcome the symptoms you are experiencing. As part of cancer therapy, patients are trained to imagine their body's defences as warriors, physically killing their cancer cells. You can use this technique to combat headaches, migraines, high blood pressure, and general aches and pains.

BREATHING TECHNIQUES

Almost all muscle relaxation programmes involve proper breathing as the key to controlling stress and anxiety. This may be simple deep breathing, yoga breathing, or deep abdominal breathing.

Most people breathe incorrectly, using no more than one-third of their lung capacity, and hardly using the abdomen at all. You can test this by standing naked in front of a mirror and seeing whether your abdomen moves when you breathe in. Most of us only use the upper part of the chest, meaning that we are depriving the body of oxygen. Try to change your shallow breathing to deep, slow breathing. Besides improving the function of your lungs and the muscles of your abdomen, it will relax your whole body.

To achieve deep abdominal breathing, place one hand on your abdomen and breathe in slowly through your nose to a count of five. As you inhale let your abdomen balloon out. The further out it goes, the more lung capacity you are using, and the more oxygen you are getting to your tissues. When you think your lungs are absolutely full, try to take a little more air in to the very bottom of your lungs, which are at the back, above your waist. Then breathe out deeply, through your nose if you can, but through your mouth if it allows your stomach and chest to collapse completely. This "oxygen fix" is wonderfully refreshing and you can do it as often as you like.

Colour Breathing This is an ancient oriental tradition used to calm the nerves and heal the body. The idea is that you imagine absorbing energy from the earth by inhaling its "colour". For example, when sitting or lying in a comfortable position, imagine that the earth beneath you is red. As you inhale, imagine that you can draw in this red colour until your whole body is suffused with it. Visualize it spreading to your head, neck, arms, legs, and feet. Now slowly exhale. You can repeat this with any colour you like.

MENTAL FITNESS AND AGILITY

Most of us are concerned about our physical fitness, but fewer of us consider our mental fitness. Women, regardless of their marital status, suffer from more mental illness than men, and can become more vulnerable around the time of the menopause. During middle age, some women feel that their freedom of choice becomes restricted, and this can lead to frustration, conflict, unhappiness, and mental trauma.

Mental fitness can be as easy to maintain as physical fitness, and we must strive to maintain a basic state of mental health so that we can rise to challenges, cope with emergencies, and have the resilience to survive stressful situations in the long-term. As we get older, we have to deal with emotional trauma, such as the loss of parents and possibly our partner.

Self-knowledge requires supreme realism: we have to learn that we are not unique in suffering, that difficult times come and go, that adversity is normal, and that some failures are inevitable. As we grow older, we should leave behind preconceptions and prejudices, and constantly be prepared to change our attitudes. We need to work with our emotions in a constructive and helpful way, and yet still be affectionate and tender with ourselves.

STAYING MENTALLY FIT

We can learn a lot by observing the qualities of people whose mental and emotional resilience we admire. The following qualities result from emotional openess, flexibility, and self-reliance.

- Independence and recognition of others' independence, privacy, and peace.
- Lack of self-pity, so that when a problem arises it is looked at objectively.
- The attitude that nothing is hopeless and problems are there to be solved.
- A sense of inner security rather than security gained from controlling others.
- Being prepared to take on responsibility for your own mistakes.
- A few close relationships rather than many superficial ones.
- A sense of realism about the goals you can set yourself.
- Being in touch with your emotions, and feeling free to express them.

Just as a muscle becomes weak if it's not exercised, so your brain will slow and become feeble if you do not think. The best mental exercise is work. An experiment performed on Japanese octogenarians showed that those who kept going into their offices, even for one hour a day, had greater mental powers than those who had retired at 60 and given up disciplined thinking.

The first tip to maintain mental fitness is daily intellectual work. It helps if your efforts are judged by your peers, but work of any kind provides mental stimuli. Interaction with other people forces you to assess what they are saying, and respond with questions and comments. Your brain has to assimilate information and your cognitive processes remain active.

As we get older, we lose the ability to form new brain connections, so we have to make certain that old and well-established connections are continually used. The only way to do this is through thinking. Thinking is not a passive process – it means engaging in, questioning, and absorbing what is happening all around us. For example, arithmetical "exercises" are often encountered in daily life and you can engage in them more actively. Anticipate your supermarket bill by totting up the cost of your shopping, or estimate how much change you'll receive. Try to judge the size and quantity of objects and then measure them to check on your judgement.

Try to add to your vocabulary by noting down each new word you see or hear on a daily basis. Keep a dictionary handy to check on meanings, and use the word in subsequent conversations. Read a daily newspaper article or watch the television news and discuss the main events of the day with a friend.

If you have the opportunity, think about taking evening classes. The range of courses available to adults is huge – there are craft courses that take up a couple of hours a week or you can take full-time courses in academic subjects such as history or English literature. Your local library is the best source of information on adult learning.

MAINTAINING MEMORY

As we get older, our long-term memory gets clearer; it's our short-term memory that may suffer. If you are worried about being forgetful, there are several exercises and techniques that will aid your short-term memory.

- When you read a book or a magazine article, summarize the plot or the points made in it to a friend. Refer to names, places, and dates.
- When you're going shopping, try to collect as many items as you can without referring to your shopping list.
- If there are several things you want to remember, try to do it with a mnemonic. For example, tasks such as ironing, making a phone call, and typing a letter can be abbreviated into a single word. Take the first letters of each task, and make them into a word, for example "PIT" (Phone/Iron/Type), which will act as a memory aid.
- If you walk into a room and forget why you've gone into it, go back to the place that you came from and don't leave until you have remembered the reason for going there.
- If you have lost something, track it down by a process of elimination. Write down the last six things you did prior to losing it and where you were for each activity. If necessary, draw a grid on a piece of paper with what you were doing along one side and where you were along the bottom. The item you've lost lies in one of those squares; just check each one out.

KEEPING FIT

If practiced regularly, these movements will encourage mobility, and preserve muscle strength and tone.

MOVEMENTS FOR THE SHOULDERS, NECK, AND BACK

These will promote flexibility of the upper body, and alleviate problems such as headaches and painfully knotted muscles in the neck and back. They will also improve your posture.

HEAD ROLLS
Starting with your chin on your chest, slowly roll your head around to your right shoulder. Hold this position and then slowly roll your head back, and around to your left shoulder.

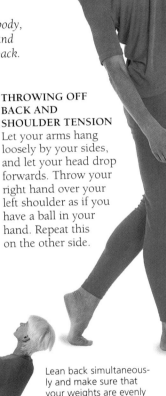

THROWING OFF BACK AND SHOULDER TENSION
Let your arms hang loosely by your sides, and let your head drop forwards. Throw your right hand over your left shoulder as if you have a ball in your hand. Repeat this on the other side.

Lean back simultaneously and make sure that your weights are evenly balanced

HANGING BACK IN A CIRCLE
This is a type of gravity inversion. Stand in a circle, hold hands with the person next to you, and lean backwards. If you do this with a mirror behind you, try and bend back so that you can see your face in the mirror. You can also do this movement with one other partner.

MOVEMENTS FOR THE FEET AND LEGS

Maintaining mobility and flexibility in your feet and weight-bearing joints is important as you get older, since it will help to prevent debilitating physical conditions, such as arthritis.

KICKING YOUR BOOTS OFF
Kicks not only increase articulation in the knees and hips, they also relieve anger and tension. Support yourself by holding on to a door frame and kick forward, as if you were kicking off shoes. The higher you kick the better. Do this several times with each leg.

Aim to kick as high as you can

BOUNCING
Stand with your feet parallel and slightly apart. Lift your arches and bounce gently up and down without bending your knees. This will improve strength and flexibility in your feet and calves.

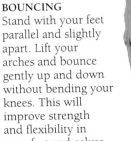

KNEE MOVES

Lie on your back, raise your right knee, and place your left palm on your right kneecap. Gently bend and stretch your leg and see if you can feel any crunching or cracking. Now move your foot round and round in a large circle, keeping your knee still, until you achieve a smooth, fluid movement. Repeat with the other knee.

Move your leg slowly, drawing as big a circle as you can with your foot

STEPPING UP AND DOWN

Stand on a soft mat with your feet slightly apart and kneel down on your right knee, followed by the other knee. Now, leading with your right foot, and keeping your spine vertical, go back to a standing position. Repeat this until your thigh muscle gets tired and then repeat with your left leg. This is the way that you should stand up after you have been sitting or working on the floor.

SQUATS

Resting in a squatting position will increase flexibility in your knees and calves, and strengthen your thigh muscles. Make sure that your feet are parallel and that your knees are on either side of your body. If you cannot stay in a squatting position hold on to a table leg to stop yourself falling backwards.

ANKLE MOVES

Sit on the floor with your legs straight and support yourself with your arms behind you. Flex and point your feet as many times as feels comfortable. Now slowly rotate your ankles, first clockwise, and then anti-clockwise. This will loosen joints and discourage puffiness.

Rest your weight on your hands or lean against a wall

Keep your feet flat to stretch your hamstrings

MOVEMENTS FOR THE WAIST, HIPS, TUMMY, AND BOTTOM

After the menopause, fat distribution changes so that more fat is laid down on the waist and the abdomen. These movements will help to keep your abdominal muscles toned and your hip joints loose and flexible.

SPINNING TOP

This move consists of a succession of quick movements and you may need to use your hands to help you at first. Kneel on the floor, shift your weight on to your bottom on the right-hand side of you, and then bring your knees up and over on to the left side. Now lift up your bottom and sit on your right-hand side again. If you repeat this movement, lifting your bottom over your feet, you should move around in a complete circle.

Move your slowly in a across your to the left

Make your movements smooth and fluid

Pull your stomach muscles in

Rest your weight on your right thigh

FULL HIP CIRCLING

Lie on your back on the floor and slowly bring your right knee over to touch the floor on the left side of your body, keeping your arms above your head. Now bring your right knee up towards your chest and hug it with your arms. Lower your bended leg to the floor, keeping it at right angles to your hip. Now slide the leg back into the original resting position. Repeat with the left leg.

Your back should stay flat

Keep your thigh at right angles to your body

Keeping the elbows raised will tone the upper arms

Return to a kneeling position

Keep your spine straight

Rest your weight on the right thigh again

Try to make your knee touch the ground when you lower your leg

Clasp your knee as close to your chest as you can

Use your hand to gently push your knee down

Support your head on a cushion

BOTTOM AND THIGH TONER

Lie on your front and cross your ankles. Keeping your knees straight, raise both your legs a short distance off the ground and hold them there for a count of ten. Now cross your legs in the other direction and repeat. (Avoid this movement if you suffer from back pain.) After this exercise, lie in the baby pose (see page 118). This is a counter movement and will prevent your back muscles from feeling strained.

BOTTOM RACING

Sit with your legs straight out in front of you and move forwards on your buttocks as fast as you can. Keep your arms stretched out straight in front of you.

STANDING SPINAL TWISTS

Stand with your feet apart, your arms loosely by your sides, and twist at the waist as far as you can. Now twist in the other direction and increase your momentum. Let your arms swing under their own gravity.

AVOIDING ABUSES

Maintaining optimum health depends not only on adopting and maintaining good habits but also on abandoning bad ones. For example, if you eat the recommended daily amount of calcium and vitamin C, and you are a smoker, this amount will not be sufficient, since smoking depletes essential vitamins and minerals (see page 150).

SMOKING

Inhaling cigarette smoke is a proven causative factor in lung cancer, bronchitis, and heart disease. For women of any age, cigarette smoking is bad for health, and it speeds up ageing of the skin. If you are still smoking, it's particularly important that you stop at the menopause. Your tissues require maximum oxygenation from the blood, and cigarette smoke prevents oxygen from being transported efficiently round the body.

Giving up smoking is difficult and some people only succeed when they have a dramatic health reason, such as heart disease or asthma. The menopause, in my opinion, is another dramatic health reason. If you really find it impossible to give up smoking completely, try to cut down by:
● Smoking less than five cigarettes a day.
● Always throwing away a long stub.
● Not inhaling.
● Always smoking low-tar cigarettes.
● Always smoking filter-tip cigarettes.
● Keeping cigarettes as far away from you as possible, so that getting one involves the maximum effort.

ALCOHOL

Although drinking can have a relaxing, mood-enhancing effect, hot flushes can be triggered by alcohol and, for this reason alone, you should keep a careful eye on your intake. Just being female significantly predisposes you to alcohol-related liver disease; statistics show that women drink more alcohol when they are premenstrual, and often over-indulge after the menopause. Alcoholism and alcohol-related problems are increasing rapidly amongst women, although the greatest increase is in younger women aged 30 or below.

A woman's response to alcohol differs according to the point she is at in her menstrual cycle. Drink for drink, she will have higher alcohol levels during the premenstrual and ovulatory phases, than at other times of the month. Because susceptibility to alcohol varies between individuals, it can be difficult for a woman to judge when to stop drinking. A woman's physiology also means that alcohol has a greater effect on her, measure for measure, than on a man of similar weight. A woman's body contains 5–10 percent less water than a man's, so the same amount of alcohol would be more concentrated in her system and thus have a greater toxic effect on the body. This means that it takes less alcohol, consumed over fewer years, to cause liver damage in women than men. Furthermore, a much shorter time elapses between early problem drinking and the development of physical illness.

Excessive drinking usually has a psychological origin and menopausal women may be more vulnerable to alcoholism, especially if they feel that their former role is being eroded (see page 18). The combined pressures of marriage, home, family, and work can prove an intolerable burden for many women, and some respond to stresses by drinking. Many women regard alcohol as a tranquilliser, and drink to escape. We may also drink heavily if we are bored or unfulfilled. At the time of the menopause, our children may have left home, we may feel in a rut with our partners, or if we are alone we may feel there is little to look forward to. Understanding why we drink heavily is the first step to overcoming the problem.

Alcohol consumption is measured in units per week. Fourteen units per week is considered the healthy amount for a woman to drink. Half a pint of beer, a pub measure of spirits, or a glass of wine is one unit. A light drinker would drink one to five units per week, and a moderate drinker would drink 6–14 units a week. If you drink more than 14 units a week, you could be damaging your health, and if you drink more than 21 units a week, you're getting into the heavy drinker category and may be verging on alcoholism. If the latter applies to you, or if you feel that your drinking is becoming a problem, you should seek medical help.

Menopausal women have particularly acute reasons for limiting alcohol intake. Alcohol is an anti-nutrient, depleting the body of vitamins A, B, and C, and it can cause depression, insomnia, and can impair your body's immune reactions, making you prone to infections. It is a powerful oxidant and can lead to premature wrinkling of the skin.

CAFFEINE

This is a xanthine compound, found in coffee, tea, chocolate, some cola drinks, and some painkillers. It is a powerful drug, which has a stimulating effect on the brain, and a diuretic effect on the kidneys, increasing the amount of urine you pass. Caffeine can be a pick-me-up and, in small doses, may result in clearer thinking and sharper sensory awareness. Larger doses, however, can give you "coffee nerves" – an anxious fluttery feeling.

Caffeine can be particularly bad for menopausal women because it causes constriction of the tiny blood vessels in the skin; it can actually trigger a hot flush because it elevates the body temperature. Caffeine also causes a temporary rise in blood pressure. Its diuretic effect may also deplete the body of essential foodstuffs and trace elements. If you have a weight problem, you should monitor your caffeine intake carefully, since too much can encourage the pancreas to release more insulin. This lowers your blood sugar, making you hungry and therefore inclined to binge.

Trying to cut out caffeine from your diet in one fell swoop may bring on withdrawal symptoms, especially if you are a heavy coffee drinker. To avoid nausea, drowsiness, constipation, headaches, and depression, wean yourself off coffee gradually. Reduce the number of cups of coffee you drink by one a day over a period of a week or more, and replace it with decaffeinated coffee. While you are cutting down on caffeine, make sure your diet is rich in fibre and drink plenty of water to help reduce the risk of constipation.

A good way to reduce your caffeine consumption is to use a mixture of both regular and decaffeinated coffee, gradually increasing the amount of decaffeinated coffee, until the caffeine part is completely replaced. You might like to try one of the grain-based, coffee-like beverages on the market. It may taste strange at first, but no stranger than your first cup of coffee. You can also try substituting hot or cold herbal teas for caffeinated drinks, but check the list of ingredients, since some herbal teas contain caffeine.

WAYS TO CONTROL ALCOHOL INTAKE

● *Try to drink an equal quantity of water with alcohol.*
● *Eliminate drinks before and after meals, such as aperitifs and liqueurs.*
● *Always eat when you drink.*
● *Offer your friends more non-alcoholic drinks, and drink more of these yourself.*
● *Skip the occasional round of drinks.*
● *Never drink on an empty stomach; eat a snack at the very least.*
● *If you have been drinking during the evening, have some water before you go to bed and put a full glass by your bedside that you can drink during the night, should you wake.*

A Healthy Pulse Rate
Exercise speeds up your pulse
rate, but you should check that
you are not pushing your body so
hard that your heart is stressed.

PULSE RATES AFTER MILD EXERTION	
Age	Pulse rate
35–39	*130*
40–44	*126*
45–49	*122*
50–54	*117*
55–59	*113*
60–64	*109*

OVERDOING EXERCISE

The 1980s philosophy of "going for the burn" did a great deal of harm. "The burn", first described by Jane Fonda, is the pain that you feel when a muscle has run out of oxygen and is no longer metabolizing normally. Abnormal muscle metabolism produces excessive quantities of lactic acid, which collects in the muscle, causing pain and cramp.

Another 1980s saying, "no pain, no gain", advocated the same philosophy – if your body isn't hurting, the exercise isn't doing you any good. Nothing could be further from the truth. In an attempt to "go for the burn", many women pushed their already unfit bodies to the point where they inflicted injuries upon themselves. With the advent of aerobic exercise, there has been a large increase in the incidence of musculo-skeletal injuries, particularly of the ankles, knees, hips, and lower back.

As we know, all the organs in the body are affected by the menopause. Tissues can no longer regenerate and repair themselves as they did when you were young. Bones may become brittle, and muscles are weaker with less stamina. No menopausal woman should take up a vigorous exercise regime without first checking with her doctor to make sure that her body is fit enough. In addition, you should not start exercising until you measure exactly how "unfit" you are. During exercise, your heart responds to the body's increased need for oxygen by beating faster, and you can measure this increase by taking your pulse. The fitter you are, the less your heart rate increases, because a fit heart pumps out more blood without being under stress.

To make sure that you don't abuse your body with excessive exercise, find out what your personal pulse rate is after mild exertion. To do this, run on the spot for 30 seconds, and then take your pulse by counting the number of beats for 15 seconds and multiplying this number by four. Compare your pulse rate with the chart above. When you exercise, your pulse should not rise above the rate that you've just calculated or above the healthy pulse rate shown on the chart. The aim of heart and lung exercise is to sustain a higher, but healthy pulse rate for about 15–20 minutes.

Research has shown that when you "go for the burn" you are not helping your body to become fitter. The best way to maintain fitness is to keep exercising at your personal pulse rate. If you're exercising at the right rate, you will feel that you could continue exercising for hours. If you get tired quickly, you are overexercising and abusing your body.

MAINTAINING YOUR APPEARANCE

Many women become conscious of the signs of ageing on their faces and bodies during the menopause. It is very important to feel comfortable with the way you look – not only will your confidence improve, but your whole outlook will benefit. A feeling of self-esteem is important as you get older, and looking after your appearance is a good way of promoting self-worth. Your body will look better if you eat a good diet and take regular exercise; you can make the most of your skin and hair if you take proper care of them; and paying attention to your figure will mean that your clothes are more flattering.

There's no secret formula for looking good. You have to think carefully and logically about how to make the most of your good points and successfully conceal your bad ones. There's no need to buy expensive cosmetics or clothes;

it's much more important to look natural and feel comfortable. The wonderful thing about reaching the menopause is that there are no prescribed roles for you to play, and no set of rules that you have to follow.

POSTURE

Shapelessness and poor posture can give the impression of age, and a relaxed, upright posture and a supple figure can make you look much younger. Make sure that you stand with your feet parallel, your pelvis straight, and your spine vertical. Your shoulders should be relaxed rather than hunched. You will not only improve your appearance by paying attention to your posture and gait, but you will help maintain the health of your spine and back muscles.

CLOTHES

If you remain in good shape, you'll carry on wearing the kind of clothes you have always worn. However, ageing inevitably brings changes to body shape, and you may want to accommodate these. Comfortable garments with flattering lines suit mature women, but you should avoid viewing your age as a constraint upon what you should and shouldn't wear.

Choose your shoes very carefully. High heels can throw your body out of alignment, and increase the likelihood of falling. Shoes that are too narrow will cramp your toes, and cause corns and ingrowing toenails. When you are at home, make a point of taking your shoes off and allowing your feet to spread and relax.

UNDERWEAR

Even if your waistline and hips start to spread, you shouldn't be tempted to wear rigid corsets. Wear light foundation garments that allow you to move and breathe freely. Lightweight garments also make hot flushes easier to cope with. If possible, wear underwear that is made of natural fibres such as cotton and

silk, since these are the most comfortable fabrics, particularly in warm temperatures. Avoid wearing harsh, coarse fabrics next to the skin, and look for fastenings that are easy to reach and operate.

All your underwear should be chosen on the basis of comfort. Choose a bra with wide straps that don't cut into your skin, and try wearing an underwired bra for extra support. Two tips to remember when you are buying a bra: if the bra rides up and sits high on your back, it is too big; if you cannot comfortably slide a finger underneath the straps at the front, it is too small. Check that there are no bulges of flesh around the cleavage, which means that the cup size is too small.

Choosing A Bra
Underwired bras give support and can prevent the appearance of sagging breasts. Make sure the wired part lies flat against your skin and extends underneath your arms.

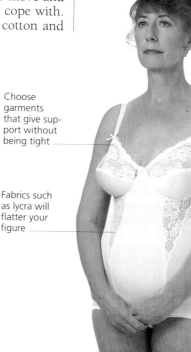

Choose garments that give support without being tight

Fabrics such as lycra will flatter your figure

APPLYING MAKE-UP

The art of applying make-up well lies in creating an overall impression. The minimum effective quantity for the maximum possible effect is all that you need, and make-up shouldn't cost a fortune. If you haven't changed your make-up in the last 12 months, start experimenting with different colours and techniques now. Try copying a look that you have seen in a magazine, particularly of an elegant, older woman. If you can afford it, go to a make-up expert who will recommend ways in which you can

enhance your bone structure using colour and contour. Take time to look objectively at yourself and choose which features you like and want to emphasize and which ones you want to disguise.

CONCEALER
Skin marks such as shadows under the eyes, broken veins, and spider naevi can be covered by light camouflage. A pigmented, solid or liquid blemish cover can be dotted over the area that you want to conceal, and blended into your skin using a fingertip or brush.

FOUNDATION
Applying moisturizer before foundation will prevent a dry, wrinkled appearance. Use a foundation similar to the colour of your skin, and apply with a dampened sponge. Leave the area below your eyes free, but take the colour over your jaw and under your chin to avoid a tide mark.

powder puff

cosmetic sponge

applicator and brushes

blusher brush

all-purpose brush   powder brush

Applicators
Using brushes and sponges to apply your make-up will improve its set and staying power.

EYEBROWS
You can enhance the shape and colour of your eyebrows by brushing colour through them with a pencil, or eyebrow powder applied with a brush. Very dark or bushy eyebrows can be set using eyebrow gel. If you pluck your eyebrows, make sure that you take the hairs from underneath the brow.

cream foundation

powder blusher

translucent face powder

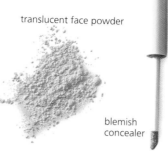

blemish concealer

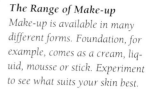

The Range of Make-up
Make-up is available in many different forms. Foundation, for example, comes as a cream, liquid, mousse or stick. Experiment to see what suits your skin best.

lipstick and mascara

neutral eye colours

POWDER
Apply translucent powder using a powder puff or a brush. If you use a powder puff, apply powder with a pressing motion; never rub or drag across the face as you will smudge or remove your foundation. Avoid applying powder to dry areas of your face, such as below the eyes.

EYE MAKE-UP
Choose muddy or neutral tones of eye-shadow. Lift the eyebrow with one finger and brush the colour into the socket of the eye. Avoid taking eye colour all the way up to the eyebrow. Separate the eyelashes with a brush after you have applied mascara.

BLUSHER
Choose subtle rosy or peachy shades rather than stronger pinks or oranges. Apply with a blusher brush along the cheek bone, creating an impression rather than a band of colour. A small amount of blusher on your chin, forehead, and either side of your nose will brighten up a pale complexion.

LIP COLOUR
Apply lip colour sparingly with a brush. If your lips are unsymmetrical, compensate by taking the colour slightly over your lip line (or use a lip pencil). Set your lip colour by blotting with a tissue and dusting with translucent powder. Choose colours that complement your natural colouring.

A Professional Make-over
Consulting a beautician is a good way to learn new techniques for applying make-up that will suit your individual face.

BEAUTY TREATMENTS

No substance or process yet known to science can permanently restore the collagen, protein, fat, and moisture that we lose from the skin as we grow older. Nor is it possible to repair the fractures that develop in the collagen within the dermis as our faces start to wrinkle. Cosmetic creams certainly cannot hold lines and wrinkles at bay, no matter what exotic ingredients they contain. However, rich cleansing creams and moisturizers may prevent the top layer of your skin from drying out. The following procedures vary in their effectiveness at rejuvenating and repairing the skin.

BEAUTY TREATMENTS AND THEIR EFFICACY

	TREATMENT	CLAIMS	RESULT
Facial	*The face is cleansed, massaged, a non-setting facial mask is applied, and the skin is toned. Make-up is applied.*	*Beauticians maintain that facial massage stimulates blood circulation in the skin; this increases natural cellular regeneration and helps to keep the skin's oil and food content well balanced.*	*Your skin can function efficiently on its own without the aid of facial massage. If you find massage soothing and relaxing there is no reason not to have it, but a feeling of being pampered is the only real benefit.*
Viennese Facial	*The face is cleansed and massaged with a high-frequency electrical current. Face mask, toner, and make-up are applied.*		
Face Masks	*A pack, gel, cream, or lotion is applied to the skin, left to dry, then peeled or washed off.*	*Said to stimulate, refine, cleanse, soothe, and nourish the skin, unblock pores, control blackheads, and moisturize the skin.*	*Face masks produce increased blood flow to the skin, and they can remove dead epidermal cells. They cannot repair ageing skin or restore collagen.*
Pressure Spray Toning (*Vaporizers*)	*A fine spray of pressurized water is directed on to the face to help remove a facial mask.*	*Water from the fine penetrating spray is absorbed into the skin, where it has a moisturizing effect.*	*Some water may be absorbed, but it will be lost in a very short time, especially in a centrally heated environment.*
Galvanic Skin Treatment	*A current is passed through a gel applied to your face, so that particles become positively or negatively charged.*	*Applying a current to the skin is supposed to make the cells of the skin expand and increase their blood supply.*	*The skin is stimulated and the pores open, but this effect is only temporary.*

BEAUTY TREATMENTS AND THEIR EFFICACY

	TREATMENT	CLAIMS	RESULT
Chemical Skin-peeling	An acid, such as trichloracetic acid, that produces a second degree burn, is applied to small areas and turns the skin a whitish grey colour. A brown crust forms within three to five days and then drops off.	Skin peeling will result in younger looking skin by removing wrinkles and blemishes.	For purely cosmetic purposes, peeling will get rid of minor blemishes, fine lines, wrinkles, and discoloured areas of skin and freckles. Although the process softens facial lines, it does not stop the ageing process. The rejuvenating effect usually wears off in a year.
Cryotherapy (*freezing*)	Substances such as ethyl chloride, carbon dioxide snow (solid carbon dioxide), and liquid nitrogen are used to freeze the surface of the skin.	Designed to permanently remove warts and other blemishes.	Freezing kills the cells on the surface of the skin and gets rid of blemishes, warts, age spots, and broken veins.
Dermabrasion	Usually done with a high-speed rotary drill and cooling techniques. After sedation, cold packs are applied to the area being treated. The skin is then frozen with a stream of cold gas and a drill breaks the skin to the required depth. Great experience and skill are needed to perform dermabrasion correctly.	Designed to remove acne scars, large flat birthmarks, stretchmarks, and wrinkles around the mouth.	The area may bleed for up to 15–30 minutes after treatment, and a non-adhesive surgical dressing is used for 12–24 hours. Crusts form over the treated area and drop off seven to ten days later. This is effective at removing blemishes.
Electro-desiccation	Skin cells are killed using an electric current, either by a spark that solidifies the skin, or by heat that coagulates it.	Designed to permanently remove minor disfigurements of an ageing skin.	This is good for treating skin tags, as several can be removed in one session without an anaesthetic. It also gets rid of broken veins on the face and legs.

LOOKING AFTER YOUR HAIR
● *Do not scrub the scalp with your fingertips when you wash your hair as you will loosen hairs from the soft wet hair follicles.*
● *Do not tug or pull at wet hair as you comb it; this will remove or tear it. Use a wide-toothed brush or comb.*
● *Do not brush or comb your hair too frequently, this may irritate the scalp and stimulate oil glands to produce more oil, making your hair look lank and dull.*
● *Do not use anti-dandruff shampoos more than once every two weeks as they contain ingredients, such as selenium, that can irritate the scalp.*

BASIC BODY CARE

Keeping your body in good condition throughout the menopausal years requires the same combination of exercise, monitoring your health, and hygiene that it always has. However, you may need to pay slightly more attention to parts of the body such as the teeth – due to recession of the gums – and the legs, which may be affected by less efficient circulation.

THE NECK

As we grow older, the skin of the neck is inclined to sag and become "crepey". This is due to a number of things; first, the neck is very mobile, so the skin is stretched more than skin elsewhere and becomes loose as a result. Second, the skin on the neck is often neglected and does not receive the same cleansing and moisturizing that facial skin does. Third, the neck is nearly always exposed to the sun, so it ages in exactly the same way as the face. We can help to reduce some of these effects by using a sunblock on the neck whenever we go out, and by cleansing and moisturizing neck skin along with the face.

THE HAIR

As you get older, new hair grows in with no pigment. Grey hair is just as healthy as pigmented hair and needs no special treatment. As far as general hair care is concerned, use the mildest shampoo you can find, and only ever shampoo your hair once – shampoos are so efficient that shampooing twice is unnecessary. Mix two teaspoonfuls of shampoo in a glass of warm water and pour it over your already wet hair. Then massage the shampoo very gently into your hair. It's not necessary to scrub hard to work up a lather, just leave the shampoo on for about a minute, and then rinse until the hair is clean. If your hair is slightly dry, you will need a conditioner; these work by coating, or softening and swelling the hair fibre. After you have washed your hair, dab it dry with a towel rather than rubbing it vigorously.

Grey hair can be hidden with temporary or permanent colouring, but, to avoid a harsh contrast with your skin, it's probably better to use a shade that is lighter than the original colour of your hair. The way your hair responds to artificial colourants depends on how porous your hair shafts are. There are several types of hair colouring.

● Restorers can be combed through or sprayed on. They work by coating the hair and may make it brittle and easily damaged.
● Temporary colours, dry or liquid, can give highlights to grey hair, but they don't last beyond one shampoo.
● Semi-permanent colours blend grey hairs into your natural colour and completely cover them. They fade over a period of time, especially in the sun, so reapplication is necessary every few weeks.
● Permanent hair colours penetrate the hair shaft itself and cannot be shampooed away. They have a chemical base that can dry out the hair. They also leave a regrowth when new hair grows in, and have to be reapplied every four to six weeks depending on the rate of growth. Try to avoid bleach, as this really strips the hair of natural oils.

Make sure your hair is regularly looked after, and pay as much as you can afford for a cut and style that really suit you. Don't feel pressured into expensive perms and colours though. Grey hair can be very attractive and you may not want to go to the trouble of regular colouring.

Hirsutism Excessive hair growth is a condition that many postmenopausal women experience. Women have two kinds of hair: the fine, unpigmented hair that usually covers most of the body, and the darker, thicker hair that responds to sex hormones. Hormone-responsive hairs can be found on the pubis, under the arms, and on the face, chest, and lower abdomen. High levels of male sex hormones (androgens), in the blood can promote the conversion of fine unpigmented hairs to dark thick hairs (stress can stimulate the adrenal glands at any age to increase androgen secretion). At the menopause, two factors can bring about hirsutism. First, oestrogen levels are falling, and the normal balance of male and female hormones is upset, so that there is a relatively high amount of androgens. Second, it seems that obesity may cause hirsutism. Facial hirsutism gets worse with age, probably due to changes in hormone metabolism induced by obesity.

There are several methods of temporary hair removal, such as shaving, plucking, waxing, and depilation, but the only permanent methods are electrolysis, which destroys the hair root by a chemical reaction, and short-wave diathermy, which destroys the root by heat. It's generally unwise to use a deodorant or antiperspirant on the underarms for 24 hours after depilation because it may irritate the skin.

THE EYES
Visual defects that occur with age usually result from the changing shape of the eye, rather than the impaired functioning of its various parts. Roughly four out of five people aged over 65, who have some form of visual impairment, can be fitted with glasses so that their eyesight returns to normal. Even if you think your eyesight is alright, it is important as you get older to have regular eye checks for acuity and conditions such as glaucoma (see page 200).

Presbyopia, or far-sightedness, becomes quite common in middle age, and develops because the lens is less able to change its shape to focus on what we're looking at. The eye becomes more oval in shape from front to back, and objects are focused behind, instead of on, the retina. As a result, our vision is blurred. Your optician will fit you with convex (outwardly curved) lenses to increase the power of your own lens, so that objects focus on the retina.

As we age, the lens can also become yellowish, which makes it difficult for us to distinguish between different colours. Blue and green are filtered out by our yellowing lens, but warm colours, such as red and orange, are easier to see.

THE EARS
By the age of 50, some of us will be less able to hear higher pitched sounds, but most of us should be able to look forward to normal hearing beyond the age of 60. Hearing loss is usually due to changes in the inner ear affecting transmission of sounds to the brain.

Sound vibrations reach the cochlea (inner ear) from the eardrum and middle ear, and are transformed into nerve impulses that are transmitted via the auditory nerve to the brain. As we get older, we tend to lose the fine hair cells within the cochlea that activate the neurons in the auditory nerve, and this is the most common cause of hearing loss – one that cannot be helped by a hearing aid. If hearing impairment is not due to damage to the auditory nerve, or to the hair cells inside the cochlea, a hearing aid can help, but it cannot restore the full range of sound frequencies.

The outer ear – the external auditory canal – is rich in sebaceous glands that produce wax. Ear wax has several useful functions: it's an antiseptic, a lubricant, and it prevents foreign substances from reaching the eardrum and the middle ear. As we get older, we tend to produce less wax. Daily washing is all that's necessary to keep the external ear clean. Wax should never be removed by a cotton bud – it will be driven down the ear canal where it will become desiccated, hard, and impacted. It can then only be removed with warmed ear drops that dissolve the wax.

THE MOUTH

The mouth is a self-cleansing organ that loses millions of cells from its surface every day. It is kept clean and healthy by the acts of talking, eating, and drinking. Mouth breathing for any length of time, or failing to eat and drink, causes a build-up of cells that coat and discolour the surface of the tongue.

Halitosis (bad breath) can be due to bad dental hygiene, mouth infection, dental decay, or smoking, but a cause cannot always be found. Regular tooth brushing is essential. Mouth washes and deodorant sprays do not compensate for bad hygiene and they only cure bad breath temporarily.

Dental Care By middle age, most of us will have dental fillings, inlays, and crowns, and we may also have a bridge or partial denture. Dental cavities are the most serious problem up to the age of 35; after 40 the most common reason we lose teeth is infective disease of the gums, or pyorrhoea.

At the menopause, the gums begin to recede due to lack of collagen, so the teeth are more exposed and appear longer (hence the saying, "long in the tooth"). The most common dental problems that affect menopausal and post-menopausal women are worn or missing teeth, teeth becoming slack in the gums, and badly fitting dentures. All of these problems can lead to changes in facial appearance. As the teeth become worn, the distance between the upper and lower jaw shrinks, so that when the teeth meet there are redundant folds of skin on either side of the mouth. This can be relieved to a certain extent by cosmetic dentistry or by fitting full-length caps and crowns.

Care of your mouth and teeth is as crucial now as it was when you were a child. The worst enemy, pyorrhoea, is largely caused by calculus, the chalky, white tartar deposited around the margins of your teeth where they enter the gum. Calculus is formed from plaque, a mixture of food debris and bacteria, which produces acids that erode tooth enamel and undermine the margins of the gums, causing pockets of infection. You can keep plaque at bay by regular tooth brushing in the morning and at night, and after eating sweet foods.

As we age, we develop spaces between our teeth and we should take care to clean in between them. Dental floss or a tiny brush with a specially designed handle are suitable. It's also worth carrying a toothbrush, so that you can brush your teeth if you're eating out. Visit your dental hygienist every three months for plaque removal, and visit your dentist every six months for checkups.

Any sore patches on your tongue, gums, or the inside of your cheeks that last two weeks or more should be seen by your doctor or dentist. A dry mouth can be a postmenopausal condition, and can be relieved by sucking a sugarless sweet or having a drink of water. Always have the sharp edge of a tooth attended to by a dentist since it could cause an ulcer. Gum shrinkage that leads to loose dentures should also be attended to.

THE GENITALS

The vagina is another self-cleansing organ, which does not benefit from excessive cleansing, in fact, it may well be less healthy. Over-zealous washing can upset the delicate bacterial balance necessary for vaginal health. It's far better to underclean than to overclean, and this applies to all parts of the body lined with delicate mucous membranes. In fact, the vagina is designed to take care of itself under all circumstances unless it becomes seriously infected. Organisms that normally live in the vagina, such as lactobacilli, keep the vagina at a slightly acidic level that not only prevents most invading organisms from growing, but also makes fertilization possible during the fertile years.

You should try to avoid using douches, antiseptics in the bath, and vaginal deodorants. Overuse can kill off the bacteria that are the first line of defence against invaders such as candida, which causes thrush. The natural vaginal smell is preferable to an artificial perfume, and plays an important part in sexual attraction. You may be less attractive to your partner if you take pains to camouflage it.

The genitals do need to be kept clean. Before the menopause, vaginal secretions can be profuse around the time of ovulation, and can have a different smell in the second half of the month when the hormone progesterone (see page 30) stimulates wetness and odour. The sweat glands in the perineal area are of the same type as those found in the armpits; bacteria on the skin break down sweat from these glands into chemicals that can be strong-smelling.

Under ordinary circumstances, bathing daily is sufficient. In hot weather, you may feel comfortable washing more frequently, and women who are particularly fastidious may want to wash every time they use the lavatory. When washing, try not to use soap inside the labia majora (the outer lips of the vulva). You can wash the anal area as much as you like – it will come to no harm – but the vulval area is much more delicate and you should treat it gently. Unless you are sweating profusely or having sex a lot, never use soap and water more than twice a day, and always use a gentle soap, such as baby soap. At other times, it's quite sufficient to use water alone. You can wet a couple of clean cotton wool balls in water and wipe them once from the front to the back of the perineal area, then throw them away. If you can't wash yourself during the course of the day, use baby cleansing pads after you've been to the toilet, again from front to back, using them only once before disposal.

THE LEGS AND FEET

To maintain an active lifestyle, we should pay special attention to the legs and feet. Hardening of the arteries and increasingly poor circulation can take their toll on the lower limbs and feet.

You'll avoid blisters, sore heels, and toes if you wear comfortable, supple, low-heeled shoes most of the time. A shoe that fits well should grip your heel and instep, and not press on your toes. Whenever you can, sit with your feet up so that any fluid can drain away and the blood can flow more easily. This will also speed healing if you get any kind of cut, abrasion, or sore place on your feet. As you get older, minor injuries take longer to heal than they did when you were young, and this particularly applies to the feet because of their dependent position. Treat cuts and sores promptly with a simple antiseptic cream. If they don't heal within a few days, consult your doctor; if you're a diabetic, consult your doctor immediately if you have a break in the skin of your

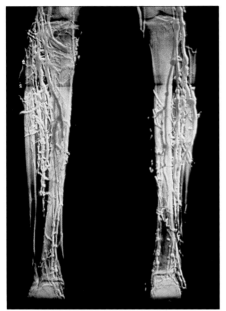

Varicose Veins

When the valves in veins become damaged, allowing blood to flow back, varicose veins appear.

legs and feet. The feet become more prone to infections with age, so never soak them in hot water as this makes the skin soggy and is a perfect medium for bacteria. You should also avoid wearing anything tight on your legs, as this will worsen circulation and hinder blood returning to the heart via the veins.

Chilblains, which are areas of itchiness, swelling, and redness, on the feet and the backs of the legs, tend to become more of a problem as you get older. You can help to avoid them by keeping your feet warm and wearing thick, woollen socks or tights, and in cold weather, fleece-lined shoes and slippers. Make sure that you choose sufficiently large shoes and boots, because tight footwear retards circulation and encourages chilblains. One way to discourage the development of chilblains is to start the day with a warm bath and massage your feet with lotion or oil, using circular movements, and then drying them with a rough towel. Never put your feet or legs near direct heat or hold them against a radiator.

Varicose Veins The tendency towards bulging, dilated, tortuous veins in the lower legs, which may be accompanied by swelling and ulcers of the ankle, runs in families. Varicose veins are most often the result of deep vein thrombosis in the leg, following pregnancy or a surgical operation.

Self-help measures include wearing support stockings or tights, avoiding tight garters or bands, keeping your legs warm, and moisturizing them after washing. Wearing support hose will certainly help to increase blood flow to the tissues and to prevent swelling of the lower legs. Try not to stand for long periods at a time, and rest the legs in an upright position whenever possible. If you can, lie down on the floor and put your legs up against the wall for half an hour, and then put on support hose. Treat abrasions, bruises, or minor infections of the lower legs meticulously, and consult your doctor if necessary.

Mild varicose veins can be injected so that they shrink and eventually scar and shrivel. If the varicose veins are extensive, they can be stripped out by a vascular surgeon. Modern vein surgery is less painful and requires less hospitalization than previously.

THE NAILS

Brittle and flaking nails can be a problem after the menopause because waning oestrogen levels result in poor quality collagen (see page 52). Hardening of the arteries and poor circulation can lead to thickening of the finger and toenails, so it's important to trim them once a week to keep them in good condition.

If your fingernails are brittle and flaky, avoid using nail varnish remover, as this can dry out the nails even more. Use an emery board in preference to scissors and metal files, and massage hand and nail cream into your cuticles every day. When you cut your toenails, you should use good-quality nail clippers and cut the nails straight across the top to the edges – never cut your nails steeply at the sides, since this encourages ingrowing toenails. If your toenails are very thick, file them frequently and try to thin them down as well as shorten them. From the menopause onwards, it's wise to visit a chiropodist on a regular basis. Not only will it keep your feet feeling and looking good, it will be a vital investment if you want to remain supple, agile, and active.

AESTHETIC PLASTIC SURGERY

These days plastic surgeons do a lot more than surgery. Collagen injections are widely used to ameliorate the effects of ageing. They can be used to give a more youthful appearance to the backs of the hands and almost any small contour in the face can be changed with collagen – frown lines, deep nose to mouth lines, smile lines, horizontal forehead lines, and facial scars can all be treated. Even the lips can be enlarged using collagen. Some women can have an allergic response to collagen so you should request a test before you have treatment, otherwise you may suffer from profound swelling and scarring that, at worst, may be permanent.

AESTHETIC PLASTIC SURGERY TECHNIQUES

Operation	In or outpatient/ Length of stay	Post-operative effects	Stitches removed	Results / Recovery time
Blepharoplasty (reshaping eyelids and removing bags)	Inpatient/ 1 night or a day's rest	Tender and bruised eyes	3–4 days	Very good/ 3 weeks
Rhinoplasty (reshaping nose)	Inpatient/ 1 night	A little swelling around the nose, and bruising under the eyes	Plaster removed after 7 days	Excellent/ 1 month for swelling to go down
Chin Augmentation	Inpatient/ 1 day	Soreness inside the mouth and a swollen chin	None	Excellent/1 month
Facelift	Inpatient/ 1–2 nights	Red, swollen face, and numbness and tension in cheeks and neck	Some after 3–7 days, the rest after 2 weeks	Generally good, should last 10–15 years. Swelling goes down after 4 weeks
Breast Augmentation	Inpatient/ 1 night	Bruising and tingling around the nipples, occasionally soreness	1 week	Very good/2 months
Breast Uplift	Inpatient/ 2 nights	Bruising and diminished nipple sensitivity	2 weeks	Good/1 month
Breast Reduction	Inpatient/ 2 nights	Swelling and bruising, and nipple sensitivity may be diminished	1 week	Excellent/1 month
Liposuction	Inpatient/ 1 night or day	Temporary bruising and numbness	1 week	Very good/1 week
Collagen Replacement	Outpatient	Slight redness for a few days	None	Very good/3 weeks
Abdominoplasty (tummy tuck)	Inpatient/ 3 nights	Temporary loss of sensation across wound	1–2 weeks	Very good/3 months

Liposuction is now fashionable and widely practiced – not always to the highest standards. It's always worth seeking out an experienced plastic surgeon of excellent reputation to perform liposuction because it can go seriously wrong. On the tops of the thighs, for instance, the result can be worse than the original condition. It is possible for liposuction to scar and leave a pitted and uneven skin surface. The best practitioners of liposuction are experienced surgeons, with the most modern techniques, who are able to extract fat from a deep level and leave a flat, even surface to the skin. An incision is made in the area from which the fat is to be extracted and a glass or metal tube is inserted. This tube is attached to a surgical device that will suck up the soft fatty tissue from the fat deposit. Liposuction usually requires a general anaesthetic, and it is common to suffer from bruising after surgery.

Quantities of fat in excess of two-thirds of a litre (approximately one pint) should never be removed on a single occasion. Fat is liquid and in "circulation" around the body. Losing more than a pint of fat is similar to losing a pint of blood and can make you ill. Fatty tissue can be removed from one part of the body and inserted at another site to change your shape. For example, liquid fat from the abdomen can be used to augment breast size.

If you decide on plastic surgery, choose your surgeon carefully. It's better to select your surgeon on the recommendation of a friend, whose results you can see, or through your own family doctor, rather than from an advertisement. Be suspicious of a surgeon who says that he or she can perform exactly the operation you require without giving a professional opinion about what you need.

I'd also be sceptical about a surgeon who is over-optimistic about the results of the operation. No good surgeon will give you a 100 percent guarantee of success. A trustworthy surgeon will always give you some idea of his or her work by showing you before and after surgical photographs. Ask your surgeon to draw exactly what he or she is going to do, and if you don't understand, ask for further clarification. If you are in any way uncertain, go elsewhere. As a general rule, you should never employ a surgeon with whom you cannot establish a good rapport.

Composite Facelift

Although surgery is one of the most extreme methods of combating the effects of ageing, it can have a dramatic affect on facial appearance. A composite facelift involves restoring fat and muscle to their former position.

8

MAINTAINING YOUR SEXUALITY

If you had an enjoyable and fulfilling sex life before the menopause, you almost certainly can afterwards. In fact, there are many advantages to postmenopausal sex, one being that you no longer have to worry about contraception and pregnancy.

A LIFETIME OF SATISFACTION

One benefit of growing older with a partner is that you share a history of past experiences with him. You know your partner really well, and you have the opportunity for true companionship. You know how to strike a balance between shared interests and privacy. A well-kept secret is that many of us lose our inhibitions as we get older. We begin to feel the freedom to enjoy sexual pleasure – to express ourselves in ways that we kept hidden when we were younger. Perhaps it's a result of children leaving home, or the feeling that we should forgo our inhibitions and fully explore our sexuality.

Activities that once took up a great deal of energy, such as looking after children, working, and domestic routines, should have been left behind to some extent, so there is more time and energy for pleasurable activities, such as sex. Furthermore, you will often find that intimate situations are now easier to control, there is more privacy, and there are fewer interruptions.

The saying "if you don't use it, you lose it" is particularly applicable to sex during the menopause. We know from studies published over several years that regular sexual activity can keep our sex organs healthy, and if we take care of ourselves, we can remain sexually active for the rest of our lives. There are, however, changes in your body, and often your partner's body, that require adjustments to your familiar sexual routine. Once we know about these changes, we can begin to adapt our lives accordingly to keep sex satisfying.

FACTORS THAT CAN PROMOTE SEX AFTER THE MENOPAUSE:
- A rewarding sex life before the menopause.
- Positive attitudes towards sex and ageing.
- A good relationship with your partner.
- Physical and emotional fitness, and an accepting attitude towards your body.
- Regular sex or masturbation will keep your genitals healthy, and will help to prevent vaginal dryness and atrophy, enabling you to continue being sexually active as you grow older.

FACTORS THAT CAN INHIBIT SEX AFTER THE MENOPAUSE:
- A history of unsatisfying sex.
- An unsupportive partner or an unhappy relationship.
- Problems such as vaginal dryness or soreness (see page 50).
- Attitudes that equate sex with youth or having children.
- Surgical removal of the ovaries (see page 76).

VAGINAL CHANGES

During and after the menopause, the walls of the vagina become thinner, smoother, dryer, and less elastic. Even the shape of the vagina changes, becoming shorter and more narrow (although it always remains big enough to accommodate an erect penis). The clitoris becomes slightly smaller, and the lips or labia of the vagina, become thinner and flatter. The covering of the clitoris (the female equivalent of the male foreskin) may also become thinner and pull back, leaving the clitoris more exposed. This can make the clitoris extremely sensitive to touch, and you may find that you need quite a bit of lubrication before it can be stimulated with the fingers.

In young women one of the first signs of arousal is the wetness produced by the walls of the vagina. Droplets of fluid form a slippery coat in the vagina and on the vulva, making penetration easy and pleasurable for both partners. Falling oestrogen levels mean that vaginal cells may not be able to lubricate so quickly. You may feel aroused but it takes several minutes for your vagina to "catch up" and lubricate. If this is the case, explain to your partner that you need to take things slowly, and spend more time on foreplay. Hormone replacement therapy (HRT; see chapter six) can improve vaginal health by restoring oestrogen and increasing blood flow to the vagina, resulting in improved lubrication of the vagina.

In young women, thick vaginal walls serve as a cushion during intercourse, protecting the bladder and the urethra from friction. As the vagina becomes atrophied, you lose this cushioning and your urinary tract is no longer so well protected, and it is common to feel a strong urge to urinate after sex. If this is the case, you should empty your bladder promptly. Some menopausal women also complain of a burning sensation during urination that can persist for several days, especially after a long sex session. Drinking plenty of water can relieve this (see page 91).

Although vaginal dryness is very common during the menopause, sexologists, Masters and Johnson recorded that a small number of women (all 60 years or over) still lubricated rapidly when aroused. The likely reason for this is that these women continued to have sex once or twice a week throughout their adult lives. This supports the belief that regular sex can promote vaginal health.

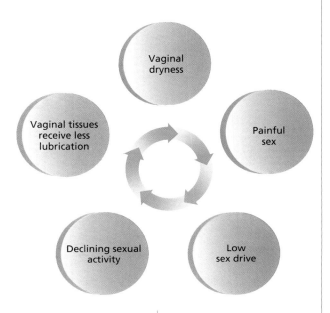

The Vicious Circle Of Vaginal Dryness

The vagina and vulva become prone to thinness and dryness after the menopause, which can make sex painful. Ironically, if you abstain from sex, the problem may get worse.

HORMONAL CHANGES

Sex drive is hormonally related, and there are many studies that have shown that women experience heightened sexual desire around the middle of the menstrual cycle, which is the time that they usually ovulate. Women are more likely to masturbate, fantasise, have sexy dreams, and initiate lovemaking with their partners during their midcycle – on approximately the 14th day of a 28-day cycle.

Oestrogen is produced by the developing egg follicle in the ovary, and it reaches a peak at ovulation. However, ovulation is also marked by high levels of the male sex hormones, testosterone and androstenedione. High levels of testosterone are known to be responsible for a high sex drive in both men and women. During the postmenopausal years, the ratio of testosterone to oestrogen becomes greater. This is due to the fact that oestrogen levels fall while testosterone levels remain the same (or even increase).

NATURAL TREATMENTS FOR VAGINAL HEALTH

There is anecdotal evidence from women that yoghurt containing live bacteria, lactobacillus acidophilus, applied to the vagina can help to prevent infections. The yoghurt should remain in the vagina for at least two hours after application – wearing a tampon can keep it from leaking out.

Another treatment is douching with a solution of one tablespoon of white vinegar in a pint of water. This will keep the vagina acidic. (Too much sugar in your urine can make your vagina alkaline and prone to infections, such as thrush.) Alternatively, you can add a cup of vinegar to bath water or use a tampon soaked in the solution. There are also many herbal remedies available, but you should consult a qualified herbalist. If any treatment causes soreness, stop using it immediately.

Contrary to the myth of sexual decline after the menopause, some women – approximately one in six – report increased sexual desire, and this may be attributable to the relative excess of male hormone.

Research carried out on American women who had undergone hysterectomies, which included the surgical removal of their ovaries, confirmed the role of testosterone in sex drive. The women were asked to rate the intensity of their sexual desire before and after their operations. After surgery the women were given one of the following treatments:

- Oestrogen
- Testosterone
- Oestrogen and testosterone
- A placebo

The women who received a placebo reported that their sex drive, fantasies, and levels of arousal all declined after surgery. The same was true for women receiving oestrogen alone. In contrast, women taking either testosterone or a testosterone/oestrogen combination had higher levels of desire, arousal, more fantasies, and their sex drive was very similar to that of those women in a control group who had had a hysterectomy, but had kept their ovaries.

The conclusions drawn from this study confirmed that the hormonal secretions of the ovaries make an important contribution to a woman's sexual health, and that the effectiveness of testosterone in restoring sexual interest after surgical removal of the ovaries shows that male sex hormones do stimulate sexual interest in women.

For this reason, the amount of testosterone your menopausal ovaries will produce is likely to have a significant effect on your sex drive. Hormone levels vary from woman to woman: in some women, blood levels of male hormone actually increase after the menopause; in other women, they decrease by 50 percent or more. If HRT is taken, this may reduce the amount of free testosterone in the bloodstream by up to 30 percent.

If you've noticed a decrease in sexual desire that seems to coincide with your menopause – particularly if you have had your ovaries removed – it could be due to decreased levels of male sex hormones. Although testosterone replacement therapy would seem to be the answer, there are two problems. First, the ideal level of testosterone for women has not been determined. Doctors can only use blood tests as a guideline to determine how your level compares with what is normal for your age. Second, male sex hormones have potent side-effects and can cause masculinization to occur. This usually results in a lowering of the voice and hirsutism, including facial hair growth.

If you are prescribed testosterone for a low sex drive, ask to start with the lowest available dose. Injections and implants, which are inserted underneath the skin, are not reversible, and if testosterone does not suit you, you may be compelled to suffer its effects for several months. Instead, use a low-dose tablet (e.g., one 40 mg tablet of testosterone undecanoate) so that any side-effects last no longer than a day at a time.

SEXUAL CHANGES IN YOUR PARTNER

An interested partner is the most important factor for good sex at any age, and the influence of declining hormones on desire may have a relatively modest effect in comparison to the importance of a fulfilling relationship. Menopausal women usually have partners who are experiencing changes in their own sexual response and behaviour, so it's helpful to be aware of male physiology, particularly if you have a partner over 50.

Changes in your partner's sexual behaviour are easier to understand if you realise that there are changes in his hormones as well as yours – albeit in a different pattern. As men age, testosterone-inhibiting factors increase, and this has the same effect as a decrease in testosterone levels, causing a declining frequency of erection. Replacing hormones in men is not as beneficial as it is in women. Men need a minimum amount of testosterone. If they already have this minimum level, testosterone replacement therapy will not usually help.

Most young men can have an erection within seconds of being physically or mentally stimulated. For men over 50, it may take longer, and more direct stimulation of the penis may be necessary. It can take several minutes before an older man's penis becomes really firm, and you may notice that your partner's drive to ejaculate becomes less urgent. Some men find that they cannot maintain their erections for as long as they used to. This is not a problem, it just means that you have to adjust your timing where sex is concerned, so that you are fully aroused at the same time that he is ready for penetration. Mutual masturbation as part of foreplay can be helpful.

As a man ages, the volume of his ejaculate and the force with which it is expelled decrease. His penis becomes flaccid faster, and it may take longer for him to have another erection. Some men may take a very long time to get an erection of sufficient firmness for intercourse. For a man over 50, the waiting period may take 12 hours; for men in their 60s and 70s, it may take up to several days. Older men don't necessarily ejaculate during sex. If your partner doesn't ejaculate on one occasion, it doesn't mean that he will never ejaculate again. Each man is different and follows his own timetable. Your partner may be in his 50s or even his 40s when changes occur. Other men may be well into their 80s. For all these reasons, you may find your partner's interest in sex lessens, particularly if he isn't aware of why his body is changing, or that it is a universal phenomenon and not his own unique problem.

SEEKING MEDICAL HELP

If your partner has severe problems getting or maintaining an erection, he should seek medical advice. Difficulties can be physical in origin, and are sometimes caused by blood leaking away from the penis so that turgidity is impaired. If your partner is taking certain medications, these can interfere with his erection. Betablockers, which are prescribed for high blood pressure, affect sexual function, and so do antihistamines. Studies in both men and women have shown that low histamine levels may impede orgasm. In men it is well documented that the higher their histamine level, the quicker they ejaculate, and the lower the histamine level, the slower the response. Diabetes can cause damage to the nerves that stimulate erection and ejaculation.

There is a popular fallacy that ageing robs a man of his capacity for sexual pleasure. Even though this is not true, many men are anxious about their sexual performance deteriorating. If your partner does not achieve an erection on more than one occasion, he may be afraid that he is impotent and start avoiding sex altogether. This can lead to all sorts of misunderstandings: he may blame you, and you may feel guilty, or he may blame himself. It is therefore essential that you communicate honestly and frankly about your feelings.

EVALUATING YOUR SEX LIFE

Take stock of your sex life by answering the following questions. There are no right or wrong answers – the questions simply serve to help you assess your sex life and identify any areas that you would like to change. It may help if you and your partner answer the questions together.

Your Body

Are you happy with your body?

If you're not, are you prepared to improve your body by changing your diet and taking more exercise?

Are you inhibited about one part of your body?

Do you feel relaxed about undressing and being naked in front of your partner?

Your Feelings

Do you feel close to your partner?

Do you think you and your partner are well matched sexually?

Do you find it easy to talk about sex?

Can you ask for what you want sexually?

The Setting

Where do you make love?

Do you ever try to create a sexy atmosphere with lights, candles, or music?

Do you always make love in the same place?

Do you have complete privacy?

The Build-up to Sex

How do you initiate sex?

Do you give conflicting signals?

If your partner misunderstands you, how can you communicate better?

Do you spend enough time on foreplay so that you are fully aroused when you have sex?

Intercourse

Do you ever find penetration difficult or painful?

What do you do to overcome this?

Do you reach orgasm and, if so, how?

If you don't reach orgasm during intercourse, do you ask your partner to stimulate you in other ways?

Answering these questions may give you a better idea of what, if anything, you want to change or improve about your sex life. For example, you may feel that sex has become routine and predictable, or that you and your partner don't communicate very easily about sex. Below are some suggestions about how to inject variety into your lovemaking.

TECHNIQUES TO MAXIMIZE LOVEMAKING

One of the most important things you can do is make the time to create a relaxing sensual environment, and to talk intimately with your partner, so that you become fully aroused during the build-up to sex. Pay attention to mood and atmosphere, have a drink together, and take turns undressing each other. Using some fragrant massage oil, stroke your partner all over, working your way down the length of his body. When it's your turn, show your pleasure at what feels good, and be explicit about your preferences. Slowly move on to touching your partner's penis, and when he touches you, tell him what you would like him to do, or demonstrate this to him physically by guiding his hand or mouth to where you want to be caressed.

Genital touching can progress to penetration, or can bring you both to orgasm. If you choose mutual masturbation, lubricate your hands with oil or a water-based jelly so that you don't hurt your partner (don't use fragrant massage oil if you are going to use a condom because it perishes the rubber).

Although some women may be inhibited about giving or receiving oral sex, it is another good way to extend foreplay, or it can be used as an end in itself if you are not in the mood for penetrative sex. Fellatio is one of the most powerful ways of stimulating a man, and the lips and tongue are capable of producing a greater variety of sensations than the vagina. Saliva is a greatly undervalued lubricant. It's always available, you can both use it readily, and it can take the pressure off your concern about vaginal dryness.

Some couples like to increase their arousal by sharing their sexual fantasies or by reading or looking at erotic material. Arousal begins in the brain, and if you are mentally stimulated, genital stimulation will usually follow. Most men and women have erotic fantasies, and talking about them is a good way of opening a sexual dialogue.

Don't assume that because you have been making love to your partner for years, you know everything about him sexually. The secret of satisfying sex is to keep communicating with each other, asking your partner what he wants, telling him what you like, and sharing your sexual thoughts, dreams, and fantasies. Break away from your normal sexual routine – make love in a new position, in a new place, at a different time.

SENSUAL MASSAGE

Two people who have always been physically affectionate with each other are more likely to share caresses as they get older than a couple who have grown out of the habit of touching each other. There is much research that shows that the power of touch and its importance in our lives never diminishes. Even in very old age, in the 80s and 90s, the importance of physical intimacy and touch is high. Being hugged and petted would seem to be necessary for our physical and mental well-being.

A massage is not only an excellent way to relax, it also allows you to focus your senses deeply on the responses aroused in your body. You can explore your partner's erogenous zones and set the scene for sex. Use fragranced massage oil or cream to lubricate his skin – apply it to your hands first to make it warm. Begin a massage with your partner lying face down, sit astride his legs or buttocks, and run your fingertips lightly up and down his back. Progress to firmer pressing strokes, using the heels of the hands or the thumbs and paying special attention to the muscles between the shoulder blades and at the base of the neck. Next, ask your partner to roll on to his back and lightly massage his abdomen and chest, using soft stroking movements. Circle his nipples with featherlight strokes using your fingertips. Also pay attention to parts of the body that are usually neglected, such as the feet.

EXTENDED FOREPLAY

The main reason for extending foreplay is that both you and your partner may have slower sexual responses. Build up to sex very gradually by petting and stroking each other, and slowly move on to kissing. Prolong the moment when you touch your partner's genitals by giving him a sensual massage with fragranced oil. Other foreplay techniques include having a bath or a shower together, sharing and enacting your fantasies, and exploring your partner's erogenous zones by lightly nibbling and licking them. When you touch your partner's genitals, spend time slowly caressing him until you both feel completely ready for penetration.

TECHNIQUES FOR ENHANCING FOREPLAY

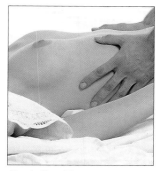

Erotic Touching
Tell your partner where you want to be touched, or demonstrate this by guiding his hand.

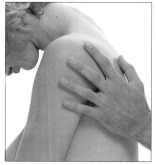

Sensual Caresses
Spend time stroking, kissing, and caressing your partner before you begin to make love.

SEX POSITIONS

You can very easily adapt lovemaking to accommodate minor sexual changes. If, for example, you lubricate more slowly than you used to, clitoral stimulation before penetration can help. You may also prefer sexual positions in which your partner can stimulate you with his hand. Woman-on-top positions are good in that you can control the pace and rhythm of lovemaking, taking the pressure of performance off your partner.

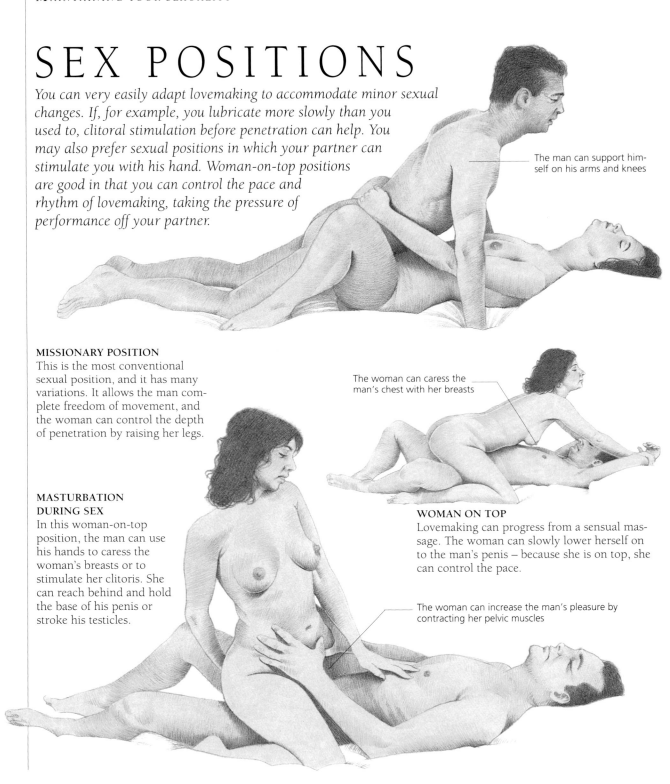

The man can support himself on his arms and knees

MISSIONARY POSITION
This is the most conventional sexual position, and it has many variations. It allows the man complete freedom of movement, and the woman can control the depth of penetration by raising her legs.

The woman can caress the man's chest with her breasts

MASTURBATION DURING SEX
In this woman-on-top position, the man can use his hands to caress the woman's breasts or to stimulate her clitoris. She can reach behind and hold the base of his penis or stroke his testicles.

WOMAN ON TOP
Lovemaking can progress from a sensual massage. The woman can slowly lower herself on to the man's penis – because she is on top, she can control the pace.

The woman can increase the man's pleasure by contracting her pelvic muscles

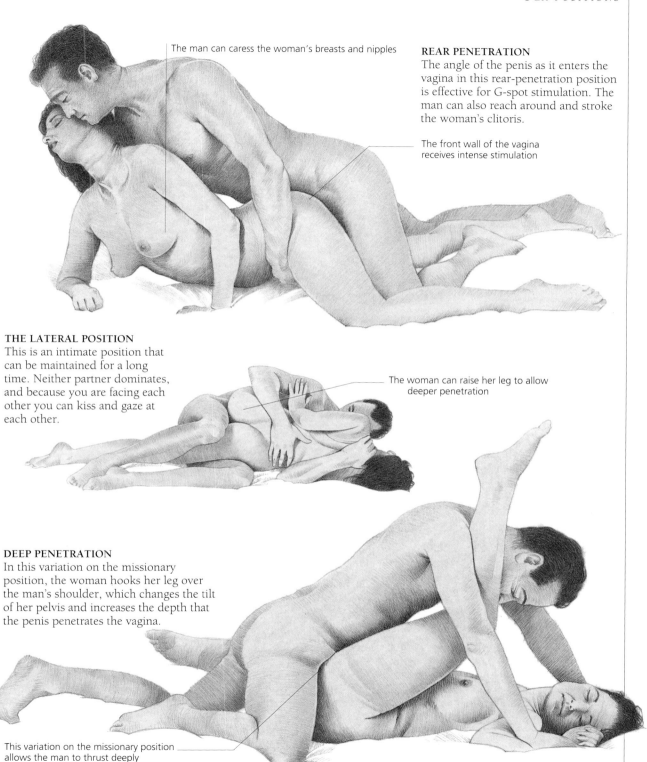

The man can caress the woman's breasts and nipples

REAR PENETRATION
The angle of the penis as it enters the vagina in this rear-penetration position is effective for G-spot stimulation. The man can also reach around and stroke the woman's clitoris.

The front wall of the vagina receives intense stimulation

THE LATERAL POSITION
This is an intimate position that can be maintained for a long time. Neither partner dominates, and because you are facing each other you can kiss and gaze at each other.

The woman can raise her leg to allow deeper penetration

DEEP PENETRATION
In this variation on the missionary position, the woman hooks her leg over the man's shoulder, which changes the tilt of her pelvis and increases the depth that the penis penetrates the vagina.

This variation on the missionary position allows the man to thrust deeply

Vibrators

You can use a vibrator to bring yourself to orgasm, or your partner can use it on you as a means of enhancing foreplay.

G-spot attachment

Standard variable-speed vibrator

Supple plastic vibrator

Egg-shaped vibrator

MASTURBATION

Self-stimulation is not only a safe form of sexual enjoyment, it is also an ideal way to explore your body and release sexual tension. If you don't have a partner, masturbation can provide vital sexual release – this can be a positive choice for many women. If you do have a partner, masturbation can complement intercourse. If you find that you become aroused very slowly, your partner can spend time stimulating you manually. Alternatively, you can masturbate alone for pleasure, when your partner doesn't want sex, or is ill.

Masturbation is extremely common. As many women as men begin to masturbate in their teens and continue throughout life. Nearly half of the women questioned in one study said that they masturbated in their 50s and a third masturbated at the age of 70 and over. These figures matched those for men of the same age.

The techniques for masturbation are different for everyone. Whatever brings you satisfaction and pleasure is fine, and you shouldn't be afraid to experiment. If you have never masturbated, choose a time when you will be totally undisturbed, and a place where you feel relaxed. Start by stroking the whole of your body, and then focus on your genital area. Some women stroke or press their entire vulva, others concentrate on stimulating the clitoral area. Stroking or rubbing movements by the fingers can provide intense stimulation, and some women use a vibrator. Other women can climax by rhythmically pressing their thighs together. Fantasizing or inserting something into your vagina may enhance arousal.

OVERCOMING SPECIFIC PROBLEMS

Problems such as a low sex drive may be due to relationship problems, stress, or boredom. Occasionally, there is a physiological basis for loss of libido, and you should see a doctor to eliminate this possibility.

PROBLEMS ACHIEVING ERECTION

The first rule in achieving an erection is for your partner to learn to relax. Most sexual problems are psychological in origin, and if your partner is anxious and afraid that he won't be able to achieve an erection, then he probably won't. Try to acknowledge the problem rather than ignoring it. If you talk about your anxieties to each other, this may help to defuse the tension and create a more relaxed atmosphere between you. If you feel that your problems are more deep-rooted and having a serious impact on your relationship, it may be helpful to receive relationship counselling.

Don't set out to make love, because this may put pressure on your partner. Spend a long time touching and stroking each other, and if your partner is aroused, concentrate on stimulating his genital area with your hands or mouth. If you use your hands, lubricate the penis with a water-based jelly and massage the shaft firmly.

If your partner's problems result from the medication he is taking, he should ask his doctor about alternatives. In severe cases of impotence, a penile implant consisting of two inflatable rods can be surgically installed in the penis. A pump in the scrotum inflates the rods, causing the penis to become erect.

LONG-TERM ILLNESS

Serious illness can be a major inhibiting factor in sex. This is particularly true if you or your partner have had a heart attack or suffer from angina. Because you are afraid of putting any extra pressure on your heart, you may abstain from sex altogether. Fortunately, doctors agree that a normal sex life can greatly benefit people who have suffered heart attacks, and they encourage a return to normal sexual activity as soon as possible.

You will be able to judge for yourself when the time is right for you to have sex: if you are feeling very tired, you have been drinking, or you have eaten a rich, heavy meal, you should probably wait until your body is less stressed – in the morning, for instance.

Arthritis can make intercourse uncomfortable, but pain can often be alleviated by some simple self-help measures, such as having a hot bath to mobilize your joints, adopting a restful position during lovemaking, and taking painkilling drugs an hour or so before you have sex. The spoons position, in which you and your partner lie on your sides, is gentle and relaxing. The woman lies on her side with her knees raised, while the man penetrates her from behind; this gives him access to her breasts and upper body, while she can stimulate herself manually. Remember that sex does not always have to be penetrative – alternatives such as oral sex, mutual masturbation, or touching and stroking can be equally stimulating.

Diabetes is another medical condition that can cause sexual problems. In women these problems include a dry, itchy vulva, and yeast infections. In men they include difficulty in getting an erection and problems ejaculating. Some drugs to treat diabetes can cause impotence, so check this with your doctor and ask about alternative medications. If diabetes is closely monitored and treated early, all these problems may be lessened.

VAGINISMUS (VAGINAL SPASM)

Fear of penetration, which is sometimes referred to as "frigidity", can lead to involuntary spasms of the vaginal muscles that make sex very painful, and often impossible. The cause of vaginismus is almost always psychological and may stem from deep-rooted fears about sex. Some women develop vaginismus after the menopause as a result of vaginal pain and dryness. They may become acutely sensitive to the stretching sensation that occurs during penetration and learn to anticipate pain – this triggers muscular contractions. If this is the case, there are several self-help measures to alleviate postmenopausal sexual problems (see page 55), and taking HRT will prevent or reverse vaginal atrophy. Alternatively, if you had vaginismus before your menopause, it may be a defensive reaction to sexual situations that you feel you cannot control. In this case it may help you to receive counselling. For women whose vaginismus is not too severe, the following exercise may help.

Using a mirror, touch the vaginal entrance with your fingers. Relax by breathing deeply, and when you feel ready, try inserting the tip of one finger into your vagina. Use a lubricant, such as oil, lubricating jelly, or saliva. Now insert your finger further into the vagina – if you feel your vaginal muscles contracting, stop, wait until you feel relaxed, and try again. Using this technique, try to get to the point where you can insert two or three fingers into the vagina. When you make love, experiment with a woman-on-top position, which allows you to control the depth of penetration.

The G-spot

This is reputed to be a small area on the front vaginal wall that can produce intense feelings of pleasure if it is stimulated repeatedly. The G-spot and the clitoris can take on an important role in sex if the cervix is removed in a hysterectomy.

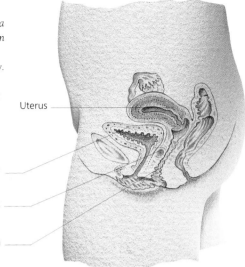

Uterus

Bladder

G-spot

Front wall of the vagina

SEX AFTER A HYSTERECTOMY

If you have had your uterus surgically removed, you should not have intercourse until you feel comfortable – around four weeks after the operation is likely to be the earliest time. When you do resume sexual activity you may notice some changes; a growing body of research shows that a hysterectomy can have a negative impact on a woman's sex drive, particularly if the ovaries and cervix have been removed. Data from Scandinavia shows that some women who have had a complete hysterectomy may experience orgasms less frequently than they did before surgery. Data from America suggests that although HRT can relieve painful sex and vaginal dryness, it may not be so effective at restoring sex drive. The reason for a declining libido after a complete hysterectomy may, in part, be due to the withdrawal of the male sex hormones secreted by the ovaries. Some women, therefore, may benefit from taking HRT combined with a daily dose of testosterone.

YOUR DIET AND SEX

Sex is improved if you are fit and eat a healthy diet. While there's no proof that certain nutrients improve desire or performance, several minerals are thought to be important.

When your zinc levels are low, your blood histamine levels are also low, which may make it slightly more difficult for you to reach orgasm. Zinc deficiency is quite common in women because significant amounts are lost during menstruation and dieting. Unfortunately, the process of refining grains and cereals removes 80 percent of their zinc content. However, you can make up for this by eating seafood, such as clams, oysters, herrings, and sardines. Seeds and nuts are also good sources of zinc. Niacin, one of the B vitamins, is another nutrient that may be associated with histamine production.

Strengthening the vaginal muscles with Kegel exercises (see page 50) may help to improve sexual enjoyment, as the better toned the muscles, the easier it is to achieve orgasm through clitoral or vaginal stimulation. Contracting your vaginal muscles during penetrative sex will also increase your partner's pleasure (bear in mind that the position that you make love in may affect your ability to contract your vaginal muscles; if you have your legs spread widely apart with your feet above your body, you may find it hard to contract the muscles adequately).

Although the cervix is implicated in vaginal orgasm, some women may be able to reach orgasm as a result of rhythmic stroking of the G-spot. Although there is no conclusive evidence that the G-spot exists, it was first commented upon by a German gynaecologist, Ernst Grafenburg, and is thought to be an area of tissue about four centimetres (one and a half inches) up, on the front wall of the vagina. The G-spot may become engorged with blood, causing it to swell in response to repeated, regular stroking movements, such as the thrusting of the penis during sexual intercourse.

9

MONITORING YOUR HEALTH

Monitoring your health is the key to continuing a healthy and active life. Observing and reading the messages your body sends, then responding to them, brings a great sense of well-being and satisfaction. Being aware of your health gives you control over your body, and helps you to spot potential medical conditions early, when they may be more easily and successfully treated.

HEALTH CHECKS

As you reach the menopause you will need to have a variety of health checks done regularly. Certain tests that you have had in the past will be carried out more frequently, while new tests may need to be done because of your changed status as a menopausal woman. There are also procedures such as colposcopy that may be necessary if routine checks reveal any abnormalities. Ideally, there will be a large team of people to help monitor your health, of whom you are the first member. The second would be your doctor, the third, your gynaecologist, the fourth, the radiologist who reads your mammogram, the fifth, the cytologist who reads your smear, and so on. Think of them all as a supportive team with whom you can interact, discuss, and make informed joint decisions.

Doctors have a responsibility to women on hormone replacement therapy (HRT; see chapter six), and, before HRT is prescribed, your doctor should carry out an examination of your pelvis and breasts, take a cervical smear, and check your weight and blood pressure. Ideally, you should have a mammogram to assess the health of your breasts, and a bone density test to predict your likelihood of developing osteoporosis. Once you are taking HRT, you should have six-monthly consultations with your doctor in which you discuss any side-effects and bleeding, and have your weight and blood pressure checked.

Medical Tests
Doctors can monitor your physical health during the menopause with a range of medical procedures.

Eye test

Blood test for hormone levels and thyroid function

Mammogram

Electrocardiogram

Blood pressure test

Blood test for high cholesterol

Urine test for diabetes

Cervical smear test

Bone density scan

SELF-CHECKS

There are several checks you can make yourself to monitor your health. For example, excess weight at 55 is much more difficult to lose than at 35, so it's worth keeping a weekly check on your weight. If you put on too much weight, too quickly, you can take immediate steps to lose it over a period of a few weeks. This way you should never have more than a few kilograms or pounds to shed.

You can also assess what stage of the menopause you have reached by keeping a detailed diary of your menstrual periods (see page 20), physical symptoms, and mood changes. This information will lead to increased self-awareness and may help you to develop strategies, including taking HRT, to cope with menopausal symptoms (you should also examine your breasts at least once a month). To prevent tooth decay, you need to pay special attention to dental care – use dental floss (see page 216), replace your toothbrush regularly, and pay periodic visits to an oral hygienist for the removal of plaque.

BREAST SELF-EXAMINATION

It is important to examine your breasts once a month. If you are still menstruating, the best time is at the end of your period when your breasts are not swollen or tender. You can do a breast examination at any time of the month if you are postmenopausal.

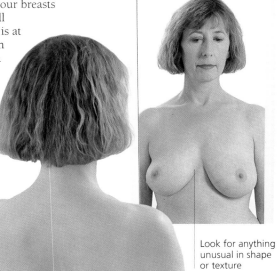

Pay special attention to swellings or lumps, a dimpled, puckered appearance, or a newly inverted nipple.

What To Look For

Stand naked in front of a mirror and observe your breasts carefully with your arms by your sides, then with them raised with your hands behind your head. Look for differences in the shape or texture of your breasts and nipples.

Look for anything unusual in shape or texture

How To Feel Your Breasts

Lie on your back with your head on a pillow and your shoulders slightly raised. Hold your fingers flat and examine each section of your breast using gentle circular movements.

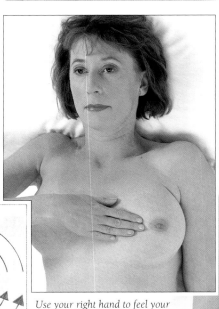

Use your right hand to feel your left breast and your left hand to feel your right breast. Keep the arm you are not using by your side.

Move your hand in a clockwise circular direction on the left breast and an anti-clockwise direction on the right breast.

Complete your examination by extending the arm you are not using behind your head and checking for lumps along the collar bone and in your armpits

MAMMOGRAPHY

This is a type of X-ray that shows up changes in the consistency of breast tissue, including cysts and tumours. Mammograms, known as "soft" X-rays, penetrate only a few centimetres, and are harmless. A radiologist uses them to locate any areas of increased density, possibly even calcification, which may indicate abnormalities or cancer.

HOW IS IT DONE?

To have a mammogram, you will need to be naked from the waist upwards and stand in different positions so that your breasts can be X-rayed from various angles. In order to photograph every angle, the breasts may sometimes have to be gently compressed between two X-ray plates; although you may find this uncomfortable, it is not painful.

Mammography is particularly reliable for the examination of large breasts, because accurate pictures are obtained and there is a high degree of contrast between normal and abnormal structures. A radiologist will be able to use a mammogram to discern extremely small cysts and tiny tumours, which you would not be able to feel or notice yourself during your monthly breast examination.

Mammograms are likely to be less revealing if you have had breast implants, as these can obscure the view of the breast tissue. Mammograms also tend to be less accurate on small-breasted women.

FREQUENCY OF PROCEDURE

It is recommended that women should have a mammogram every two years from the age of 45, or earlier if they have a family history of breast cancer.

Because mammography detects minute tumours before they have the chance to spread, it is the most important procedure for the early detection of breast cancer. Research data shows that close to 90 percent of breast cancers detected by mammography emerge in the first "baseline" reading. If your baseline reading is clear, it is less likely that any tumours will be found in subsequent mammograms. They will, however, show up any later changes.

RECOMMENDATIONS

If you have not had a mammogram performed in the last year, and you are planning to take HRT, your doctor may suggest you have one done before you start treatment. Every time you ask for your HRT prescription to be repeated, you can ask your doctor to perform a manual examination of your breasts in addition to the one you carry out yourself.

Since breast cancer is regarded by some doctors as a contraindication for HRT, if your mammogram reveals a lump you will probably be advised not to take HRT until the cause of the lump has been diagnosed. Alternatively, some gynaecologists will tailor the dose and route of administration of HRT to your individual needs, placing you at minimal risk.

DETECTION OF BREAST CANCER

Mammography is a specialized X-ray procedure that shows up cancerous changes in breast tissue. It is very effective in detecting abnormalities that are too small to be felt manually.

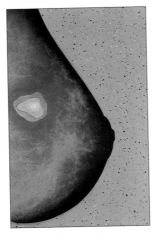

Tumour Deep In Breast
The yellow core in this colour-enhanced mammogram indicates a cancerous tumour deep in the tissue of the breast.

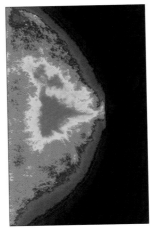

Tumour in Mammary Duct
The red area indicates a large malignant tumour in the mammary duct, probably containing dense fibrous tissue.

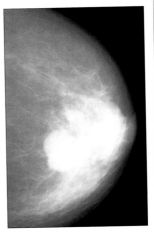

Calcified Tumour
The large irregular white area is a calcified cancerous tumour. Calcification is a typical feature of malignant tumours.

CERVICAL SMEAR TEST

Although cervical cancer is comparatively rare in postmenopausal women, the cervical smear test is so effective in the prevention of cervical cancer it is an important gynaecological test for women of all ages. Before cancer develops there is a precancerous stage that is symptomless and does not produce signs that are visible to the naked eye. However, there are cellular changes in the cervix and by taking a sample of cervical cells, staining them, and examining them under a microscope, doctors can identify abnormalities and decide upon treatment.

If abnormal cervical cells are discovered as the result of a smear test, they are classified as mild, moderate, or severe. In the first case, a repeat smear test will be recommended in three to six months' time, as sometimes abnormalities can simply disappear. If the cell changes are moderate or severe, a colposcopy, which allows your doctor to see a microscopic level of detail on your cervix, is likely to be recommended. Occasionally, women may be called back for a repeat smear – not because there are any abnormalities, but because the smear is "unreadable". This may be because there were blood or inflammatory cells present (you should not have a smear test while you are bleeding or if you have a gynaecological infection), or because the cells were collected from the wrong part of the cervix.

The area of the cervix that is affected by abnormal growth is called the transformation zone, and its exact location depends on the age of a woman. In postmenopausal women the transformation zone moves up into the cervical canal, making it less accessible during a smear test. This is remedied by the use of an endocervical brush, which can be gently inserted into the cervical canal.

A common reason for abnormal changes in the cervix is the genital wart or human papilloma virus (HPV). Some types of HPV can cause changes that show up in a smear test, but up to a third of these abnormalities can disappear spontaneously. For this reason, if you have a history of genital warts, you should make sure that you have a smear test annually. Other women should have a smear test every two or three years.

HOW IS IT DONE?
A smear test entails an internal examination in which a speculum is inserted into the vagina. The speculum holds open the vagina and allows your doctor to gain access to the cervix and note any abnormal changes. A thin layer of cells from the cervix and some mucus are collected. A smear test is carried out when you are lying down with your knees apart. Although you may feel a mild scraping sensation, the procedure should be painless.

RESULTS OF A CERVICAL SMEAR TEST
To help you understand the results of a smear test, this is a breakdown of the mild, moderate, or severe microscopic changes that can occur.

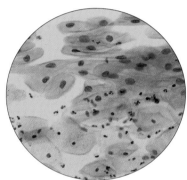

Mild Inflammatory Changes
Slightly abnormal cells have larger-than-normal nuclei. A repeat smear test will be recommended.

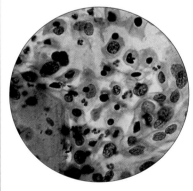

Moderate Abnormality
The nuclei are large and contain heavy clumps and strands. A repeat cervical smear test will be recommended as well as a colposcopy.

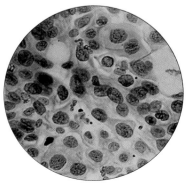

Severe Abnormality
Cells are smaller, and have very large nuclei containing coarse clumps and strands. You will need a colposcopy, and a biopsy to remove all of the abnormal cells.

COLPOSCOPY

If a smear test reveals any abnormal cells, this is a further non-invasive procedure that a specialist will use to decide on an appropriate treatment.

Using apparatus resembling a pair of binoculars on a stand, a microscopic level of detail can be seen on the surface of the cervix. Expert colposcopists can recognise chronic inflammation, infection, polyps, and areas of pre-invasive cancer.

If your colposcopist finds something that appears abnormal to the eye, he or she may recommend laser treatment, a cone biopsy, or loop excision.

CONE BIOPSY

This is performed if a colposcopy shows the presence of cancerous cells in the cervix, or if colposcopy is inconclusive. The latter is likely to be the case for women over 35, as less of their cervical tissue can be seen due to retraction caused by age.

Under general anaesthetic, a piece of the cervix in the shape of a cone is removed using a laser or scalpel. The base of the cone is on the outside of the cervix and the apex is deep in the cervical tissue. This cone is then finely dissected so that the exact extent of disease can be determined. The area will be stitched to reduce bleeding, although diathermy (electrical stimulation), or freezing is also effective.

LOOP EXCISION

This is the most recent procedure for removing abnormal cervical cells. The technique is very straightforward and involves the removal of tissue using a heated wire loop. Loop excision is advantageous in that it can be carried out in the outpatient department of a hospital without the need for a general anaesthetic. It also removes a smaller amount of tissue than a cone biopsy.

CARDIOVASCULAR TESTS

If you have no symptoms, you exercise several times a week, you are not overweight, and don't smoke, it's very unlikely that you have any cardiovascular disease, and occasional check-ups will be sufficient. Heart checks include listening to your heart, measuring your blood pressure, and possibly having an electrocardiogram (ECG), and a blood test. If you have raised blood pressure or high blood

TESTING YOUR BLOOD CHOLESTEROL LEVEL

High blood cholesterol can provide an early warning of heart disease and allow you to take preventive measures, such as modifying your diet. Simple home test kits are available that allow you to test a small sample of blood from your finger. If a home test reveals high blood cholesterol, you should seek medical advice.

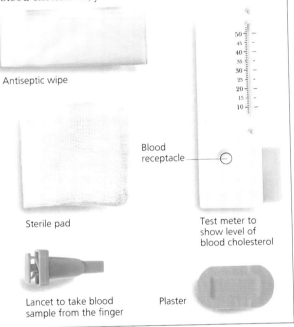

Antiseptic wipe

Blood receptacle

Sterile pad

Test meter to show level of blood cholesterol

Lancet to take blood sample from the finger

Plaster

cholesterol, a family history of heart disease, you are overweight, you smoke, or you rarely exercise, you should have annual heart check-ups from the age of 35. You should not need an ECG unless your doctor finds an abnormality.

HOW IS IT DONE?

An ECG provides an early warning of cardiovascular disease and can be carried out in a doctor's office, at home, or in a hospital. Electrodes connected to a recording machine are applied to your chest, wrists, and ankles. Electrical signals, which record the contractions of the heart muscle, are charted and displayed as a trace on a moving graph or a screen. To an expert, this tracing reveals detailed information about the health and functioning of your heart. Minute changes on the tracing reflect potentially dangerous changes in your heart function.

In conjunction with an ECG, you may be given an exercise tolerance test. You will be asked to perform a set exercise, such as walking on a motorized treadmill, and a reading will be taken that will record your heart's response to the additional strain.

BONE DENSITY SCANS

In the first few years after oestrogen secretion declines, many women go through a phase of rapid bone loss. Oestrogen is crucial in maintaining bone repair, a process called remodelling, and without sufficient oestrogen you lose more bone than you build up, resulting in fragile bones and osteoporosis. Within a few years of the menopause, the rate of bone loss slows down, but by that time, damage could be irreparable.

A bone density scan provides a window on your skeleton. It's based on the principle that X-rays cannot penetrate hard structures such as bone; the whiter your bone X-rays are, the more dense and healthy your bone. The darker the X-ray, the less dense your bones are, and the more brittle they are likely to be.

A bone density scan is useful both as a diagnostic tool – to reveal osteoporosis for the first time – and as a tool for monitoring progress after treatment for osteoporosis has begun. Experts suggest that one bone density measurement around the time of the menopause can predict your future risk of osteoporotic fractures. Women can be divided into two risk groups: those with low bone mass and high risk of future fracture, and those with high bone mass and low risk of fracture.

HOW IS IT DONE?

A bone density scan is a simple procedure that can be carried out in hospital X-ray departments, menopause clinics, well-woman clinics, and consultants' surgeries. Your bone density is assessed by a radiologist.

Dual energy X-ray absorptiometry (DEXA) is currently the most precise and widely used method of assessing bone density. In this non-invasive procedure, you lie on a table and a radiation beam is passed over you. The density of the spine and the femur (thigh bone) usually provide a good indication of bone health throughout the body. In a similar technique, called single photon absorptiometry, the bones in your wrist are measured. You place your arm between a beam of low-level radiation and a detector. Your X-rays will be rated on a specially devised scale, which correlates the appearance of bone X-rays with bone health.

RECOMMENDATIONS

In my opinion, all women with menopausal symptoms, but particularly those suffering from bone, muscle, back, and joint pain, should have a bone density scan performed. This is best done when your symptoms first start, but any time during the menopause is sufficient.

ASSESSING BONE DENSITY

In these colour-enhanced X-rays of the spine, decreased bone mass can be seen very clearly. Areas of orange show bone that is dense and healthy, areas of blue and green show bone that is weak and prone to fracture.

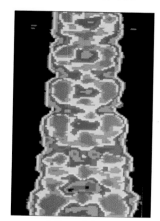

Normal Bone Mass
The orange and yellow colours indicate a normal lumbar spine, with bone that is healthy.

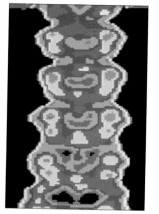

Below Normal Bone Mass
This is bone on the verge of osteoporosis. Any further weakening could lead to fracture.

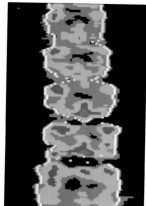

Osteoporotic Bone
The high proportion of blue and green areas indicates osteoporotic bone that will easily fracture.

HORMONE LEVEL TEST

Specialized hormone tests require laboratory equipment and are more likely to be carried out by gynaecologists than by GPs, although you may find that hospital departments adapt some procedures slightly.

Profound changes happen to your sex hormones at the menopause (and then again in your 70s and 80s). The two major oestrogen hormones, oestradiol and oestrone, plummet after the menopause, and oestradiol stays low for the rest of your life unless HRT is taken. Oestrone follows a slightly different pattern. During a woman's 50s, 60s, and 70s, levels decline, but after that oestrone begins to increase. Low levels of oestrone or oestradiol in midlife mean that the menopause is imminent. This shows up in a blood test as high levels of follicle stimulating hormone (FSH) and luteinizing hormone (LH).

If you go to see your doctor when you are symptomless, before the onset of the menopause, it's unlikely that you'll convince him or her of the need to carry out hormone tests. If, however, you have early symptoms of the menopause, like the occasional hot flush, back pain, or slight dryness of the vagina, it could be that you're on the rising part of the curve, and this could easily be confirmed by performing a blood test for FSH or LH.

RECOMMENDATIONS

I feel that information about hormone depletion is crucial for women who are approaching or going through the menopause. It gives you knowledge

Rising Hormone Levels

During the menopause, the levels of the hormones FSH and LH rise dramatically. If a blood test reveals high levels of these hormones, it is likely that your menopause is imminent.

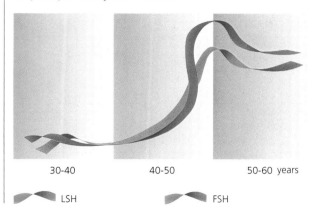

30-40	40-50	50-60 years

LSH   FSH

about what's going on internally, which can help you to understand the symptoms that you may be experiencing. It also means you can plan ways of dealing with the menopause. For example, you can argue your case for HRT if, having consulted the table on page 133, you feel you are a candidate for it and would benefit from it. If you have a family history of heart disease or brittle bones, low blood hormone levels of FSH and LH will support the case for your taking HRT before the onset of the menopause.

PROGESTOGEN CHALLENGE TEST

Women who are taking HRT, and who have not had their uterus surgically removed, may have a withdrawal bleed in each HRT cycle. This is provoked when they stop taking the hormone progestogen in each cycle of therapy. In the 1980s it was proposed that this effect of progestogen could be exploited as a screening test for endometrial cancer.

The theory behind the progestogen challenge test is that if you take hormones cyclically, with 12 days of progestogen each month, and don't experience a withdrawal bleed after three months, it will be safe to eliminate the progestogen for three months. In other words, if the uterine lining does not respond to progestogen with a menstrual flow, you can assume that it is not being overstimulated by the oestrogen you have been taking, and there is little risk of uterine cancer.

Although the theory behind the progestogen challenge test is correct, it has not been widely adopted among doctors prescribing HRT because uterine or endometrial cancer is rare. Some doctors who are using unopposed oestrogen therapy may carry out a progestogen challenge test annually, and will do an endometrial biopsy if bleeding occurs.

RECOMMENDATIONS

This test can be an important tool for women who experience progestogenic side-effects, such as depression, irritability, bloating, and weight gain, in that it provides a way of cutting down the number of times you expose your body to progestogen.

However, if you are very overweight you will have high oestrogen levels because you will be producing a lot of oestrogen from fat cells. Therefore, it is probably not a good idea to take unopposed oestrogen, not even in the progestogen challenge test.

UTERINE CURETTAGE

This procedure is used to determine the contents of the uterine cavity and is also referred to as a dilatation and curettage (D&C). It can diagnose the many causes of irregular or heavy bleeding, or bleeding after the menopause. For instance, menorrhagia can be caused by fibroids, endometriosis, or polyps. Curettage can also exclude uterine cancer and, sometimes, simply removing the endometrium can cure the bleeding.

A curettage may be performed under anaesthetic in a doctor's surgery or a hospital. A speculum is inserted into the vagina and the cervical canal is dilated using graduated metal rods. The next step is to introduce either a metal curette (a spoon-shaped instrument) or a plastic tube (catheter) into the uterus. The endometrium is removed using an up-and-down scraping motion or by suctioning out the tissue through the plastic catheter. A sample of the removed tissue is then analyzed under a microscope to determine the cause of bleeding.

Your doctor or gynaecologist can also perform a mini-curettage or endometrial biopsy in the surgery. This is a very quick, simple procedure in which a small sample of endometrium is removed using a fine suction curette. The cells are then examined microscopically to determine the cause of bleeding.

The Curette

This is a long, thin metal instrument with a spoon-shaped end. A curette is inserted into the uterine cavity after the cervix has been dilated. It is used to remove the uterine lining.

Fine Suction Curette

An endometrial biopsy can be carried out without anaesthetic using a fine suction curette. The inner tube is pulled down and a small sample of tissue is sucked into the outer tube.

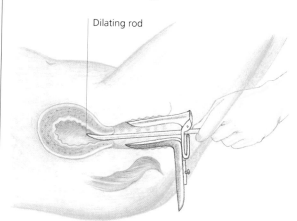

Dilating The Cervix
After an anaesthetic a speculum is inserted into the vagina to gain access to the cervix. The cervical canal is then stretched using a series of progressively bigger metal rods.

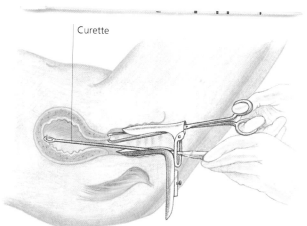

Scraping The Endometrium
The curette is inserted into the uterus to scrape the lining. A sample of endometrial tissue will be retained and examined under a microscope. A D&C can be curative as well as diagnostic.

THE BLEEDING DAY TEST

This test is a gauge of endometrial health and can determine if women taking progestogen as part of their HRT regime are getting a sufficient amount of this hormone. Progestogen is usually taken for 12 to 13 days of the month. If you count the first day of progestogen therapy as day one, and bleeding does not begin before you have taken the 11th tablet, then you're not at risk of endometrial disease because your endometrium isn't being overstimulated. However, if bleeding begins before the 11th day, you are not taking enough progestogen. You can delay the bleeding by increasing either the dose or the duration of the progestogen supplements. Dose control and methods of HRT are being improved all the time, and while no HRT regimen can guarantee against endometrial disease, this particular test can lower the risk dramatically.

BLOOD TEST FOR OVARIAN CANCER

Recent research has revealed that the presence of a hormone called inhibin may be a forewarning of ovarian cancer. Although research is still at an experimental stage, inhibin may soon be able to be identified with a simple blood test – which is a more straightforward and less traumatic procedure than a laparoscopy (inserting a tube through the adominal wall). Inhibin appears very early in the course of the disease – as much as 20 months before the actual cancer shows – making early diagnosis possible. This is a potentially great advance in the management of ovarian cancer, because tumours can grow quite large and spread before they cause symptoms. Cure rates are directly related to early diagnosis, so this test could increase survival rates significantly. Monitoring inhibin levels also reveals whether treatment is working, but this test is likely to be available at only a few specialized centres.

OTHER HORMONE TESTS

Both diabetes mellitus and hypothyroidism (underactive thyroid) result from hormone deficiency and are more common during and after the menopause.

Diabetes mellitus (see page 97) can be regulated by losing weight and taking medicines to lower blood glucose. To spot diabetes early, you should have your urine tested yearly, or immediately if you develop an itchy vulva or you start drinking or urinating excessively.

Two main symptoms of hypothyroidism are fatigue or depression. If either of these persist, ask your doctor for a thyroid test. You should have a simple blood test for thyroid function once a year after the age of 55, especially if you suddenly start to feel the cold and your hair begins to thin.

CANCER WARNING SIGNS

You should be familiar with the early potential warning signs of cancer. When you are 20 years old there is little likelihood that you will develop cancer by the age of 30. But your risk of developing cancer doubles between 30 to 40, and doubles again for each decade thereafter. A woman who dies in her late 80s may die of a condition that is unrelated to cancer, but a postmortem may reveal small cancers of the internal organs that

---

CANCER CHECKLIST

Coughing up bloody phlegm

Blood in the urine

Blood in the stools – either fresh and red, or black and tarry

A bloody discharge from the nipple

Vaginal bleeding or spotting beween periods, after the menopause, or after intercourse

Rapid weight loss without apparent cause

Any ulcer, sore or scab that fails to heal within a few weeks

A mole that enlarges, itches, becomes red, loses its original shape, or bleeds

Severe recurrent headaches

Sudden difficulty in swallowing

Sudden loss of the voice or persistent hoarseness

Persistent abdominal or pelvic pain

A sudden change in bowel habits

A lump in the breast or a change in breast shape

---

never caused symptoms. For example, the majority of elderly men have small localized cancers of the prostate gland.

If cancers are unchecked, they can grow bigger, and spread to other sites of the body to form secondary tumours. If any of the above persist beyond a week, they should be investigated by your doctor so that cancer can be eliminated. The earlier that cancers are detected, the better the chance of them being cured. Treatment for many cancers is very advanced and cure rates continue to improve.

EYE TESTS

In the postmenopause, women sometimes become clumsy and ill-coordinated, making falls and fractures more likely. For this reason, it is essential that your eyesight is checked periodically and that you have new glasses if necessary. As we get older, drainage of fluid from the inside of the eye can become restricted. This leads to a rise in pressure within the eye, which is a condition called glaucoma. Untreated glaucoma can lead to loss of sight and eventually blindness. It is recommended that women over the age of 40 should undergo a routine eye examination annually. This should include a visual field test, measurement of eye pressure, and an examination of the back of the eye.

10
BEYOND THE MENOPAUSE

Now that women are expected to survive into their 80s, we live a substantial portion – in some cases half – of our lives after the menopause. This means that it is crucial to develop positive strategies to deal with ageing. Fortunately, with the right attitudes and a combination of body care, exercise, and diet we can continue to live productive lives indefinitely.

POSTMENOPAUSAL LIFE

Technically, the term "postmenopause" refers to the years between your last menstrual period and the end of your life. Although you may experience classic menopausal symptoms, such as hot flushes and night sweats, for months or even years after your last period, your body will finally adjust to its lowered oestrogen levels and settle into a new and consistent hormonal rhythm. The physical changes that you notice from now on will be related to a long-term deficit of oestrogen and to the natural ageing process, and the majority of them are under your control.

CHANGING FOR THE BETTER

As you grow older, you may go through a period of major reassessment. You may have a nagging feeling about something in your life you would like to change, but, consciously or subconsciously, you have deferred making changes because the time was never right. You may be dissatisfied with your job situation. You may feel that you don't spend enough time doing the things that you want to do. Your marriage may feel claustrophobic, and you may want to make some changes in your relationship, or even arrange some time away from your partner. If any of the above apply to you, confront your feelings and try to be honest with yourself. Talk over your thoughts with your partner, with friends, or perhaps even with a counsellor. If you let people know what you are looking for – whether it be a job or a new friendship – communicating your thoughts may open the door to new opportunities.

COMMIT YOURSELF TO ACTION

Once you've made up your mind about what you want to change and how to go about it, you must take the leap and commit yourself. This doesn't have to mean walking out of your job or filing for divorce, it just means taking a step in the right direction, whether it be registering with an employment agency or spending more leisure time away from your partner.

Try to avoid thinking of yourself as selfish – others close to you, such as your partner, can benefit from any changes that you decide to make. For instance, if you have spent most of your life at home bringing up a family, a new part-time job or a course could increase your sense of independence and make you feel more fulfilled, and this can have a positive effect on your relationship. You may have always wanted to follow a career and, as your husband approaches retirement, you could suggest swapping roles. Alternatively, you may be looking forward to a restful retirement.

Remember, you have already made many decisions and experienced many changes in your life and you're well equipped to cope with new experiences. Think of retirement as a period of self-renewal and it shouldn't be the crushing change that people often perceive it to be.

When asked what they miss most about working life, many people mention money and the social environment of work. However, there are very many advantages to retiring: you can follow your own body clock – eating, sleeping, and studying when you feel like it; you no longer have to comply with authority; you have more time to spend on your family, friends, and hobbies; and being out of the rat race can dramatically reduce your stress levels.

Pre-retirement
- Other people can dictate your life.
- Your life is structured around work.
- Your leisure time is limited.
- Your tax burdens may be heavy.
- You worry about getting ahead.

Post-retirement
- You can live life as you please.
- You can set your own pace.
- You can choose your own friends.
- You have fewer expectations.
- You have time to be with your family.

PREPARING TO GIVE UP WORK

People usually start to prepare for retirement when they are in their 50s. You may start to reduce your job workload, seek financial advice, or you may even decide to move to a smaller house. On a personal level, you may start to place more emphasis on your personal relationships.

Whereas some people find retirement a natural transition, others, particularly women who have had fulfilling careers, may find it harder. We must prepare for this time because there may be little space for adjustment if we don't.

Retirement preparation is now a widely recognized need. Many firms, voluntary organizations, and adult education centres give advice or run courses about financial planning, buying and dispersing personal property and assets, attending to health needs, and organizing leisure time.

FINANCIAL PLANNING

It is worth taking the best advice you can to make your money work for you during your retirement years. Several years before you retire, you should be thinking about investments, insurance, mortgages, and a will. An accountant or a bank manager will be happy to give you advice. Try to work out a comprehensive budget based on what your income will be after you leave work.

As a practice run, it is a good idea to start living on your projected retirement income about six months before you or your partner retire. If you ease into retirement this way, before you are under the strain of other changes that go with retirement, financial adjustments will be easier to cope with. You will also have saved up the money that you didn't use in the previous six months, which will give you a nest egg and a sense of security.

ORGANIZING YOUR TIME

If your partner retires and you carry on working, or vice versa, you will find that your days are suddenly out of sync. Instead of both getting up early in the morning and going to bed at the same time, one of you will be tired while the other is still raring to go. If this becomes a problem, talk about it and find a solution that works for you both. Make a point of doing things together at weekends when your body clocks become synchronized again.

If you find yourself at home with time on your hands and you feel at a loss, you are probably having problems making the emotional transition to retirement. Your partner may be able to help by adapting his routine slightly. Discuss a rota for the chores. Make a list of friends and relatives who are free at certain times during the week (perhaps people whom you haven't seen for several years), and share your interests with these people. Think up new projects and revive old hobbies. If you have lots of spare time, spend some of it pampering yourself. Sleep in late, meet a friend for lunch, read in the afternoon, and put your feet up whenever you feel like it.

Retirement doesn't mean that you have to devote yourself to domestic tasks. Adjustments need to be made, and a benefit of retirement is that you can put off chores and do them when you feel like it.

If your partner is retired and you are still working, try to be sensitive to his moods. While you may envy the amount of leisure time he has, he may envy the fact that you still have an income and are part of a working environment. How your partner adjusts to a slower pace of life will have a crucial effect on how you adapt. If he has had a high-powered job for the last 30 years, he may find it hard to reduce his commitments. Taking courses to prepare for retirement will enable more men to enjoy their retirement years.

Working fewer days in the week or less hours each day, taking longer holidays, or working from home are just a few ways in which you can make the move from paid work to retirement. If retirement could be less of a cut-off point and more of a transition, this might help to improve emotional stability and lessen the social stigma of retirement.

The loss of relationships at work following retirement, the departure of your children, or even the death of your partner, all mean that you may become more reliant on your friends and the younger members of your family. Friendships are important and likely to become more so as you grow older.

YOUR CHANGING BODY

Society often equates older age with ill health or disease, believing that fitness is not compatible with an ageing body. This is another example of negative stereotypes. Provided that we take care of ourselves, we can remain fit well into old age. Ageing should not be synonymous with disease: we don't necessarily become ill as we grow older; it is only certain bodily functions that are less efficient. Many changes can be accommodated if we are able to anticipate them.

TISSUE REPAIR

When we are injured or infected, body cells take action to repair or replace the damage. The healthy cells take over by becoming bigger or by producing replicas of the lost cells. However, this function slows down as we get older, with the result that cuts and broken bones take a longer time to heal.

Some cells, such as brain and nerve cells, do not have this self-repair mechanism, and when they are destroyed, they are never replaced. This explains why memory loss is such a common aspect of ageing.

BONES AND MUSCLES

One of the classic signs of ageing in women is a decrease in bone density, which, in its most severe form, leads to osteoporosis (see page 66). This causes compression of the bones in the spinal column, resulting in back pain, and eventually a spinal curvature (see page 70). Water is lost from the discs of cartilage between the spinal vertebrae and the sufferer begins to lose height. Weakened bones may fracture under only slight stress.

Like brain cells, muscle cells do not reproduce themselves and so, as we age, they decrease in number. This can be compensated for if the size and power of the remaining muscle cells are increased by exercise. Body composition also changes with age, so that there is more fat in relation to muscle and lean body mass. A well-balanced diet and regular exercise is essential after the age of 50.

SKIN AND BLOOD VESSELS

Ageing causes the skin to become thinner and appear more transparent. Small blood vessels are not so well supported and rupture more easily. Even minor knocks can cause bruising, and a severe fall can cause bleeding into deeper tissues. If large amounts of blood are lost from the circulatory system, we may go into shock or collapse. It can sometimes take weeks or even months for blood levels to become normal again or for blood to be re-absorbed from the tissues back into the general circulation. This is why an injured elderly person can feel very tired and take a long time to recover. If we don't allow for this, the recovery period can be frustrating, depressing, and it may make us anxious.

Gradual changes to connective tissue are most easily seen on the backs of the hands, but are widespread throughout the body. Connective tissue becomes stiffer and loses its elasticity, resulting in conditions such as arthritis, hardening of the arteries, reduced lung capacity, and loss of skin tone.

BALANCE AND POSTURE

As we get older, we may find it harder to maintain an upright posture. Posture is maintained by the contraction of opposing muscle groups, and if we lose our balance we compensate immediately and subconsciously through a sensory mechanism built into the skin, muscles, joints, and even bones. This mechanism is called proprioception. As soon as proprioceptors in the nervous system sense that our centre of gravity is altered, our position is corrected by opposing muscle groups. Posture is maintained against a background of swaying motion, and due to the slowing down of nerve conduction as we age, the sway increases and we can easily lose our balance if we are bumped or knocked. Moreover, if we stumble, we are more likely to fall.

BLOOD PRESSURE

Other self-regulating mechanisms are lost as we age, such as the maintenance of blood pressure during changes in posture. This may result in giddiness, and a tendency to lose our balance when we have to get up suddenly, especially from a horizontal position. Such symptoms are caused by gravity pulling blood to the lower part of the body and depriving the brain of an adequate supply. This doesn't happen when we are younger because corrective reflexes throughout the body immediately increase the heart's output, causing more blood to go to the brain. Loss of elasticity in the blood vessels also means that it is harder for oxygen to reach the tissues, and this increases the workload of the heart.

LUNGS

Cells in the lungs may be affected by age or disease. There is a decrease in the surface area of the air sacs in the lungs, so that gaseous exchange is less efficient. This accounts for the breathlessness that you may experience on exertion. Exercise can play an important part in combating this problem – medically supervised exercise can improve the efficiency of your lungs.

KIDNEYS

These organs are affected by the deterioration of the circulatory system. The rate at which blood is filtered slows down and valuable minerals are reabsorbed more slowly. Worn-out kidney cells are not replaced, but there are ample resources in just one healthy kidney.

EYESIGHT

We become much more prone to sensory deterioration as we age. Certain parts of our eyes, such as the lens and the cornea, begin to wear out and change shape slightly. In fact, this is such a normal part of the ageing process that it's possible for specialists to estimate a person's age quite accurately by looking at the back of the eye with an ophthalmoscope.

THE AGEING SENSES

As we grow older we may notice that our senses, to varying degrees, become impaired. However, we should not assume that deteriorating eyesight or hearing are the inevitable consequences of ageing. For instance, problems with eyesight may be the result of an underlying condition such as diabetes, which can cause damage to the retina. Conditions such as glaucoma also become more common with age. Any sudden or severe changes should be reported to your doctor.

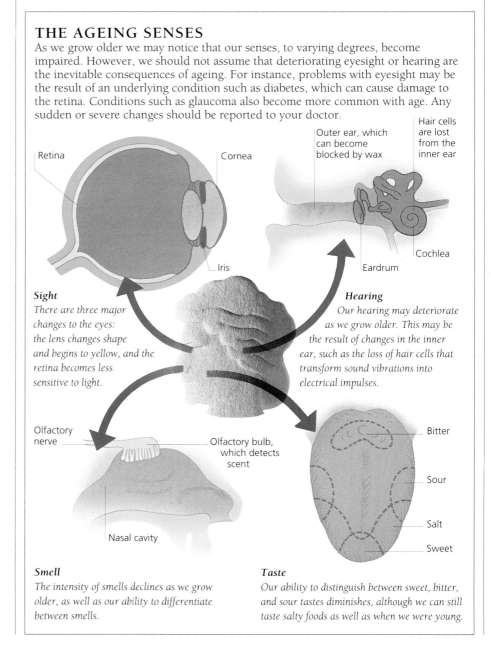

Sight
There are three major
changes to the eyes:
the lens changes shape
and begins to yellow, and the
retina becomes less
sensitive to light.

Hearing
Our hearing may deteriorate
as we grow older. This may be
the result of changes in the inner
ear, such as the loss of hair cells that
transform sound vibrations into
electrical impulses.

Smell
The intensity of smells declines as we grow
older, as well as our ability to differentiate
between smells.

Taste
Our ability to distinguish between sweet, bitter,
and sour tastes diminishes, although we can still
taste salty foods as well as when we were young.

When the lens changes shape the ability to focus images on the retina is reduced, a deficiency that can be easily corrected with glasses. If you notice your vision deteriorating, you should have your eyes tested as soon as you can.

The cells of the retina also become less sensitive to light as we age, and it can become more difficult to read or see when light levels are low. On average, an 85-year-old woman needs about eight times as much light as a young person in order to see as well. This is why rooms, stairs, and steps need to be very well illuminated.

HEARING

Our sense of hearing becomes less acute as we age, and a carefully prescribed hearing aid can make a big difference to your ability to cope. If you have an impairment at a comparatively early age it is easier to adapt to a hearing aid when you can still discriminate between different sounds and pitches, than to wait until your deafness has become more acute. When you are older, it will be harder to adjust to the device. Since neither hearing nor sight remain static, you should have both checked regularly.

TASTE AND SMELL

Our sense of smell nearly always diminishes with age, and because smell accounts for at least half of taste, this explains why foods may seem to lose their flavour as we get older. We may find we need more and more salt or added herbs and spices in order to give food flavour and character.

STRESS AND BODY FUNCTION

The effects of ageing are always more apparent when the body is stressed than when it is at rest. Stress can be psychological or it can be physical. For example, the digestive system may be perfectly efficient until it is physically stressed by a high intake of sugar.

Changes in our hormone system are also more common under stress. The thyroid gland in the neck, for example, controls the body metabolism and is less efficient if we are stressed.

THE BRAIN AND MIND

Because brain cells do not reproduce themselves, their function and number decrease as we grow older. The result of this is most apparent when it comes to memory, particularly when committing new experiences to memory. Elderly people find it easier to remember the distant past than the recent past (which may explain the stereotype of old people living in the past). The number of brain cells we lose, however, is miniscule in proportion to the number that remain – a more significant cause of declining mental function is likely to be oxygen deficiency due to the stiffening of bones, cartilage, and muscle.

Opinions and attitudes can also become more rigid, so that the acceptance of new ideas or information can become progressively more difficult. However, as long as mental skills are exercised continuously, they should not decline to any significant degree. It is, however, not so easy to master complex new skills.

Although intellectual deterioration is considered to be a result of ageing, it is actually a physical process that begins around the age of 16. For most of our adult lives, we do not notice any deterioration, mainly because we gain new experiences and knowledge, which compensate. This is why an alert mind and a willingness to embrace new ideas, opinions, and situations will keep us mentally healthy. Just as an unused muscle wastes away, so does an unused mind. It is important to keep thinking and planning for yourself. Age itself should not bring any marked intellectual decline.

POSTMENOPAUSAL RELATIONSHIPS

Retirement can sometimes put a strain on marriages. Couples who can live together quite happily in the evenings and at weekends find that it can be hard to talk to and tolerate each other all the time. You might encounter problems that you never anticipated. Your partner might compensate for his loss of power and prestige at work by demanding excessive attention, and you might respond by nagging. Alternatively, a man and a woman who are wrapped up in work and children respectively may find that when he leaves his job and the children leave home, they have fewer things in common than they imagined. The following suggestions may help alleviate stressful situations.

- Plan separate, as well as joint, activities.
- Try to arrange your home so that you both have a place to escape to, for instance, a television room and a study room.
- Respect each other's friends, conversations, and routines.
- Develop a common interest, such as a shared hobby, a small business venture, or an evening class.
- Keep talking to each other. Your partner can be your closest friend.
- Maintain a wide circle of friends; you'll need to plan not only for today, but for the future, when one of you may be alone.
- Plan your finances together.

If a marriage has never been good and problems have never been resolved, the situation will be dramatically intensified when two people are thrown together for the greater part of every day. Emotional strain at this time can be great – but it is preventable if you tackle problems early on.

A full life includes physical love. The capacity to respond to your partner sexually need not decline as quickly nor as completely as fertility. If the frequency with which you and your partner make love declines, try to examine the reasons why. Some people believe that sex is dirty, indecent, or at the very least, aesthetically undesirable for older people. Sexuality in old age can be a taboo subject and often meets with strong disapproval. This attitude may spring from the belief that sex for enjoyment is wrong – carnal pleasure has long been the subject of religious strictures. These days, however, intercourse takes place more for pleasure than for procreation. We know from many recent surveys that people in their 70s and beyond need and, indeed have, active sex lives. Sadly this is often kept secret. We must realise that, as we age, we still have the capacity for physical love as much as we did 20 or 30 years before, and this is the ideal time to cast aside taboos and inhibitions.

Many older couples find that sex is better in the morning, when they are refreshed, than in the evening, when they are more likely to be fatigued. In fact, a man's highest sexual hormone level occurs between four o'clock in the morning and noon, and his lowest around eight o'clock at night.

Masturbation should be actively encouraged, particularly for single women and women whose partners are infirm. No matter how frequently it is practised, masturbation has no harmful effects (see page 188).

DIVORCE

Marriage break-up gets harder as people get older. In the aftermath of divorce, many women feel that they are too old to be attractive, and fear that no one will desire them again. Some dislike going alone to social events after years of being accompanied by a partner. Some women are bitter because they are left alone after 20 or more years of marriage.

Financially, women may be very dependent on maintenance payments, particularly if they haven't been trained for a job, or feel they are too old to begin a career. Some women can feel very short-changed, both financially and emotionally, after many years of bringing up a family and helping a husband achieve success in his career.

However, bitterness and pessimism can end up making women believe that divorce is the end of their lives. But having lived through the despair, pain, self-pity, and even self-hatred, many of us find that life improves after divorce. Some women get their first full-time job, some feel self-confident enough to go out with other men. Some women even enjoy sex for the first time after leaving a claustrophobic marriage: they have mistakenly believed that they have a low sex drive, and then feel reborn after divorce when they find a fulfilling relationship with a new, more sympathetic partner.

If you go through a divorce in midlife, try to remember that there are many years ahead in which to enjoy yourself. If you are postmenopausal you don't need to worry about getting pregnant, and if you have children, they are likely to be growing up and able to take care of themselves. Your biggest concern should be how best to maximize the potential of the years ahead.

SINGLE LIFE

If you are on your own, you have a variety of lifestyles open to you. You can live alone, sublet a room of your house, rent a flat and let your home to tenants, buy a bigger house and rent out rooms to other singles. You could even set up a commune; some 60-year-olds in Florida have gathered together and live in four homes as families, paying a younger couple to manage the homes and do the domestic work.

CHANGES IN FAMILY ROLES

The structure of the family is constantly changing. For many of us, the time when we really need stability and continuity may be the very time when we have to cope with a major upheaval in the family, such as divorce, remarriage, and new relations with various children and children-in-law. We may have to face changing relationships with former sons- and daughters-in-law of whom we are very fond. As we get older, we may have to decide with whom or near to whom we are going to live.

The extended families that can arise from divorce and remarriage may include children and young adults who have grown up with the idea that their parents are fixed points in the universe. Suddenly they may acquire new grandparents. Similarly, grandparents may find themselves with new grandchildren. At first, this may be difficult to deal with, but, as with many other aspects of changing family patterns, people often overcome these difficulties through love and generosity. Newly formed family ties can be just as strong, and sometimes stronger than the old.

CARING FOR ELDERLY PARENTS

Although family relationships have changed radically in the last century, one thing that has remained fairly consistent is the way in which younger members of a family assume responsibility for older members. There is no doubt that this can place severe emotional, physical, and economic stress on us. The mobility of today's society means that the family is not always gathered in one place. Even a few minutes travelling time can make support difficult, especially if we have other commitments, such as work.

Sometimes the combined responsibilities of looking after a home, a husband, and aged parents, as well as dealing with postmenopausal symptoms, can seem overwhelming. Try to delegate as much as you can. Enlist the help of your partner, your children, and your siblings. If you have a very old or infirm parent, you and your family may have to take the decision to house him or her in sheltered accommodation. No family should feel guilty about doing this – it's a highly responsible option, ensuring that your parent is well cared for.

THE MOTHER/DAUGHTER SYNDROME

There are several documented scenarios in which the interaction between different family members can cause friction and anxiety. The mother-daughter syndrome is one example.

A daughter grows up with her mother, adores her, and is dependent on her. As the mother grows older, however, the relationship becomes strained due to a gradual reverse in status. The daughter may reluctantly assume command and tensions arise as a result of the daughter taking responsibility.

THE FALLEN DICTATOR

It is usually a father or husband who falls into this role. He would be described as powerful, domineering, good at his job, respected at work, but overbearing, and tyrannical at home. As such a man gets older, ill health, and loss of income and status at work can undermine the basis of his power. He then attempts to exert authority inappropriately, often causing a crisis and even rejection by the rest of the family.

THE "IDEAL" HUSBAND

This is the opposite scenario to the fallen dictator – a man who has always been egalitarian becomes manipulative in midlife. This man has always been a model husband – constantly helping in the house and sharing financial control with his wife. He takes great pleasure in doing what his wife and children request. When he is older he becomes an invaluable family member, but then as his health begins to fail, the way he conducts himself changes. For the first time, every minor illness demands the attention of the whole family. When he gets better, he will have learned that he has the power to be the centre of attention, and to direct people's feelings. He may not be willing to return to his former "humble" position in the family.

Although these three scenarios do not apply to everyone, they do illustrate the changes and upheavals that can occur during middle and later life when we give up work, face changes in status, and come to rely more upon our partners and families. If we allow ourselves time to adapt, and make an effort to communicate honestly with the people close to us, then such problems do not have to be inevitable.

BECOMING A GRANDPARENT

One of the joys that many people have in store for them in midlife is becoming a grandparent. Once past childbearing age, many women begin to look forward to their second chance at mothering and find that few experiences compare with spending time, learning from, and teaching their grandchildren. In my opinion, grandparents are an important part of the family in that they can teach a child how to relate to older people. Grandparents, by virtue of their age, may be more philosophical, tolerant, and sympathetic than parents. Long practice means they have learned the knack of handling children with ease. These qualities enable children to develop in a relaxed, familiar environment.

It's sometimes said that grandparents spoil their grandchildren. This must be a misuse of the word "spoil". If spoiling a child means giving explanations instead of dismissals, suggesting alternatives instead of negatives, and helping instead of ignoring, then grandparents do indeed spoil children. As a grandparent you are in a position to share your passions with your grandchildren, whether they be gardening, sewing, sketching, or swimming. As grandchildren grow up, you can be a valuable confidante to them. You, of all people, are best-equipped to teach them how to cope with change, having lived through some of the most drastic changes the world has known. You have a valuable historical perspective on employment, politics, and social change. Recount your past experiences and encourage them to ask you questions.

You can provide a positive role model of middle and old age for your family. You can be independent. You can also listen. Parents don't always have a lot of time for this, but you are in a position to listen to family members without giving advice. You can tell your family about your own experience and what it has led you to believe.

You may find that you have much more in common with teenage grandchildren than you had imagined. At opposite ends of life, you are both likely to be experiencing changing identities and both asking the same questions: Who am I? What do I really want? How do I get it? Very often adolescents can have more in common with grandparents than they do with parents, who are often too busy to be self-aware and introspective. Grandparents can give a unique kind of loving and caring, and grandchildren relish knowing that they hold a special place in their grandparents' lives.

Mothers
- May have to juggle home life with a job or career.
- Concerned with organizing the day-to-day practicalities of life.
- Have continual day-to-day contact with their children in the context of a normal homelife.
- In the case of first children, may be anxious or inexperienced about childrearing.
- May be influenced by current trends and attitudes about childrearing.
- May have little time for seeing friends and going out.

Grandmothers
- Have free time to spend talking and listening to grandchildren.
- Can spend time on activities that are fun, rather than routine.
- May live apart from grandchildren enabling the children to feel they have a second home.
- Can provide personal information to daughters or daughters-in-law from their own experience.
- Can have an overview about general child care.
- Can create more time for mothers by taking care of children.

LOOKING AFTER YOURSELF

There are three factors that influence our health and fitness. The first of these is heredity, the second is our environment, and the third is our own personal behaviour. To neglect exercise and diet is to reduce your chances of longevity. By incorporating exercise into your life, you promote heart and lung health, and muscle stamina. Other benefits include sounder sleep, freedom from headaches, appetite suppression, and reduced blood cholesterol. By eliminating habits such as smoking, you can reduce the likelihood of serious disease.

The two basics of body maintenance after the age of 50 are diet and exercise. You should eat fresh food, with the emphasis on fruit and vegetables, pulses, wholegrains, and cereals. Cut down on dairy products; drink skimmed or semi-skimmed milk, and eat fish at least twice a week, poultry when you like, and red meat no more than once a week. As you get older and your sense of taste becomes blunted, stimulate your appetite with an apéritif or a glass of wine.

Although it may be tempting to eat snacks and convenience foods, try to make the effort to cook nutritious meals for yourself. Plan menus in advance, and if you can, cook in bulk and freeze the surplus. If you have a disability that makes cooking difficult, such as osteoarthritis of the hands, seek advice from organizations such as the Disabled Living Foundation, and invest in specially designed cooking aids.

WALKING

Like other good habits, exercise should be undertaken regularly and be a lifelong habit. As W.C. Fields said, "If I knew I was going to last this long, I'd have taken better care of myself". Don't fall into the trap of taking less and less care of yourself, otherwise your muscles will get slacker, and your heart and lungs will be less able to deal with exertion.

Doing a reasonable amount of walking – 20 or 30 minutes or so each day – is a good habit to develop, and you can build this up over a period of months. This kind of routine becomes important after retirement, when most people use up less energy but carry on eating and drinking the same amount.

Tips For Walking

- Do some gentle flexibility exercises before you go out (see page 160).
- Begin by walking on level ground and progress to hill-walking as you become fitter.
  - Don't get too out of breath to talk.
  - Never push yourself further than you feel you can comfortably go.

Walking

Going for a brisk three mile walk every day will maintain your physical stamina and cardiovascular fitness.

- Try to increase the distance or the time you spend walking, rather than the speed at which you walk.
- Don't walk into the wind as this will require more effort. If you suffer from heart disease, you should be able to walk quite comfortably for one or two miles in calm weather, but walking into the wind may cause angina.
- Aim to walk for three miles in about 40–55 minutes, without stopping.

TAKING CARE OF YOUR BODY

There are various simple measures that you can adopt to improve the health of different parts of your body. There are also some day-to-day health hazards, such as intense sun and prolonged loud noise that should be avoided, in order to keep yourself in good condition.

Looking After Your Skin As you grow older, the activity of the oil and sweat glands declines, causing your skin to become dry, wrinkled, and itchy. Skin loses its former elasticity and tone, and liver spots, skin tags, and moles may appear. However, age doesn't cause the most deterioration in appearance – the biggest culprits are sunlight and weather. You can help to preserve your skin by staying out of the sun, and wearing a sunblock on exposed areas such as your face and the backs of your hands. Even small periods of exposure to the sun can make your skin leathery. The sun is also the prime cause of skin cancer, such as malignant melanoma.

Don't wash your skin too often, and try to avoid harsh soaps or detergents that strip the skin of oil and make it dry. Stop bathing daily; once every other day is enough, and when you do bathe, use bath oil. Replace lost oils with emollient creams and use soothing lotions that you can use on any part of the body that feels dry or itchy. Use a handcream containing silicone on your feet.

Looking After Your Eyes If you suffer from eye problems, it is worth consulting an ophthalmologist. An ophthalmologist is a doctor who is not only qualified to test your eyes and prescribe glasses, but can also treat and operate on your eyes. An optician can examine your eyes and fit glasses, but will not be able to treat underlying problems.

Keep eye trouble to a minimum by keeping your hands, towels, and flannels clean, so that you don't carry germs to the eyes. Sleep and rest is important, and you should limit the amount of close work you do to prevent eye strain. Rest your eyes periodically by focusing on a distant object. When reading, make sure that you have a lamp of at least 100 watts, slightly to the back and to one side of you, with the light angled to avoid glare.

Looking After Your Hearing We usually lose our sensitivity to certain sound waves as we age, and it can be extremely difficult to follow conversations where there is a lot of background noise. Disease, drugs, blows, and falls may damage the auditory nerve, in which case deafness may be irreversible.

You should never put anything into your external ear canal, not even to remove wax. Even cotton buds impact the wax and push it deep into the ear canal, and only syringing will be able remove it.

Try to avoid noise. Anything over 90 decibels, such as pneumatic drills, jet aircraft, and rock music can have a detrimental effect on your hearing. If people always seem to be mumbling, have your hearing checked.

Skin Care
Ageing skin is prone to dryness and wrinkling – moisturizers and sunscreens will help to protect it.

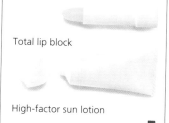
Total lip block

High-factor sun lotion

Lip salve

Body lotion

Emollient cream

Silicone-based handcream

Moisturizing soap

Good Posture
Stand with your feet apart and parallel, and your spine straight. Avoid tipping your pelvis forwards or backwards, or resting your weight on one leg.

Keep your spine straight and your hips aligned

Take the weight on your thigh muscles, not your back

Lifting Heavy Weights
Instead of bending down at the waist, bend at the knees, keeping your spine and neck straight.

Looking After Your Back Exercise, especially swimming and walking, is the best way of protecting your back. There are also specific exercises designed to strengthen the muscles in your back.

- Lie on your back on the floor, squeeze your buttocks together, and tighten the abdominal muscles. Now flatten your back against the floor. Hold this position for a few seconds, relax, and repeat.
- Lie on your back on the floor, bend your knees up, and then drop them – aim to touch the floor on either side of you with each knee. Try to keep your back in contact with the floor.

Be very careful how you lift heavy objects. Try to take the weight on your thigh muscles rather than your back muscles. Place your feet close to the base of the object, bend your knees, grasp the object, and then push up with your legs, keeping your spine straight. Keep the object close to your body – the further away the object, the greater the strain on your back.

When you are getting out of a chair or bed, use your arms to lift yourself. Choose a straight-backed chair in preference to an easy chair, to keep your back erect. Reclining chairs that keep your legs propped up also help. Try not to sit with your legs crossed and don't sit in one position for too long, and when you're on a long plane or train ride, get up every half-an-hour or so to stretch and take the pressure off your back. The most relaxing position for your back is lying flat on your back with your knees bent.

Good posture will also keep your back healthy, so make an effort to walk with your feet parallel and your head, chest, pelvis, and feet aligned. Lead with your thigh rather than your foot. Good posture when you're standing involves holding your shoulders firmly, but not rigidly, backwards, with your head up and your stomach pulled in. If you find it difficult at first, imagine that you are balancing a book on your head. After a while, it will become a habit. You should look relaxed rather than rigid.

Looking After Your Feet Your feet are the part of your body furthest from your heart, and therefore the most poorly nourished. Diseases such as arthritis and diabetes often show up in the feet first because their nourishment is compromised and fluid tends to pool there. Untreated foot problems can result in tension headaches, fatigue from muscle over-compensation, and lower back and shoulder pain. Warning signs of serious foot disorders include cramp in the calf muscles, pain in the arches and toes, and unusually cold feet, particularly if the skin has a bluish tinge. Brittle or thickened toenails, burning, tingling, or numbness may also signal circulatory disease or illness. Diabetes may first manifest itself as a foot ulcer; arthritis can cause swollen, tender, and red joints of the foot. Heart, liver, and kidney disease may cause swelling of the feet and ankles.

Older people need to pay careful attention to footwear. The best shoes have a broad base across the instep, a moderately low heel, and should extend about two centimetres (one half to three-quarters of an inch) beyond the longest toes. Don't buy shoes in the morning – feet swell during the day and shoes that fit in the morning may be too tight to wear at night.

FIVE-STEP PEDICURE

You can ensure that your feet stay healthy by paying regular attention to them at home and following the steps in this simple pedicure. You should also visit a chiropodist periodically.

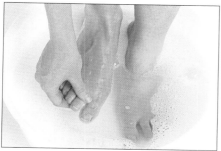

Soak The Feet

Wash the feet using warm water and liquid footbath. You can also add essential oil to a footbath (see page 109).

Trim The Toenails

Using a pair of toenail clippers, cut the nails straight across. Don't try to shape them at the sides, since this can cause ingrowing toenails.

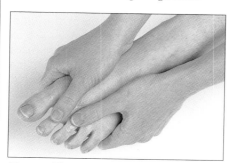

Massage The Feet

Apply a moisturizing or refreshing foot gel all over the feet to invigorate the skin, and to prevent the formation of hard skin.

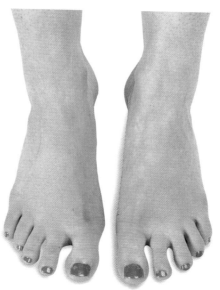

Prevent foot problems with a regular pedicure

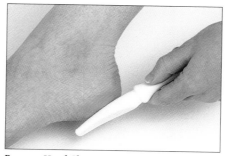

Remove Hard Skin

Using a pumice stone or hard skin remover, gently rub areas of the feet, such as the heels, which are prone to hard skin.

Paint The Toenails

As an optional finishing touch, use a toe separator while applying two coats of nail polish and one coat of nail hardener.

Foot Care

When collagen levels decline after the menopause the toenails may become thick or brittle, and need special care. You should avoid the build up of hard skin on the feet.

Nail varnish

Nail strengthener

Toe separator

Hard skin remover

Emery boards

Nail clippers

Liquid footbath

Dental Hygiene
Gum recession as we age means that we should take good care of our teeth. Disclosing tablets and dental floss help get rid of plaque.

Antibacterial mouthwash   Toothpicks

Electric plaque remover

Electric toothbrush

Straight-handled toothbrush

Angled toothbrush

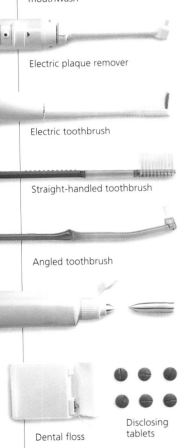

Dental floss   Disclosing tablets

You can help prevent foot problems by giving yourself a pedicure once a month. After bathing your feet, dry them thoroughly and massage them with silicone hand cream, and use medicated powder for fungus infections, such as athlete's foot. Trim your toenails straight across, and never too short. Keep your feet warm and dry, and in the winter wear woollen socks and fur-lined boots if your feet get cold. You should also see a chiropodist once every few months.

Looking After Your Teeth Periodontal disease (disease of the gums) becomes particularly prevalent in postmenopausal women, and can extend to the bones of the jaw and the tooth socket. Gums start to recede, which exposes the sensitive dentine of the teeth below the protective enamel, and eating sweet, hot, or cold foods can become painful. Gum recession can also cause teeth to become loose in their sockets.

MAINTAINING DENTAL HEALTH

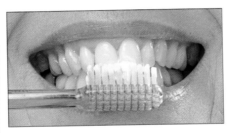

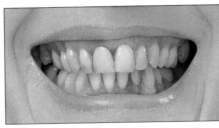

Brushing And Disclosing
Brush the teeth using a rolling motion from the gum. Using disclosing tablets after brushing will reveal any areas of plaque that you have missed.

Flossing The Teeth
Use unwaxed dental floss to remove plaque and food particles from between the teeth after you have brushed them.

After the age of 50, dental hygiene should be absolutely meticulous and you can prevent tooth problems by brushing after every meal. Use a soft brush at a 45° angle to vibrate along the gum lines. You can gently brush your tongue too, as it harbours tooth-decaying bacteria. A salt-water rinse helps to retard bacterial growth and toughens up soft gums. Fluoride toothpaste will strengthen tooth enamel. If you lose a tooth, have it promptly replaced, so that adjacent teeth don't drift.

Looking After Your Genitals The vulval area is constructed of very delicate skin, and after the menopausal decline of oestrogen it becomes prone to dryness, thinness, and cracking. The use of soap should be kept to a minimum as it dries out the skin and will exacerbate any genital symptoms. If you do use soap, choose the gentlest you can find, or dissolve a capful of baby bath soap in several pints of warm water and make a mild lather. Try to avoid washing inside the labia with soap, and be meticulous about rinsing. At other times, you can simply cleanse the genital area with pure water or with moist toilet tissue. Avoid any perfumed products, such as talcum powder and vaginal deodorants, and wear cotton underwear.

Pessaries containing oestrogen can relieve vaginal symptoms, and perfume-free moisturizers will combat dryness. If the genital area itches or you have a discharge, particularly if it is foul-smelling, consult your doctor immediately.

ENHANCING SLEEP

Our need for sleep diminishes as we get older. Whereas a new-born baby needs up to 16 hours a day, adults can function on seven. We can survive on an hour less every decade until we may need as little as four hours a night in our 60s. By the time we reach our 70s, it's quite common for us to sleep for just two or three hours and then to doze intermittently for the rest of the night. As a general rule, our need for sleep runs parallel to our growth rate.

Sometimes, just one hour of sleep in the late afternoon, or even 15 minutes of deep sleep during a catnap, can make you feel more refreshed than several hours of light, fitful sleep.

If you find yourself habitually lying awake at night, don't lie there feeling frustrated and allowing resentment to build up. It is better to be constructive about insomnia and take advantage of it. Get out of bed, go into the kitchen, and make yourself a milky drink. Find a book to read or do a job that you have been wanting to do for ages. Try and think positively about the few hours you have gained and make the best of them. After all, this is the one time in your life when you may not have to get up to go to the office by a certain time. The following may help to relieve insomnia:

- Do something quiet and relaxing before you go to bed, such as going for a walk, practicing yoga, or reading a book.
- The temperature of your bedroom should be comfortable – if possible, have the window open to allow the air to circulate.
- Make sure that there are no distracting noises to keep you awake. Mend dripping taps, close doors, and if you have radiators that knock, bleed them to get the air out of the system.
- Invest in the best mattress you can afford. A lumpy, uncomfortable mattress will exacerbate back problems.
- Wear loose-fitting nightclothes made from natural fibres.
- If you have a partner, take turns to give each other a back and neck massage before you go to bed.
- Have a warm bath last thing at night. This diverts blood from the brain to the skin and makes you feel sleepy.
- Have a warm milky drink.
- Herbs, such as camomile can be soporific. Try sleeping on a herb pillow.
- A low-fat carbohydrate snack, such as cereal or low-fat crispbread taken about half an hour before bedtime, can help induce tiredness.
- Cut down on your hours of sleep to improve their quality.
- Avoid stimulating or worrying thoughts before you go to bed. Think of relaxing images – my own tip is to think of black velvet. You could also practice the relaxation methods on page 156.

THE AGE TO WHICH YOU SHOULD LIVE			
45	78.1	63	81.3
46	78.2	64	81.6
47	78.4	65	81.8
48	78.5	66	82.1
49	78.6	67	82.4
50	78.8	68	82.7
51	78.9	69	83.0
52	79.1	70	83.4
53	79.2	71	83.7
54	79.4	72	84.1
55	79.6	73	84.4
56	79.8	74	84.8
57	80.0	75	85.3
58	80.2	76	85.7
59	80.4	77	86.2
60	80.6	78	86.6
61	80.8	79	87.1
62	81.1	80	87.1

Staying Active
Exercise such as cycling and walking is an excellent way of staying fit in the postmenopause.

THE BEST OF TIMES?

There are a lot of positive things to be said about being older. Older means being wiser, more experienced, and knowledgeable. Older means being less likely to develop many diseases, as well as having a greater life expectancy than a baby's. In fact, the older you get, the longer you can expect to live. A newborn baby may have an average life expectancy of 75 years, but a 75-year-old woman can expect to live for a further 12 years.

Many women find their greatest happiness in middle and older age, which is good news, considering that we can live more than a third of our lives after the age of 50. By the time a woman is postmenopausal, she probably knows herself better than in any other period in her life. Not only does she know who she is, but she will probably have a clear idea of what she needs and how to achieve it. With more leisure time and fewer family responsibilities, she has the time and self-knowledge to pursue what she wants. Satisfaction in the postmenopausal years will probably be derived from different things than in earlier decades. Change is, and should be, the keynote of our later years. Our bodies change and so does our outlook on life.

I can guarantee that many new and exciting opportunities will present themselves; even when you maintain your current interests, you will find that the way you engage in them will be different, and that they will please you in different ways. Each age has its own pleasures and excitements, and for many, these are the golden years.

Being postmenopausal means that we have successfully negotiated the changes brought about by the climacteric and we now have the freedom to enjoy our sexuality, without worrying about contraception. If we have children they are likely to be grown up and living independent lives. Our partners usually have more free time so we often develop more companionable relationships with them. Alternatively, the postmenopause can be a time when some of us find the courage to end unsatisfactory relationships.

Because we have more time to spend on ourselves, we can concentrate on maintaining our physical health and perhaps exploring our spiritual sides. Our later years should be characterized by a lack of self-repression and a greater tolerance towards others. Nature ensures that there is plenty of life left to us after the menopause – it is up to us to make the most of it.

USEFUL ADDRESSES

Women's Health
52–54 Featherstone Street
London EC1Y 8RT
Tel: 071 251 6333

Information on most aspects of women's health, including menopause. Telephone helpline (available Mon, Wed, Thur, Fri): 071 251 6580.

The Amarant Trust
Grant House
56–60 St John Street
London EC1M 4DT
Tel: 071 490 1644

Information on menopause, HRT, and other treatments; list of menopause clinics available on request.

National Osteoporosis Society
PO Box 10
Radstock
Bath BA3 3YB
Tel: 0761 432 472

Advice on osteoporosis (send sae).

Relate
Herbert Gray College
Little Church Street
Rugby
Warwickshire CV21 3AP
Tel: 0788 573 241

Offers counselling on all aspects of relationships, including sexual problems. Has a large network of local branches – see local phonebook for nearest one.

Faculty of Homeopathy
Hahnemann House
Powis Place
Great Ormond Street
London WC1N 3HT
Tel: 071 837 9469

Send large sae for information pack and list of registered homeopaths.

British Heart Foundation
14 Fitzhardinge Street
London W1H 4DH
Tel: 071 935 0185

Offers postal advice on coronary health and related matters.

Family Planning Association
27–35 Mortimer Street
London W1N 7RJ
Tel: 071 636 7866

Provides written information on sexual and reproductive health, and operates a telephone helpline (weekdays 10.00 to 3.00).

Age Concern
Astral House
1268 London Road
London SW16 4ER
Tel: 081 679 8000

Provides information and advice by post or by phone (ask for Information Department) on coping with old age.

Institute for Complementary Medicine
PO Box 194
London SE16 1QZ

Compiles the British Register of Complementary Practitioners and provides information on methods of natural health care. For information send an sae and three first class stamps.

Open University
Central Enquiry Service
PO Box 200
Milton Keynes MK7 6YZ
Tel: 0908 65 3231

Open University courses, including degree courses, are open to everyone, regardless of previous academic qualifications or lack of them. Ask for the brochure titled: Studying with the Open University.

Breast Cancer Care
15–19 Britten Street
London SW3 3TZ
Tel: 071 867 8275

Offers advice, information, and counselling on all aspects of breast cancer and its treatment. Telephone helpline: 071 867 1103.

Women's Heart Foundation
Suna House
128-130 Curtain Road
London EC2A 3AR
Tel: 071 228 3170

Offers written advice in ten languages on cancer screening and treatment, and operates a telephone helpline service on 071 729 2229 between 9.30 and 4.30, Mon to Fri.

Marie Stopes Clinics
108 Whitfield Street
London W1P 6BE
Tel: 071 388 2585

Provides written information on sexual and reproductive health, and operates menopause clinics in London and elsewhere.

National Institute of Medical Herbalists
9 Palace Gate
Exeter
Devon EX1 1JA
Tel: 0392 426022

Send sae for list of members.

National Back Pain Association
The Old Office Block
Elmtree Road
Teddington
Middlesex TW11 8ST
Tel: 081 977 5474

Send sae for information pack.

Women's Nutritional Advisory Service
PO Box 268
Lewes
East Sussex BN7 2QN
Tel: 0273 487366

Offers advice on dietary matters in connection with menopausal problems and premenstrual syndrome. Send sae for information.

INDEX

ACKNOWLEDGMENTS

Carroll and Brown Limited would like to thank:

Photography:
Jules Selmes, Steve Head (assistant)

Illustration:
Tony Graham, Aziz Khan,
Sue Sharples, Joanna Cameron,
Joe Lawrence, Howard Pemberton,
Coral Mula

Paper Sculptor:
Clive Stevens

Medical consultant:
With thanks to Nicholas Siddle MB
ChB MRCOG, for checking the text
and illustrations

Additional consultants:
Neil D Cox FBCO FAAO
Sami Girling MCSP SRP PGDSP
C J Hilton FRCS
Diana J Mansour MRCOG

Juliette Kando devised and
performed the movements on pages
118-119 and 160-163
Kando Studios
88 Victoria Road
London
NW6 6QA

Film outputting:
Disc To Print (UK) Ltd

Typesetting:
Deborah Rhodes, Debbie Lelliott,
Rowena Feeny

Additional editorial assistance:
Patricia Shine, Alison MacTier,
Laura Price, Jemima Dunne,
Annelise Evans

Additional design assistance:
André Scott-Bamforth

Proof reader:
Ann Vinnicombe

Models:
Juliette Kando, Sylvia Newton,
Barbara Cogswell, Heather Johnston

Make-up:
Julia Biddlecombe

Equipment:
Ann Summers, Boots, Braun UK,
Colourings by The Body Shop,
Kays Shoes, Marie Stopes Clinic, Neal's
Yard Remedies, Rigby and Peller,
St Bartholomew's Hospital

Additional Photography:
116, 185: Ranald Mackechnie

Index:
Anne McCarthy

Picture Credits:
19: SPL
21: top centre right; Frank Spooner
Pictures
21: others; Rex Features
26: top left; B&C Alexander
26: centre; Adam Woolfitt; RHPL
26: bottom left; Adam Woolfitt; RHPL
26: bottom right; Martin Burton;
Raleigh International; RHPL
27: top; RHPL
27: right; Carol Jopp; RHPL
27: bottom left; RHPL
27: bottom right; RHPL
36: Professors P Motta & J Van
Blerkom; SPL

39: Dr Brian Eyden; SPL
42: David Scharf; SPL
51: CNRI; SPL
52: Prof. P Motta, Dept. of
Anatomy, University "La Sapienza",
Rome; SPL
54: Manfred Kage; SPL
57: National Medical Slide Bank
67: Prof. P Motta, Dept. of
Anatomy, University "La Sapienza",
Rome; SPL
67: Secchi, Lecagne, Roussel,
UCLAF, CNRI; SPL
67: Prof. P Motta, Dept. of
Anatomy, University "La Sapienza",
Rome; SPL
70: Mehan Kulyk; SPL
79: CNRI; SPL
84: CNRI; SPL
85: Hank Morgan; SPL
87: CNRI; SPL
88: Chris Bjornberg; SPL
89: AVC Dept, St Mary's Hospital
Medical School
95: Ultrasound Dept, Queen Mary's
University Hospital
97: SPL
176: CNRI; SPL
178: The National Hospital for
Aesthetic Plastic Surgery
194: left; Chris Bjornberg; SPL
194: centre; J Croyle; Custom
Medical Stock Photo; SPL
194: right; Breast Screening Unit,
King's College Hospital, London;
SPL
195: SPL
197: J C Revy; SPL
218: Zefa

Picture researcher:
Jackum Brown